Reporting the Nat

Press-Government Relations during the Liberal Years, 1935-1957

During twenty-two years of unbroken rule in Ottawa, the Liberal government shared power with key elements of the Canadian press. Five men of outstanding journalistic ability formed an influential coterie: Grant Dexter, George Ferguson, Blair Fraser, Ken Wilson, and Bruce Hutchison.

The significance of these five can best be understood in the context of the growth of bureaucracy in Ottawa and a new role for the state during and after the Second World War. As they tried to explain the formulation and administration of government policy, these editors and reporters were responsible not only for reporting the governments of Mackenzie King and Louis St Laurent but also for creating them.

Patrick Brennan takes a balanced view of the close connection between press and government. He points out that the Canadian people, reading reports by these journalists, were better informed than they ever had been. He observes that political partisanship does not adequately explain the allegiance of these men to the Liberal government; rather, they were attracted to the style, personalities, and ideas of the Liberal-bureaucratic team. All five had similar nationalist and internationalist sympathies, and were impressed by the expertise, commitment, and vision of government experts, whether civil servants or cabinet ministers. All shared a respect and affection bordering on hero-worship for Lester Pearson. And, despite political disclaimers, all considered the Conservative party a threat to the continuation of moderate, progressive government.

Journalists of a later generation will be astounded by the closeness of the relationship.

PATRICK H. BRENNAN is a member of the Department of History, University of Calgary.

Reporting the Nation's Business

Press-Government Relations during the Liberal Years, 1935–1957

Patrick H. Brennan

UNIVERSITY OF TORONTO PRESS
Toronto Buffalo London

ISBN 0-8020-2977-9 (cloth)
ISBN 0-8020-7434-0 (paper)

Printed on acid-free paper

Canadian Cataloguing in Publication Data

Brennan, Patrick H. (Patrick Harvey)
Reporting the nation's business : press-government
relations during the Liberal years, 1935–1957

Includes bibliographical references and index.
ISBN 0-8020-2977-9 (bound) ISBN 0-8020-7434-0 (pbk.)

I. Government and press – Canada. 2. Mass media – Political
aspects – Canada. 3. Liberal Party of Canada – History –
20th century. I. Title.

PN4914.P6B7 1994   070.4'08'8328   C93-094473-9

This book has been published with the help of a grant from the
Social Science Federation of Canada,
using funds provided by the
Social Sciences and Humanities Research Council of Canada.

To Clare and Winnie

Contents

Preface

During their unbroken twenty-two-year span in office from 1935 through 1957, the Liberals, assisted by a competent, self-assured bureaucracy, coped ably with a succession of domestic and foreign policy challenges. An image of efficient competence came to surround this Liberal-bureaucratic team, one that worked so obviously to the Liberals' political advantage that they came to be seen by a great many Canadians, themselves included, as the 'Government party.' The degree to which this image became part of the English-Canadian consciousness was also the result of the cooperation both the Liberals and the civil servants were able to count on from key elements of the press.

Considering how extensively they rely on journalists' writing as a primary source, Canadian political historians have had little to say about editors, reporters, and publishers, either individually or as a group. Certainly there are few well-researched studies of journalists active during the middle decades of the century, when, despite the advent of competition from radio and television, the importance of the print media in helping to shape opinion and convey information reached its apex in Canada. Nor have the stream of popularly written (and generally mediocre) biographies and memoirs filled the void.

This study focuses on the wartime and postwar emergence of a special relationship between a small but increasingly prominent group of English-speaking journalists on the one hand and the senior bureaucrats and more dynamic, forward-looking Liberal politicians on the other, a relationship that defined the dominant model of public affairs journalism during the period. Revealingly, the participants, if asked years later to define the relationship, invariably chose the words 'responsible' and 'civilized.'

For the journalists involved, taking Walter Lippmann and J.W. Dafoe as their models, it was 'professional' to report public policy accurately, comment on it intelligently, and, in the process, exercise influence on the government and the public alike. This role did not represent a departure in journalistic style per se; similar ideas had been steadily gaining ground among Canadian reporters and editors at least since the First World War. In the context of the emergence of a vastly expanded bureaucracy and a fundamentally altered role of state, however, the 'responsible, civilized relationship' represented more than just another stage in the professionalization of Canadian journalism.

Reporting accurately, commenting intelligently, and exercising influence required that journalists develop and maintain the confidence of those in government who could provide the background knowledge on the formulation and administration of policy in what was, by the Second World War, a complex public policy environment. Increasingly, the sources of this knowledge were the senior civil servants rather than the politicians. Given that they developed and maintained that confidence to an extent never seen in Ottawa before or since, these journalists became extraordinarily well informed, emerging as 'authoritative voices.'

This status naturally enhanced their credibility with the very readers the mandarins and the Liberals were hoping to influence. The result was a group of influential journalists who certainly exhibited sympathy for the policies and personalities of the Liberal-bureaucratic establishment, yet not the political subservience to the former of which they were increasingly criticized.

Inevitably, of course, these men were compromised by inherent by-products of the responsible, civilized relationship: the depth of their ties to party and civil service insiders as well as the blurring of roles which was allowed to occur, at least in their own minds. All of them underestimated the dangers to their independence which both of these factors represented. Still, as long as the Liberals governed well, this relationship also functioned well and was, by and large, in the public interest. Bureaucrats, in particular, used their press allies primarily to reveal, rather than conceal, government activities. When the Liberals began to show signs of losing their vision, not to mention their manners and sense of responsibility, however, this special relationship began to unravel as well.

Liberal ministers and senior bureaucrats had no difficulty in singling out those they considered the ablest among the press corps, men who, as a result of their preferred treatment, came to be identified as a 'Liberal press establishment.' The five central figures of this group included three leading Ottawa editors: Grant Dexter of the *Winnipeg Free Press*, Ken Wilson of the

Financial Post, and Blair Fraser of *Maclean's.* The other two were Bruce Hutchison, who wrote at one time or another for all three of these publications, and George Ferguson, who served first as Dafoe's assistant at the *Free Press,* then temporarily as his successor, and finally as the editor of the *Montreal Star.* Their careers in and around the centre of power at Ottawa defined the responsible, civilized relationship and constitute the core of any examination of press-government relations during the 1935–57 period.

Operating in a very political environment, these journalists liked to see themselves as 'independent Liberals.' Traditional partisanship, though to varying degrees a factor in their outlook, cannot adequately explain the 'allegiance' they displayed to the Liberal government and the bulk of its policy initiatives. More significant was their attraction to the style, the personalities, and the ideas of the Liberal-bureaucratic team. All five journalists were passionate nationalists and committed internationalists. All were deeply impressed by the expertise, dedication, and vision of the mandarins and the cabinet members who supported them. In particular, all shared an affection and respect bordering on hero worship for Lester Pearson, the most charismatic of the postwar internationalists and the Liberal who for them combined high-minded politics with bureaucratic expertise. Finally, all were convinced that Canadian Conservatism, as epitomized in the person of George Drew and the party's 'uncivilized' and 'irresponsible' Toronto power-brokers, was a threat to the continuation of moderate, progressive government.

The style of journalism they practised began to crumble during the succession of Liberal débâcles that began in 1955. Circumstances called less for informed analysis than for outright criticism. These establishment journalists felt a responsibility to join in, but it was difficult to attack longtime political friends and contribute to their defeat. But defeated the Liberals soon were, and the succeeding Diefenbaker era brought with it a steady deterioration in press-government relations. This deterioration both led to and was the result of the ascendancy of a new approach to political journalism which repudiated the special relationship as too civilized and not responsible enough and replaced it with unvarnished adversarialism.

What follows is both a political and a journalistic history, one that explores the two environments as well as the clear linkages and distinctions between them. In settling on an approach, I have chosen a combination of biography and case studies as the most appropriate. The study consciously sets out to explore developments from the perspective of the journalists rather than those they wrote about. In the process, I hope, it conveys to the reader a sense of how these reporters and editors saw themselves, their work, and the events and individuals they reported and commented upon.

Certainly the preconceptions that Fraser, Dexter, Hutchison, Wilson, and Ferguson brought to their task offer unique insights into one of the important avenues by which English Canadians' perceptions of their government, their national identity, and their place in the world were shaped during two decades of far-reaching change.

Acknowledgments

While this study is a work of original research and the product of a single person, it could not have been completed without the generous and timely assistance of friends and associates. Professor J.L. Granatstein of York University deserves special thanks. From the outset of this project, which began as a doctoral dissertation under his supervision, he provided me with encouragement, assistance, and constructive criticism, and, in the process, taught me much of what I have mastered of the historian's craft. The insightful comments provided by Professors Ramsay Cook and Fred Fletcher of York University and Paul Rutherford at the University of Toronto were most helpful. A considerable debt is also owed to Gerald Hallowell of the University of Toronto Press for his help in revising and improving the original dissertation. Certainly the timely and boundless encouragement which both he and his colleagues Laura Macleod and Agnes Ambrus provided was much appreciated. And I shall always be thankful for the superb editorial assistance of Rosemary Shipton. Laurel McCartney of Calgary generously aided in reading the proof.

My research would have been impossible without the generous cooperation of many individuals. Glen Allen, Floyd Chalmers, Wilfrid Eggleston, David Ferguson, Graham and John Fraser, Arthur Irwin, Michael Sifton, the Hon. Paul Martin, Alice Dexter, Jean Fraser, Norma Gordon, Elizabeth Pound, and Ruth Wilson graciously permitted me to examine collections of papers under their control. Similarly, both the Liberal Party of Canada and Maclean-Hunter Limited granted me access to their records. As well, David Mackenzie generously allowed me to use material in manuscript from his recently published *Arthur Irwin: A Biography*. The many individuals who agreed to be interviewed not only spoke, for the most part, with candour, but also displayed warmth and courtesy. I thank them. Archivists and librarians from British Columbia to Quebec assisted me in many ways, with George Henderson of the Queen's University Archives deserving special mention. Responsibility for errors, omissions, and any other inadequacies, of course, lies exclusively with the author.

Gratitude is also extended to two individuals who took a personal interest in this work and its author and never failed to place both in their proper perspective: my brother, Professor Bill Brennan, and David Ambrosi.

Finally, there are two people whom I can never begin to thank sufficiently: my wife and my mother. They stood by through the high points and the low, prodding or sympathizing as the occasion required, always encouraging, and helping to pay the bills.

Grant Dexter and George Ferguson (standing, left to right); Victor Sifton and
J.W. Dafoe (seated, left to right). 'If the editorial offices of the *Free Press* were
a Dafoe-Ferguson monopoly, then the Ottawa bureau was Dexter's, leaving
publisher Victor Sifton on the outside looking in.'

George Ferguson at his editorial desk at the *Montreal Star.* 'Norman Robertson called Ferguson the ablest newspaperman in Canada, a verdict few of the mandarins would have questioned.'

War Committee of the cabinet, 1943. 'As Dafoe's resident envoy in Ottawa, Grant Dexter possessed a permanent entrée into the inner circles of the Liberal government.' Angus Macdonald (standing, far left) and Chubby Power (seated, far left), Tom Crerar (seated, second from left), and James Ilsley (seated, far right) were among his most important cabinet confidants.

The grim state of Cold War relations in 1946 is all too clear on the faces of the Canadian delegation at the Paris Peace Conference. The meetings gave Blair Fraser ample opportunity to draw closer to key players in the Ottawa foreign policy establishment such as Norman Robertson (far left) and Arnold Heeney (far right).

William Mackintosh and Brooke Claxton at a UN conference in 1946. One of the leading mandarins, Mackintosh (left) frequently channelled the bureaucracy's economic views to the *Financial Post*'s Ken Wilson and others.

Mackenzie King signs the Canada–United Kingdom loan agreement, February
1946, while Clifford Clark, deputy minister of finance (far left), and his assistant,
R.B. Bryce (second from left), watch approvingly. 'Ken Wilson's relations with the
Department of Finance, with its well-deserved reputation during Clark's tenure
for the artful use of "selective disclosures," ensured he would emerge as an
authoritative voice on the government's economic policy.'

Mike Pearson conducting foreign policy from his Ottawa office. 'Probably the most popular man in Canada, among those who know him at all,' Pearson kept in close touch with favoured journalists and never shied from promoting his own career in the process.

C.D. Howe and Louis St Laurent at the 1948 leadership convention
that selected the latter as Mackenzie King's replacement.

Mike Pearson and Escott Reid. 'The master of press relations, Mike Pearson
encouraged senior colleagues like Escott Reid to cultivate the abler
members of the press corps.'

'Finance Minister Doug Abbott had a knack for handling newspapermen
that came close to matching Pearson's calculated affability.'

Prime Minister Louis St Laurent (right) shaking hands with J.W. Pickersgill.
'Prime minister St Laurent approached the press with supreme self-confidence
and the considerable talents of the ubiquitous Jack Pickersgill
never far from his side.'

Pearson holds a press conference in Ottawa during the Suez Crisis, October 1956.
'The fact that Pearson was a charmer, with a natural talent for influencing people,
gave him a huge advantage in the press-relations game.'

Setting a course towards the Liberal-bureaucratic vision of Canada,
Blair Fraser (left) and Ralph Allen (right) plot strategy in the
editorial offices of *Maclean's*.

Prime Minister St Laurent at the official opening of the new headquarters of
the National Liberal Federation in Ottawa, 1957. 'H.E. Kidd (second from
left), the mastermind of Liberal party publicity, went out of his way to
ingratiate himself with those journalists who were "prepared to help us."'
Party president Duncan MacTavish stands beside Kidd.

Graham Towers, governor of the Bank of Canada. 'Towers had little use for most reporters and was always cautious, even of those few who were in favour. Fortunately his attitude was not rigidly copied by all his senior officials.'

Bruce Hutchison at the Liberal leadership convention, January 1958,
'commentating with some degree of impartiality.'

Reporting the Nation's Business

Press-Government Relations during the Liberal Years,
1935–1957

Introduction

The Changing Landscape of Politics, Government, and the Press

At the beginning of the twentieth century the daily popular press was not only well established in Canada, but held an unchallenged monopoly in mass communications. Despite the rhetoric of many publishers and editors, and the efforts of a few notable individuals, the great majority of these publications retained a specific political allegiance. By the 1960s, however, partisan allegiance was largely a memory. Radio and especially television had successfully challenged the pre-eminence of newspapers and other periodicals as shapers of the national consciousness, and print journalism itself had undergone a thorough professionalization. Finally, the prevailing ethos of the fourth estate had become wedded to a quasi-adversarialism which made for a different style in the reporting and analysis of public affairs than had prevailed sixty years earlier.

Although these changes in print journalism were significant, they had evolved only gradually. A clear transition from partisanship to professionalism had begun early in the century, had accelerated during the Great War and the interwar years, and had become fully developed during the Second World War and the postwar decade. This last period roughly coincides with the uninterrupted twenty-two-year span of Liberal rule under Prime Ministers William Lyon Mackenzie King and Louis St Laurent. These same years witnessed the emergence of a civil service mandarinate and a 'Government party,' the two elements which together directed Canada's transformation from a parochial, quasi-colony to a confident middle power. These changes in turn gave impetus to a style of public affairs journalism that many contemporary reporters and editors deemed appropriate to the new age.

At the height of their influence during the 1940s and early 1950s, this group collectively saw themselves as Canada's first generation of professional journalists. In their view, the increasing complexity of government and public policy dictated a more sophisticated approach to their craft, if the public interest was to be served, an approach emphasizing informed comment and analysis over mere opinion. Unquestionably, their goal was to speak with an authoritative but independent voice, and their models were J.W. Dafoe, the renowned editor of the *Winnipeg Free Press,* and Walter Lippmann, the leading figure in American political journalism during the period. A central defining characteristic of those who embraced the new journalism was that they shared the world view of many of their contemporaries who were rising to prominence in the Liberal party and the bureaucracy, one based on common nationalist and internationalist sympathies and a belief in an enhanced role for the federal government. Contacts between the three groups, and particularly between the journalists and the civil servants, grew increasingly intimate, both professionally and socially. The resulting responsible, civilized relationship between journalist and source was supposed to ensure that Canadians would be objectively and thoroughly informed. In the end, the new political journalists were swept up in the pervasive postwar Liberal consensus to which they had made no small contribution. Indeed, the process was sufficiently obvious that critics inside and outside the profession began to question whether these establishment journalists could distinguish between the national interest and that of the Liberal-bureaucratic axis – whether they, too, had become 'Ottawa men.'

This special relationship embraced most of the ablest English-speaking journalists of their time. Foremost among them were Grant Dexter, from 1946 through 1954 editor of the *Winnipeg Free Press* and both before and after that their man in Ottawa; Blair Fraser and Ken Wilson, the Ottawa editors of *Maclean's* and the *Financial Post,* respectively; George Ferguson, Dafoe's right-hand man at the *Free Press* and, after 1946, the editor of the *Montreal Star;* and Bruce Hutchison, a prolific contributor on public affairs to the *Free Press* (where for a time he served as associate editor), *Financial Post,* and *Maclean's,* among other publications. The most obvious omission from this group is Grattan O'Leary, editor of the *Ottawa Journal.* However, O'Leary's Conservative sympathies clearly set him apart from the establishment journalists of the 1940s and 1950s who, if not all Liberals, were certainly not avowed Tories. The same could be said of John Bird, who spent much of this period in Ottawa as chief of the Southam bureau, and I. Norman Smith, O'Leary's *Journal* colleague and a future editor of that newspaper. Michael Barkway, who replaced Wilson at the *Financial Post* after Wilson's untimely death in an air crash in 1952, had become a fully fledged member of the Liberal press establishment by the mid 1950s. Arthur Irwin, the editor of *Maclean's* during the late 1940s and thereafter a civil servant and diplomat, certainly could be included along with his successor, Ralph Allen. So could Wilfrid Eggleston, a much-respected freelance writer and social intimate of the elite journalists, who, during the postwar decade, increasingly devoted his energies to the Carleton College journalism program he had founded. While a dozen journalists might be considered for inclusion, the careers of Ferguson, Dexter, Hutchison, Wilson, and Fraser best exemplified the evolution and operation of the responsible, civilized relationship. As historian J.L. Granatstein has observed, these five 'were so close to the Liberal government during its postwar ascendancy as to form something approximating a federal department.'[1] Certainly, they were the ones with the largest following among businessmen, intellectuals, and others whose opinions counted most with the senior Liberal politicians and civil servants in the Government party era.

During the period of their ascendancy, these five journalists exercised considerable influence, not on government policy-making, where their impact was usually slight, but on public perception and acceptance of those policy initiatives. Influence, of course, is difficult to measure, but as historian Paul Rutherford has pointed out, the attention politicians and elites in general have paid to the media gives ample evidence of the importance these groups have ascribed to it. Editors and correspondents may have spoken chiefly to the converted, but, as one contemporary publisher put it, those audiences were often both large and influential.[2] Exploring the journalists' actual role, then, something Canadian historians have rarely done, should clearly contribute to a more balanced understanding of the dramatic wartime and postwar expansion of government and bureaucratic influence in Canada.

To appreciate the attitude of the dominant group of editors and reporters towards the coverage of public affairs during the 1940s and 1950s, it is important to understand the tradition they were attempting to replace. At the turn of the century, partisan politics was certainly the grist, and in many instances the *raison d'être,* of Canadian newspapers. Although revenues from commercial advertising, especially for those newspapers with the largest circulations, were steadily diminishing the significance of government patronage, it remained an important consideration economically.[3] For politicians there were obvious advantages in controlling both the news and the editorial content of newspapers. Any turn-of-the-century politician would have sympathized with John A. Macdonald's lament that while everyone was bound to support him when he was right, what he needed was someone to support him when he was wrong.[4] A 'reliable' daily newspaper could serve the political party in many roles, including undermining the credibility of political opponents, strengthening party discipline and morale, and, most crucially, 'educating' voters by constantly bombarding them with the party line.[5] Yet from the point of view of editors and publishers, at least those who were not politicians themselves, the question of who did the bidding of whom was a constant source of tension. And for those journalists who aspired to put into action their fine-sounding rhetoric about professionalism and public trust, employment at a party organ during the late nineteenth and early twentieth century was a permanent reminder of just how far their reality fell short of their expectations.

It was John S. Willison, the brilliant young editor of Victorian Canada's foremost Liberal daily, the *Toronto Globe,* who is credited with the first attempt to establish some standard of political independence for Canadian journalists. Initially Willison had found his role as a party journalist congenial enough. In an assessment that would find its echo among members of a different Liberal press establishment half a century later, he readily admitted that 'the principal measures of the Laurier Government's first ministry made the endorsement of them an agreeable duty.'[6] But as powerful Liberals placed more demands on Willison and increasingly ignored his counsel, the relationship between editor and party soured noticeably. Clearly, Willison's efforts to practise independent Liberalism were a sham under these conditions. In one heated exchange with his most persistent adversary, Sir Clifford Sifton, Willison left no doubt about his growing frustration. 'Personally,' he noted, 'I resent the assumption of every Liberal politician that I am his hired man, that he has the right to criticize and condemn me, and that he has the right to dictate or shape my course as a journalist.'[7]

In 1902 Willison had had enough of 'political servitude' and, lured by the promise of real editorial independence, he quit the *Globe* to become editor of a new Toronto daily financed by industrialist J.W. Flavelle. But as fellow journalist A.H.U. Colquhoun observed of his friend's move, 'the public does not demand a very high voltage of intellectual content in daily newspapers, and for this reason the courageous experiment ... was handicapped from the outset.'[8] Despite Flavelle's determined backing, the *Toronto News* was unsuccessful. After a few years, the paper came into the hands of Conservative interests and Willison once again found himself a party journalist, albeit on the opposite side.

Despite this apparent setback, Willison's strong views on the need for a politically independent press committed to reliable, objective news coverage found attentive listeners, as did his calls for a better educated, more professional class of journalist. Of course, Willison was not acting out of anything more than self-interest, though admittedly a high-minded one. As a journalist committed to the professionalization of his occupation and the increased prestige and influence of the press, he was simply recognizing the obvious – that 'no public journal can be influential as the mere mouthpiece of a [business or party].'⁹ Or as *Toronto Star* editor Joseph Atkinson, a stalwart Liberal who sympathized with Willison's ideas, put it: 'A newspaper is a good ally, but soon becomes useless as the subservient organ of a party.'¹⁰ Among more forward-thinking journalists, it was no longer acceptable for the press simply to misrepresent political opponents; the arguments of the latter would have to be confronted intelligently. When the circumstances justified, that kind of journalism would also require a readiness to criticize government openly. On such occasions, as Willison liked to point out, 'knowledge [would be] power.'¹¹ The desirability of a more objective, professional journalism was recommended by larger imperatives as well, specifically the need to appeal to, or conversely not offend, the ever larger audiences that daily newspapers needed to attract if they were to survive.

Of course, the existence of any form of party press had also placed restrictions on the scope of reporters covering national affairs in Ottawa. A formally organized press gallery, self-governing though funded by parliament, had been established around 1880. In the absence of a national news service, gallery reporters' chief responsibility was to provide routine coverage of political goings-on in Ottawa. The drudgery of obtaining verbatim accounts of debates occupied the largest part of their time, at least when parliament was in session. In this early period, their newspaper's allegiance shaped everything about their job. The government treated its own news like patronage, with ministers awarding it to the loyal. Other perks ran the gamut from free stationery to appointments as part-time sessional clerks, a remunerative sideline for those lucky enough to be chosen. Even gallery seating was routinely allocated along straight party lines, with the least desirable spaces reserved, revealingly enough, for those representing the independent, not the opposition, newspapers.¹²

Opposition reporters had to scramble for what scraps they could pick up from disgruntled government backbenchers, the opposition benches, or civil servants. If that failed, they could fall back on the numerous politicos, job-seekers, and hangers-on who frequented the capital's many public houses and hotels. Though frequently shunned by ministers and their deputies, most of the opposition men felt they were actually more fortunate than their government opposites, whose connection effectively prevented them from reporting anything unfavourable to the current administration.¹³

Regardless of which party his paper supported, it was a rare reporter who arrived in Ottawa without explicit instructions on what was appropriate to write and when to write it. If by chance he harboured any doubts about these guidelines, party emissaries soon set those to rest. Those who were daring enough to disobey or who hinted that their commitment to the cause was weakening could soon find themselves looking for another employer.[14] Still, despite the enormous pressures applied to ensure party conformity, and the willing connections between party and newspaper, politicians were never able to dominate the press completely.[15] Moreover, regardless of the level of 'flackery' (as distinct from 'straight' journalism) in which the typical turn-of-the-century press gallery reporter indulged, the quality of the men working the Hill was well above the average found in their profession. Editor and reporters alike regarded a gallery appointment highly. Indeed, for a bright, ambitious young reporter, it was a sure sign that he had been earmarked for editorial responsibilities. The list of future editors and publishers who had served their stint in the prewar gallery included such journalistic luminaries from the 1920s and 1930s as Joseph Atkinson, P.D. Ross, E. Norman Smith, Grattan O'Leary, Arthur Ford, Charles Bowman, Paul Bilkey, John Bassett, Sr, and J.W. Dafoe.

To the extent that the Conservative and especially the Union government sought to mobilize public opinion behind the national war effort, the Great War was an impetus for change in party-press relations in Canada. The worst of the harassment opposition reporters had endured came to an end as political necessity induced ministers and their advisors to treat all reporters more or less equally. Prime Minister Robert Borden set a personal example by dutifully holding Teddy Roosevelt-style press conferences with leading correspondents. For patriotic reasons, after 1916 there was a notable willingness among the English-language press to suspend partisanship. The 1917 conscription crisis, which among other things shattered the vaunted unity of the Liberal press for all time, was a clear sign that changes were occurring.

By 1920, for these reasons as well as others related to the changing shape of the newspaper and magazine industry (with the never-ending need to maximize circulation being front and centre), the party organ was fast becoming an anachronism in Canada.[16] Of course, that did not mean newspapers opted for political neutrality; this rarely happened. But their relationship with their favoured party had evolved from outright subordination to association – and an arm's-length association at that. In 1929, when Atkinson explained the new orientation of the *Toronto Star* to one of his young reporters, he said that the paper, while broadly Liberal, was no party organ. Rather, its function was to develop and support liberal opinion quite independently – and, when appropriate, in advance – of the Liberal party's own actions. Where the opinion or policy of the *Star* and the Liberal party diverged, the former would take note and criticize, but in such a way as not to harm the latter.[17] This Atkinson defended as a legitimately independent Liberal editorial approach. Whether it was independent Liberalism or independent Conservatism, this was the form of ideological commitment or alliance which, by the 1920s, held sway with most publishers and editors in English Canada. For the majority, it was convenient to couch this role in the rhetoric of a unique public trust between newspapers and their readers. While it is true that some editors, particularly the older men, would always have difficulty maintaining even a semblance of political impartiality, their numbers during the interwar years were steadily declining.

No editor epitomized the shift from party to independent journalism more clearly than J.W. Dafoe of the *Manitoba* and (after 1931) *Winnipeg Free Press*. Steeped in the Victorian style of party-organ journalism, Dafoe had demonstrated a partisanship which sometimes even *Free Press* publisher Sir Clifford Sifton found disconcerting.[18] Yet in keeping with his strong nationalism, a reformist liberalism (which included reforming his own profession), and growing personal prestige, not to mention a sympathetic publisher's granting of an increasingly free editorial rein, Dafoe was swept up in the independent press enthusiasm of the first decades of the century. Under his direction, the *Free Press* developed independent Liberalism into a fine art, even if the nuances of his achievement tended to be lost on the recipients of his editorial barbs. As an independent Liberal, he tolerated no overt partisanship in *Free Press* news columns, and his editorial page was renowned for the high intellectual plane of its partisan and non-partisan arguments. After his wartime Unionist experience, the Liberal party had to earn Dafoe's support on the merits of the issue. Increasingly, he strove to use the combination of Liberal sympathies and editorial independence to influence the Liberal party along lines he considered more conducive to the national interest.

During these latter years of his remarkable career, Dafoe had a naïve but unshakeable faith in the power of his own editorial eloquence. In his considered opinion, the editorial was fundamental to any self-respecting newspaper's role as an educational forum, not to mention to its prestige. At a time when critics were bemoaning the declining intellectual quality of the typical daily's editorial page – and not without reason since most publishers were convinced that high-level editorializing seldom influenced circulation – the brilliance of Dafoe's page earned plaudits and a committed following, particularly among English-Canadian intellectuals.[19]

The Dafoe style of providing objective news reporting and original, independent editorial comment placed an enormous premium on political intelligence gathering. Under such circumstances, the role of the parliamentary reporter took on an entirely new importance. Dafoe had recognized this problem from the outset. In 1924 he posted Grant Dexter, his ablest young reporter, to monitor political developments in Ottawa full time, an unheard of extravagance for newspapers of that period. The press milieu in which Dexter operated during the 1920s and 1930s had changed remarkably little in certain basic ways since the prewar years. An appointment to the gallery was still highly prized, though not reflected in the calibre of some of the incumbents. Most members were now older men with considerable experience in Ottawa and very set in their ways, many of them remnants of the hard-drinking, hard-nosed whiskey generation of political reporters.[20] Interested in politics in the traditional sense and in little else, they cultivated a few sources, usually political cronies, and could subsist on the scraps of information provided while awaiting a memorable 'scoop.' Dogged pursuit of the real story behind government activities – the investigative reporting that would become the staple of a subsequent generation of journalists – was virtually unknown. Pay was chronically low and, to compensate, most, Dexter included, hired themselves out as 'stringers' for the many Canadian dailies that had no reporter in the capital.

The major sources of political news a recent arrival was expected to tap were the prime minister's office, cabinet ministers and their private secretaries, deputy ministers, and other civil servants. The simple truth was that government administration was unsophisticated and Ottawa itself a backwater capital. When parliament was in session, all important announcements came from the House of Commons; departments could be and were safely ignored. Few newspapers detailed a reporter to cover Ottawa year round for the simple reason that when parliament was not in session, and that was seven or eight months each year, it was thought there was no news worth reporting. During the sessions, however, life for the thirty-five or so reporters in the press gallery was a hectic scramble to get out the detailed story of the day's sitting, a task that left little time for thoughtful analysis or for gathering background material.[21]

Significant changes were coming, however, and a new type of reporter was more frequently observed on the Hill. Some, like Arthur Irwin and Bruce Hutchison, spent only a short stint in the gallery: it was still considered important experience for would-be editorial staff to have under their belts. A few of the newcomers were university-educated, and all were ambitious and considered themselves more professional than their tradition-bound colleagues.[22] They remained generalists – a one-man bureau could hardly afford to be otherwise – but they wanted to be thought of as more knowledgeable generalists. To that end, they were prepared to 'do their homework,' a phrase they would later use as a badge of honour distinguishing them from their more ordinary colleagues.

At the same time, the nature of the federal government itself was beginning to change. Throughout the 1930s the process was hardly visible, but the observant could see the handiwork of O.D. Skelton and Clifford Clark, undersecretary of state for external affairs and deputy minister of finance, respectively. These two able civil servants had begun the slow transformation of the upper echelons of the bureaucracy by a steady infusion of bright young university men, a transformation contemporary Frank Underhill called 'the greatest advance in the functioning of Canadian democratic government in our generation.'[23]

The dimensions of this bureaucratic revolution, along with its profound impact on public affairs, would become clear only during the Second World War. Suffice to say, it would transform the nature of political journalism as it did government itself. Those journalists who could adapt to and comprehend the new political geography were uniquely qualified to make it intelligible for a curious public. As such, they were destined to occupy a favoured position. Inevitably, mutually advantageous relationships developed which bound them to the leading elements in the Liberal party and the bureaucracy. All three groups would call the resulting arrangement a responsible, civilized relationship. It was one that would transform this group of able reporters and editors into authoritative voices while, at the same time, raising questions about their journalistic objectivity and independence.

I

'The bill of goods
has been sold too late'

The *Winnipeg Free Press*
and the Road to War

During the interwar years, the standing of the *Winnipeg Free Press* as one of
the leading newspapers in English Canada was unquestioned.[1] Indeed,
judged on the basis of editorial quality alone, the *Free Press* was arguably
the country's finest English-language daily. Its ability to attract the attention of intellectuals and opinion-makers nationwide was the achievement
of the man widely regarded as the most able editor of his generation, John
Wesley Dafoe. The sweep of Dafoe's nationalist and internationalist vision
guaranteed that the thundering pronouncements of the 'oracle of Carlton
Street,' if not always carrying the day, would at least be heard.

Dafoe's immediate influence was political. In his hands, the *Free Press*
was *the* Liberal voice in the West, albeit an increasingly independent one,
as well as the Prairies' national spokesman. That being so, politics and
Canadian nationalism, Dafoe-style, dominated the editorial page. However, it was his second passion – internationalism – which set Dafoe and the
Free Press apart from their rivals and ultimately guaranteed his position as
a larger-than-life figure in Canadian journalism. Ironically, most of Dafoe's
contemporaries had disagreed with, dismissed, or even ridiculed his internationalist convictions. Never was this more evident than during the course
of his impassioned defence of the League of Nations and, more particularly, the principle of collective security during the late 1930s. Some listened
to the *Free Press*'s lone voice, and many more remembered it after the fact.
Among these were many of the younger men who either were or would
shortly become committed internationalists themselves and were destined
to occupy influential positions in government, academic, and journalistic
circles during and after the Second World War. These individuals forgave

Dafoe's lapses into partisan Liberalism and his propensity to tilt at nine-teenth-century liberal economic windmills. He and his newspaper had been right about the folly of isolationism and appeasement and the necessity of collective security, and that earned Dafoe and the *Free Press* their lasting respect.

Dafoe was born in Combermere, Canada West, on 8 March 1866. Still pioneer country, the district offered a bright, curious youngster little oppor-tunity to acquire a formal education. Combermere was staunchly Tory and Protestant in equal measure, and the young Dafoe inevitably absorbed both. Not so any love of farming, however, and in 1883, after a brief and unsuc-cessful fling at teaching, the restless seventeen-year-old set off for Montreal intent on making his career in journalism. After only a year with the Mon-treal *Star,* the paper sent him to the press gallery in Ottawa, in those days a sure sign that his potential had been recognized. His brief stint there had a profound effect on the impressionable young reporter: Conservatism lost its lustre and the seeds of a lifelong commitment to Liberalism were planted. Thereafter, Dafoe followed the then standard career path of newspapermen – on-the-job training marked by frequent shifts from paper to paper as more challenging (or at least better-paying) positions beckoned. His considerable talents ensured a rapid rise and, during the next fifteen years, most of them spent in Montreal, he was rarely far from an editor's desk.

In 1898 Clifford Sifton, Laurier's western lieutenant, had purchased a controlling interest in the floundering *Manitoba Free Press* with the idea of transforming it into a powerful Liberal voice. Dafoe had already established a solid reputation as an editor, and his views on Laurier, the Liberal party, separate schools, and a host of other public issues had caught Sifton's approving eye. In 1901 Sifton offered Dafoe the editorship of his new paper. It was a challenge to be sure, but Sifton's terms were favourable and Dafoe promptly accepted.[2] Under his able direction the prestige and profitability of the *Free Press* grew steadily. By the end of the Great War he was not only acclaimed as a great editor but had emerged as a leading national figure in his own right.

To maintain the editorial page's high standards and Dafoe's even high-er expectations required a strong editorial team. By the mid 1920s its key members were already in place, and ten years later the organization was functioning with machine-like efficiency. Dafoe had always been on the lookout for suitable candidates to train in the *Free Press* style of journalism. The qualifications were simple: enthusiasm, intelligence, and an aptitude, however unpolished, for newspaper work. With Dafoe as 'dean,' the crowd-ed, cluttered editorial offices on Winnipeg's Carlton Street did double duty during the remaining years of his life as an informal graduate school of journalism for a generation of Canadian newspapermen. Two of these men went on to play especially important roles at the *Free Press:* George Ferguson and Grant Dexter.

George Victor Ferguson was born in Scotland on 20 April 1897. His father, a Presbyterian minister, emigrated to Canada in 1904 with his wife and three children, settling in the rough-and-ready mining town of Nelson, British Columbia. The Rev. James Ferguson, a passionate Gladstone Liberal and a 'free thinker' who had sided with the progressive faction during his church's fierce debates over Darwinism, was close to his children. He made sure they developed a respect for the value of education and the courage to take unpopular stands when a principle was at stake. In 1915, much to his father's satisfaction, George enrolled at the University of Alberta, but the timing could not have been worse. His older brother would soon enlist (and within months be killed in action), and George, swept up in the war fervour, felt that he, too, should volunteer. After finishing a restless freshman year, he signed up. Rushed to France with other infantry reinforcements after the heavy losses at Vimy, Ferguson spent four harrowing months in the trenches. He might have remained there but for some extraordinary good fortune that likely saved his life. A young British staff officer courting Ferguson's sister (unsuccessfully, as it turned out) arranged his transfer to an intelligence unit behind the lines. Ferguson polished his rough school-boy French with understandable haste; 'no one,' he later observed wryly, 'has ever learned a language faster.'[3] Within a month he was sufficiently fluent to begin carrying out his new responsibilities – ferreting out spies among the many displaced French civilians behind British lines. Amid the squalor, mud, and endless casualties, the 'romance' of soldiering had quickly worn thin and he learned to swear, drink, and hate war with equal passion. Like so many of his Canadian-born comrades, Ferguson was swept up in the nascent nationalism of the Canadian Expeditionary Force, emerging from his wartime experience with an appreciation of what it was to be a Canadian first and a member of the British Empire second.

After demobilization, Ferguson returned to the University of Alberta to complete his BA in economics, then sailed for England, this time as an Oxford-bound Rhodes scholar. At Christ Church College he enrolled in 'Modern Greats,' a recently introduced honours course that emphasized the new discipline of political economy. Ferguson worked hard, and on the social side gravitated naturally towards the company of other young Canadians at Oxford and Cambridge, in the process forming lifelong friendships with several destined for prominent careers as academics or public servants, including King Gordon, George Glazebrook, Graham Spry, and Arnold Heeney.[4] Ferguson found the Oxford experience enormously enjoyable and, while it left its mark on him in many ways, two influences in particular stand out. He experienced firsthand the 'imperial mentality' – that ingrained and grating sense of superiority that pervaded the British elite's every word and mannerism toward the lesser colonial breeds – and confirmed his anti-imperialist and nationalist sentiments.⁵ And he first met Dafoe – at a debate entitled 'Imperial Relations from the Canadian Point of View' at All Souls in 1923 – when facing an overwhelmingly hostile audience, the Prairie editor more than held his own and, in the process, deeply impressed Ferguson. It was not just what Dafoe said – after all, given Ferguson's own views he was bound to find Dafoe's opinions agreeable – but how he said it: straightforwardly and with conviction.

Much to Ferguson's surprise, the London *Times* offered him a copy-reading position when he left Oxford. He quickly found that he liked newspaper work, particularly when the paper's illustrious editor, Sir Geoffrey Dawson, encouraged him to believe he had a bright future with the *Times*. Ferguson was tempted, but the desire to return to Canada remained too strong. During a Christmas trip home in 1924 he made inquiries at various newspapers along the route. The results were discouraging; 'too damned much education!' was the managing editor of the Montreal *Gazette*'s dismissive comment, a verdict to which Jack Sifton, now overseeing the family interests at the *Free Press*, subscribed and which Ferguson spent his early career trying to live down. Dafoe, however, not only remembered Ferguson but wanted to hire him, and promised an answer over the holiday. As the *Free Press* editor later recounted with obvious satisfaction, 'we saw to it that the *Times* did not have him and that we did.'⁶ Ferguson's editorial, writing, and management talents quickly blossomed under Dafoe's discerning if sporadic tutelage. By 1934 he had risen to managing editor at the then impressive salary of $3900 and was Dafoe's right-hand man and confidant. As advancing age took its physical (if not mental) toll on Dafoe, the latter increasingly relied on his trusted protégé, thus blurring the normally clear distinction between editor and managing editor. By the 1930s no one challenged Dafoe's editorial prerogatives, least of all the paper's owners, Victor Sifton and his brother Clifford, Jr, but in practice Ferguson's input was considerable.⁷

As Dafoe's nickname – 'the Chief' – would imply, his employees held him in a mixture of awe, admiration, and affection. Certainly, it rarely crossed anyone's mind to dispute his pronouncements, at least openly. On the contrary, for most of the staff, thinking or doing something in the 'Dafoe way' became its own justification. Day-to-day operations, however, increasingly fell to Ferguson, a man blessed with a rare talent for marrying efficiency and informality. Gruff externals masked a sensitive, loyal interior which endeared him to subordinates. Ferguson's intellectual powers certainly matched Dafoe's, and the two men were in sympathy on most major issues. On the rare occasions when they were not, Ferguson deferred gracefully and bridled at the mere suggestion that he was suppressing his own personality or views.[8] The bonds of mutual affection and respect which developed between them over the years were strong indeed.

Dafoe's manner was always grandfatherly, soft-spoken, and amiable, and in his sixties and seventies he was still maintaining a work schedule which would have exhausted many men half his age. Ferguson, with his passion for whiskey and a working vocabulary that would have made a stevedore blush, was equally hard-driving. His manner could be (and frequently was) brusque to the point of rudeness, especially with the pretentious, and first impressions were usually intimidating. Yet in the informal confines of the *Free Press* editorial offices, colleagues remembered him as a patient, sentimental, warm-hearted man. The invariable mucker's pose – 'What do you think? I think it's crap!' – was simply a useful ploy to force others to think.[9]

The *Free Press* editorial team took enormous pride in working for what they all believed was Canada's most influential editorial page, and even experienced newcomers quickly found themselves swept up in the surge.[10] The Dafoe-Ferguson style ensured that the humblest writer or reporter felt important and that those with talent blossomed. What made everyone's situation infinitely more tolerable, of course, was the realization that they were being directed by individuals they respected personally and professionally, and not, as was usually the case, by someone whose principal qualification was ownership of the newspaper.

Alexander Grant Dexter, the third member of the *Free Press* triumvirate, was born at St Andrew's, Manitoba, on 3 February 1896. His father, once a prosperous and well-connected lawyer, had been ruined during one of the periodic collapses of the Winnipeg real estate market shortly after his son's birth. In the aftermath of this financial and social débâcle, the father moved to New York in an unsuccessful effort to re-establish himself. Meanwhile, Grant's mother and the children stayed on with relatives for a time before moving to Hamilton. The father's death some years later reduced the family to poverty. Grant, the youngest of the five Dexter children, could never accept this situation and blamed his father for all the family's troubles. By 1910 their situation had become impossible and they trooped back to Manitoba, again to live with relatives. Fortunately, the new surroundings proved much happier for the youngster, who not only enjoyed farm life but found in his uncle the father figure he yearned after. At the age of fourteen, he enrolled at Brandon College, a small Baptist school, but withdrew after only one year when he discovered that his mother was paying the tuition out of the small amount his father had left her. Not long after, a family friend who happened to be an acquaintance of Dafoe's managed to get him a copy boy's position at the *Free Press*.

Dexter's job at the paper consisted of rounding up members of the early morning shift who were a little the worse for wear. In one of those Horatio Alger–style strokes of luck, a mid-summer thunderstorm and some runaway circus elephants abruptly changed his status. With no one available sober enough to cover the story, Dexter 'cooked' a report. The initiative, if not the copy, caught Dafoe's eye, and he promptly promoted Dexter to 'cub' reporter, a jack-of-all-trades apprenticeship. As with so many other young men, however, the call of king and country soon interrupted his budding career. Enlisting in the Fort Garry Horse in 1915, Trooper Dexter spent the following summer and autumn standing behind the line at the Somme, waiting for the breakthrough that never came. He didn't ever see action, and he passed the final year of the war in England recuperating from 'trench fever' and an ear problem.

Dexter arrived back in Winnipeg just in time to put his cavalry skills to use as a 'special' during the general strike. When the strike collapsed, Dafoe assigned him to cover the trial of the ringleaders. Finally, in 1924, after having served his apprenticeship as a political reporter covering the Manitoba legislature, Dafoe posted him to the press gallery in Ottawa where he spent all but nine of the remaining thirty-seven years of his life, in the process becoming the standard by which his generation of parliamentary reporters were judged.[11] Maintaining a full-time bureau in Ottawa was a considerable expense, all the more for a Prairie newspaper, but Dafoe was convinced it would pay real dividends. Events proved him right. As the years passed, Dexter became more and more proficient at obtaining the high-grade political intelligence that was so valuable to Dafoe as he mapped editorial strategy. In part, this was a tribute to Dexter's superb reporting skills, but, as he readily admitted, much of the information came his way simply because he represented Dafoe and the *Free Press* at a time when their political influence was at its zenith.[12]

Dexter was a tireless and painstaking researcher, and, like his mentor, he amassed a prodigious collection of files on every conceivable subject. Naturally curious and a voracious reader, he would feverishly pursue one topic after another. Apart from being obvious requirements of his job, these formidable efforts at self-education reflected both a deep-seated consciousness of his lack of formal schooling – he had gone only as far as grade 10 – and the emotional insecurity he never completely overcame. These factors also explain his tendency to be too impressed by strong arguments and personalities and, more generally, they account for his elevation of Dafoe into a father figure of heroic proportions. Certainly, none of Dexter's ideas ever diverged far from Dafoe's, and most were clearly derivative. For his part, Dafoe, with strong paternal instincts and disappointing sons, understandably took a fatherly pride in the achievements of his '*Free Press* boys,' including Dexter, though among this group there is no question that Ferguson occupied the first place.[13]

From an editorial perspective, however, the real significance of this history is that mutual affection, professional respect, and, to a remarkable degree, a shared world view bound the three men together. The result was a formidable editorial team clearly superior to that of any other contemporary English-language daily. And nowhere were the combined talents of the three more clearly revealed than in their approach to the appeasement politics of the late 1930s.

The events of 1917–19, in which Dafoe had been a central participant, profoundly shaped his view of Canada and its role in the world. As a nationalist, he recognized that Canadian sovereignty would be an empty achievement without national unity. And as an internationalist, he strongly believed that his country must exercise its newly won sovereignty in the cause of world security. Unlike many of his contemporaries, he saw no incompatibility between the two objectives. Even during the depths of the Depression, when its Prairie readers had more immediate concerns and much of the popular enthusiasm for the League of Nations was waning, the *Free Press* never ceased editorializing on the critical importance of a strong internal organization and the need for unwavering Canadian support of its activities. As far as Dafoe was concerned, collective security, whatever its inherent inadequacies and risks, held out more hope of preserving the peace than any of the alternatives, and the *Free Press* would support it unreservedly.[14]

Although Dafoe's conception of internationalism[15] found limited sympathy among either the influential or the general public, the support of his *Free Press* associates was never in question. Ferguson was a firm disciple of the collective security doctrine, although for obvious reasons he tended to be more sensitive to the perspective of the young Canadians who would have to fight any future war. Dexter had overcome some earlier doubts and absorbed the Dafoe gospel completely, and the same process of intellectual osmosis had won over the Siftons.[16]

Many (though by no means all) members of the Canadian Institute of International Affairs also echoed the views of the *Free Press* on collective security, and the links between the two organizations were close. Patterned after the British Royal Institute of International Affairs and, like it, intended to draw upon an elite membership from the senior echelons of business and the universities, the CIIA had been founded in 1928 to serve as a centre of research, education, and lobbying on foreign policy matters. Its members were of a high calibre intellectually and most were in their forties or younger. Dafoe's practical interest in the CIIA was obvious: as with the *Free Press,* he could use it to educate Canadians about their international responsibilities. The heart of the organization was the Winnipeg chapter, which Ferguson aptly characterized as 'the people I respect in the town together with a few lousy millionaires who give the dough.'[17] It was dominated by the two most influential figures within the CIIA's councils, Dafoe and his close friend and confidant, Edgar J. Tarr, an insurance executive who served for many years as the institute's national president, *éminence grise,* and driving force.

During the 1930s, as the deteriorating international situation led to a resurgence of power politics and the League's increasing irrelevancy, the *Free Press's* staunch and, among Canadian dailies, frequently solitary defence of the institution never slackened. Italy's invasion of Ethiopia in 1935 placed the Canadian government in an embarrassing situation, for as soon as the League formally condemned the Italians as aggressors the question of economic sanctions automatically arose. When Canadian delegate W.A. Riddell, who had been left without specific instructions from Ottawa, committed his country to support such a move, the newly elected Mackenzie King government was aghast. Although it moved hastily to clarify any misconception as to where Canada stood, the political damage had been done. Dedicated Canadian supporters of the League like Dafoe saw the Ethiopian war as the last good chance to put some teeth into collective security, and they bitterly resented Ottawa's retreat.[18]

The publicity surrounding the Ethiopian crisis and the Italian sanctions fiasco had spawned a renewed public interest in peace through the League. French-speaking Canada remained profoundly isolationist, however, and in most of English-speaking Canada commitment to League principles, revived or not, fell well short of the iron standard the *Free Press* advocated.[19] Most English-speaking Canadians were prepared to go to war for the mother country if it came to that, so could hardly be classed as 'isolationists,' but among them the feeling was widespread that Canada should watch from the sidelines, hoping for the best, and not be looking for opportunities to intervene. Dafoe, for whom such passivity was categorical proof of a weak mind, deplored such views. While privately he despaired to friends that collective security was impotent, at least for the time being, publicly he continued to argue that a coalition of socialists, imperialists, weak-kneed politicians, and civil servants were conspiring to emasculate the League against Canadians' wishes.[20] Of all these groups, the ones he loathed the most were the 'ready, aye, ready' ilk of Anglo-Canadian imperialist, the 'butler type,' as he acidly dismissed them, who seemed to gloat over every setback the League suffered. Unfortunately for Dafoe, their mindset remained the dominant one among the leading lights of English-Canadian economic, social, and political life.

The following autumn, Prime Minister King travelled to Geneva and 'piously reaffirmed Canada's devotion to the League principles' while simultaneously repudiating the whole collective security concept.[21] Dafoe responded scathingly, but he was out of touch with majority Canadian opinion and he knew it. Canadians, after all, had traditionally viewed the League as an agency for the *peaceful* resolution of disputes. A real system of collective security, which implied a willingness to use force, was likely to involve the country in some distant and unpopular war, and the domestic implications were unpleasant to say the least. This was a political fact of life which the prime minister grasped firmly, and his so-called betrayal of the League followed from that recognition plus an appreciation that great powers could invariably be counted upon to ignore the opinions of their smaller neighbours as soon as it suited their interests.[22] Nothing could convince Dafoe and the *Free Press,* however, that the small powers, including Canada, could not and should not have shown more initiative and promoted the principles of collective security more assertively.

Dafoe looked ahead with foreboding. He was satisfied that the *Free Press* had made its points clearly, and for now there was nothing else to say. But when the next crisis broke, he wanted Dexter in London to serve as his eyes and ears. In the meantime, Dexter would be able to provide him and the paper's readers with reports free of the anti-League bias that coloured most of the English and American press accounts of the international situation. Dexter's initial reaction to the move was a combination of annoyance and trepidation which even some well-timed praise from Dafoe failed to extinguish entirely. Arrangements were speedily completed, and in October 1936, Dexter, still 'groaning heavily,' joined the tiny contingent of full-time Canadian correspondents on Fleet Street.[23] Undoubtedly with an eye to influencing his reports (and Dafoe's editorials), the ever-cautious prime minister had arranged a meeting with Dexter before the latter left Ottawa. During their session, King had patiently stated and restated his argument that foreign affairs, as the principal threat to national unity, had to be downplayed at all costs. Needless to say, the discussion left Dexter unmoved.[24]

The *Free Press* had maintained a loose arrangement with the *Manchester Guardian* for many years and it was out of their editorial offices that Dexter now operated. Certainly the *Guardian* connection had its uses. For instance, Frederick Voigt, their temperamental but able diplomatic correspondent and no friend of the new Germany, proved to be a particularly obliging source when Dexter was willing to pick up the tab for a meal and drinks. Such professional outlays, though money well spent, quickly threatened to reduce Dexter to a hand-to-mouth existence. Fortunately for him, Ferguson appreciated that they could not operate in London on an Ottawa budget and he slowly managed to apprise Victor Sifton of the fact.

Despite his financial difficulties and the appalling weather of his first English winter, Dexter's greatest initial disappointment was the attitude displayed by most of the Englishmen with whom he regularly dealt. When confronted with a Canadian, he regaled Ferguson, they would infuriatingly 'pontificate, high hat, talk you down to rat-hole dimensions and, finally, urinate on you and go their way.' The only noticeable distinction, he noted bemusedly, was that while some believed 'to [the] core that Canadians will seize spades, pitchforks, axes [and] crowbars and rush headlong to interpose themselves between any and all enemies of the good old Motherland,' others 'disdainfully inquire as to why we still hold onto the apron strings.' Even worse than these encounters, however, were those with the numerous anglicized Canadians 'who ape the Englishman like so many monkeys in a zoo.'²⁶ Despite these early difficulties and disappointments, Dexter found his new beat an exciting challenge and soon settled in. The weeks passed quickly and, before long, he was churning out the reams of first-rate copy that Dafoe and Ferguson had expected, the bulk of them dealing with either trade matters or foreign policy. They were much relieved to note that their man had not been seduced by the Tories, a danger against which one could never take too many precautions.²⁷

Dafoe, of course, had long been suspicious of Whitehall's policy towards the dictators, and with good reason. Whereas Mackenzie King had been merely 'open and callous in his denial of Canada's obligations [to the League] ... the British [had] been treacherous, two-faced and tricky beyond even their own records.'²⁸ Both Ferguson and Dafoe looked ahead to 1938 convinced that the next twelve months would force Canadians 'uneasily and reluctantly' to confront the consequences of collective security's failure, with the responsibility of the *Free Press* being to do 'whatever we can ... to demonstrate the folly of isolation.'²⁹ But with Dafoe preoccupied with his work on the Royal Commission on Dominion-Provincial Relations and consequently absent from Winnipeg for weeks on end, Ferguson would be the man on the spot.³⁰

Dexter, in contrast, was now so thoroughly enjoying his work that he happily endured even the rigours of the club, luncheon, and dinner party circuit. Participation was socially *de rigueur*, but, more to the point, provided excellent opportunities to make useful contacts and catch the latest political gossip.³¹ At these get-togethers, Dexter frequently bumped into the counsellor of the Canadian High Commission, Lester 'Mike' Pearson. Although the two men were already on a first-name basis – they had been neighbours in Ottawa – their friendship really blossomed in London. Pearson was an energetic, able, and extremely ambitious young diplomat with an endearing, outgoing manner that proper Englishmen tended to associate with the more democratic sort of colonial. His relations with his boss, Vincent Massey, were cordial enough, but as the commission's ranking professional he inevitably found working in the shadow of a diplomatic amateur like Massey frustrating. As for Pearson's understandable desire to do real diplomacy, opportunities were scarce. The last thing the prime minister needed was an act of diplomatic derring-do by one of his eager young foreign service officers. Discussions of the menacing developments in Europe which somehow might be even obliquely perceived as an official position were, to say the least, discouraged, a position with which Dr O.D. Skelton, the undersecretary of state for external affairs, was in full sympathy. As a result, Canadian diplomats abroad, with Riddell's fate etched clearly in their minds, were to 'say nothing and do nothing.'[32] Indeed, to prevent his being ensnared in the 'Whitehall web,' Pearson had actually received explicit instructions not to become too well-informed about what was going on.[33]

By the beginning of 1938, Pearson no longer had any faith that disarmament and League-style collective security could ensure the peace and he was deeply concerned where Britain was leading and Canada following.[34] Since the *Free Press* strongly favoured a public debate on Canadian foreign policy options, the newspaper gave Pearson a potentially wide audience for his personal views. Moreover, Pearson knew from experience that Dexter was trustworthy and discreet. From Dafoe's point of view, the young diplomat's opinions might still be too isolationist for the *Free Press's* taste, but at least they were strongly nationalistic and any information he leaked would be an invaluable intelligence coup for the paper. Pearson did not hesitate; soon he began priming Dexter with the gist of virtually all the information to which he had access, whether from the Department of External Affairs or the Foreign Office. In doing so, Pearson was taking a considerable, if calculated, risk. To distance himself from suspicion, he warned Skelton that Dexter 'was a new type of Canadian journalist ... energetic, independent and intelligent,' and, by implication, presumably difficult to put off. It certainly suited Pearson's purposes that Dexter and 'other responsible Canadian journalists [be briefed] fully' by External officials who would still be able to make it clear to them 'which of our remarks were confidential and which were not,' and such was his candid advice.[35] But Skelton had already cautioned Pearson about his associations with newspapermen, and one suspects was rather more sceptical about Dexter and the trouble he could cause. Thus, when a report embarrassing to the government – namely, anything dealing with Canadian foreign policy – graced the pages of the *Winnipeg Free Press* during the ensuing months, it was hardly surprising that eyes in Ottawa turned in Pearson's general direction. Dexter covered his friend's trail as best he could – well enough, indeed, that Pearson never received anything stronger than a scolding from his superiors – but the two men were to have some close scrapes.

Dexter, for his part, was almost apologetic every time one of his stories stirred up the political waters at home. After one report had apparently raised 'an incredible amount of hell' in Skelton's office, he confided sheepishly to Ferguson: 'Here I am, a good grit [sic] who did what I could to advance the cause of the [Liberal] party and who has any number of friends within it, doing nothing but making trouble for them.'[36] A few weeks later, referring to another column he was preparing to send, Dexter remarked only half-jokingly to Ferguson that 'Mike and the others faint[ed] when they had gotten a peek.'[37] While Ferguson recognized the necessity of preserving confidences, even a suggestion that Dexter might be softening his stories to protect his civil servant and Liberal friends left him less than amused. Dexter's job in London, Ferguson bluntly reminded him, was to help the *Free Press* provide its readers with the truth, and if that meant exposing a Liberal government's failings from time to time, so be it. Dexter was chagrined, especially at the implication that he had weakened on the Dafoe-Ferguson foreign policy line. He had merely been worried that some injudicious comment in the paper would tip their hand prematurely and give King a chance to muzzle their source. 'The government's foreign policy is wrong [and] we need only be patient and events will play into our hands,' he explained to Ferguson. Then, 'we will get clean shots, not shots through the hedges.'[38] Both men wrote off the incident as a misunderstanding, but in fact it illustrated only too clearly Dexter's difficulty in distinguishing between the Liberal and the national interest and the perils associated with his being on such friendly terms with his sources.

On 11 March 1938 German troops marched unopposed into Austria. As Dexter noted gloomily in his diary a few days later, 'the situation ... has been going from bad to worse and worse to terrible.'[39] The *Free Press* responded with predictable outrage, wondering aloud whether Czechoslovakia would be the next victim of Nazi Germany's 'naked aggression' while leaving no doubt that collective security was the only hope of the democracies. Needless to say, such 'stirring up in the ... press of the minds of the people' was the last thing Mackenzie King desired.[40]

However clear developments might be to Dafoe, Ferguson, and Dexter, neither Manitobans nor Canadians in general were much moved by such plain speaking, or at least they were not moved in the *Free Press*'s direction. Doubtless, a great majority of readers found the worsening European situation alarming, but continued to hope against hope that somehow war could be avoided. That was appeasement's very attraction, after all, and explains why it had such broad support in Canada as in Britain and France. In contrast, the *Free Press*'s continual hectoring on collective security seemed no better than warmongering to Canadian isolationists and, because it questioned the wisdom of exclusive reliance on Britain, patent disloyalty to the imperialist element.[41] Even the *Free Press* acknowledged bitterly that the prime minister's quasi-isolationist policy of drift might be what the majority desired. But to Dafoe and his adherents, isolationism in any form – and that included appeasement – was dangerously naïve and had to be firmly resisted.[42]

Shortly after the *Anschluss,* Ferguson sailed for England to assess the situation firsthand. He spent several weeks in and around London renewing old acquaintances and meeting with informed sources Dexter managed to line up, including, Pearson. Ferguson wanted to clarify two points in particular: the current attitude and the future posture of British policy-makers towards the dictators. He arrived prepared to hear the worst and was not disappointed. Everyone seemed to agree that appeasement, which violated all Ferguson's principles of international relations, not to mention international morality, was the favoured policy and that its support in influential circles was growing. After returning to Winnipeg, Ferguson proceeded to set down his thoughts about 'the Problem,' roundly condemning appeasement and appeasers in ten lengthy articles which, as Vincent Massey lamented to the editor of the *Times,* served to confirm that Ferguson 'appears to be incurable in his suspicion of British policy.'[43] Seldom had the Canadian high commissioner made a more astute observation. When Ferguson uttered similar criticisms on his regular foreign policy commentaries for CBC radio, he caused such a furore among prominent Canadian Conservatives – an indignant Arthur Meighen denounced them as 'scandalous and reeking with ignorance' – that an embarrassed network abruptly cut him off the air.[44] This development, of course, moved Ferguson not an inch, and, with Dafoe's approval, he made sure that Dexter's grim reports, along with every wire service account of Nazi thuggery he could lay his hands on, received front-page play.

During the last days of summer, as the situation in Central Europe continued to deteriorate, there was plenty to be grim about. Using the fate of its German-speaking minority as a pretext, Hitler was casting a covetous eye on Czechoslovakia. By now, Pearson had become thoroughly disillusioned with Anglo-French appeasement and his own government's acquiescence to it.[45] As the High Commission's political officer, he was shown most of the pertinent Foreign Office files for his job of making summaries of them and passing these accounts on to Massey for his perusal and forwarding to Ottawa. These were the summaries he let Dexter read, and which Dexter promptly mailed or cabled in memo form to Winnipeg.[46] The advantages to the *Free Press* were obvious: Ferguson and Dafoe could anticipate developments that were now changing rapidly and respond editorially in anticipation of the event or, if after it had occurred, then at least with considerably more forethought than their newspaper rivals. 'Newshunting here is tough business,' a frustrated Dexter moaned. Through Voigt and other contacts he had nurtured at the *Guardian*, he had some idea of what was going on. Still, without Pearson he would often have been left in the dark, and he knew it.[47] But as the leaks became more flagrant, shielding Pearson became a very sticky problem. Fortunately, Massey was more interested in the social perks of his post and preferred not to think about what might be going on behind his back between Pearson and Dexter, but handling Skelton and King was another matter. While Dexter continued to forward the less urgent material by mail, he now began disguising the content of cables as much as he could, using a crude but satisfactory code drawn up by Ferguson. Even here, the managing editor's contempt for the Nazis showed through – in the new *Free Press* scheme, Hitler became 'Cohen.'[48] For some time, and presumably with Pearson's agreement, Dexter had also been passing on much of his intelligence to Voigt and his editor, James Bone. Apart from his wanting them to know what was happening, stories based on Pearson's briefings appearing in the *Guardian* would deflect suspicions in Ottawa by suggesting a direct Foreign Office leak to Fleet Street. Dexter was counting, too, on the fact that any material sent to Winnipeg would not show up on Ottawa desks for several days after publication, and Pearson's bosses, he assumed, were now far too busy to read any but the most recent newspapers very carefully.[49] As the Czech crisis deepened, Pearson began briefing Dexter almost daily; as a result, Dexter's knowledge of what was happening during the next critical days was as complete as and certainly more up to date than that any official in Canada could claim. No editor could have asked for better reporting, and Ferguson was the first to acknowledge it, as well as Pearson's courage for taking such risks.[50]

Dafoe now believed, or at any rate had convinced himself, that *Free Press* readers were finally conscious of the seriousness of the situation. More significantly, he thought the public were 'pretty much convinced that we have been and are on the right track,' that 'people will read what we say and believe it, too, which adds to our responsibility.'[51] Having concluded that war was now inevitable, and determined to set the record straight before it broke out, Dafoe hurried back to Winnipeg in early September. The ensuing broadside pulled no punches. 'Who were the warmongers,' he asked rhetorically, 'the upholders of the principle of collective security or the believers in unilateral understandings between the democratic countries and the dictators?'[52] During the succeeding week, the *Free Press* editorial page alternately castigated the appeasers and cheered the British government's apparently new-found willingness to stand up to Hitler, all the while firmly reminding Ottawa of its obligations under Article XVI of the League Covenant to participate in any collective defence effort.[53]

In mid September, just when war seemed imminent, British prime minister Neville Chamberlain temporarily defused the crisis by offering to negotiate the Sudeten question directly with Hitler. Dexter had known what was afoot and suspected the resultant concessions would only whet Germany's appetite, an estimate Dafoe and Ferguson agreed with completely. The *Free Press* dismissed the settlement with its plebiscite forced on the hapless Czechs as a complete fraud. By contrast, most Canadians, Mackenzie King included, greeted the news with relief and even some optimism.[54] Yet, as the *Free Press* predicted, the 'settlement' promptly began to unravel.

On 22 September, Chamberlain returned to Germany for another meeting with Hitler. The idyllic surroundings of the spa at Bad Godesberg might have struck some as an appropriate spot for Europe to take the cure, but Hitler was in a truculent mood and the talks failed miserably. Looking back, it is often difficult to appreciate just how fearful ordinary people were of war in September 1938. The Great War's endless slaughter was still a fresh and painful memory, and another clash promised to be even more drawn out and bloody with the added horror of civilian casualties on an enormous scale. On 26 September, to celebrate their wedding anniversary, the Dexters went to a concert, somewhat ironically an all-Wagner program. In his diary entry for that evening, Dexter poignantly captured the terrifying sense of unfolding tragedy:

> Alice looked down on all the young men on the promenade floor wondering what would happen to them. Driving home through Hyde Park – gangs of men swinging picks and shovels, digging air raid shelters and gun emplacements. Search lights set about 3' above the ground – shadows thrown grotesquely on [the] grass beyond – low hanging branches edging out light – russet leaves – dying and glissening with dew. Fearsome scene. Al[ice] cried. So we drove along – sand bagging operations underway – trenches being dug in every park – guns with their snouts pointing skywards – RAF machines circling about above London.[55]

The following day, fearing the worst, a shaken Dexter made plans to move his family to the relative safety of North Wales.

On 28 September, the same day the Royal Navy mobilized, the British government accepted Hitler's surprise proposal for a four-power conference at Munich and Chamberlain flew to Germany for the third time in a fortnight. Thanks to Pearson, Dexter knew that Hitler had moderated his claims on Czechoslovakia and that the much relieved British were bent on accommodation. So the Czechs would be thrown overboard after all. Dexter immediately cabled his scoop to Ferguson, but with the recommendation that they use the information only in a 'generalized way' and then only if 'Stone' [Pearson] could be 'absolutely protected.'[56] There was no way Ferguson would sit on the story; it was far too important not to publish, and not least to the paper's reputation. A special edition of the *Free Press* hit the streets at 9:15 AM, 28 September, less than an hour after Dexter's cable had reached Ferguson's desk. To protect Pearson, he refrained from specifically mentioning Hitler's invitation, but his front-page account clearly indicated that new German proposals had broken the deadlock and in all likelihood averted war. Minutes after the 'Extra' went on sale on Winnipeg street corners, Foreign Office press officers in London made the story official.

In the early hours of 30 September, a four-power accord was reached and the Sudeten crisis ended. To most Canadians, the achievement was a diplomatic *tour de force* by the government of Prime Minister Neville Chamberlain and a complete vindication of its appeasement policy.[57] Not surprisingly, however, the general mood of relief and approval did not extend to the *Free Press,* where anger and revulsion seemed decidedly more appropriate feelings. Dafoe's sentiments hardly need explaining. As for Ferguson, even during the darkest moments of the crisis he had clung to his belief that Germany feared war and, when faced with a little British resolution, would back down. This made the result all the more bitter for him to accept, and his contempt for Chamberlain and every other appeaser now became, like Dafoe's, almost pathological. To Dexter, the sellout of the Czechs was a moral outrage that left him completely depressed.[58]

Dafoe, despite being in Ottawa attending to his Royal Commission duties for most of the month, had been in daily contact with Ferguson by telephone since the crisis had broken. He now quickly penned what has become his most famous editorial. Provocatively entitled 'What's the Cheering For?' it was a calm, lengthy, almost academic recapitulation of two years of Nazi 'guarantees' and the fruits of their 'bloodless aggression.' When he summed up his thoughts, the depth of his revulsion for what had transpired and the implicit shame he felt for the attitudes of many of his countrymen spilled out:

The doctrine that Germany can intervene for racial reasons for the 'protection' of Germans on such grounds as she thinks proper in any country in the world which she is in a position to coerce, and without regard to any engagements she had made or guarantees she had given, has now not only been asserted but made good; and it has been approved, sanctioned, certified and validated by the governments of Great Britain and France, who have undertaken in this respect to speak for the democracies of the world. This is the situation and those who think it is all right will cheer for it.[59]

This was definitely not the sort of conclusion likely to endear Dafoe or his newspaper to the great majority of its readers, and reaction to the editorial was prompt and overwhelmingly negative. Among the imperialist element, criticism of the mother country in her moment of peril was cowardly and disloyal. Isolationists, regardless of their stripe, were more firmly convinced than ever that a European war was none of Canada's concern and that the last thing Canada needed to be doing was agitating to become involved in one. To the vast majority, who were loyal to Britain but considered themselves Canadians first and did not want to fight a war for 'abstractions' even if they supported the idea of collective security, the *Free Press*'s stand was incomprehensible and unwarranted. In Winnipeg, copies of the paper were burned in the street or torn up and returned, and within a week irate customers had cancelled more than 12,000 subscriptions, about one-sixth of the paper's total. Some local businesses discontinued advertising and the editorial offices were bombarded with critical letters. Longtime cronies of Dafoe at the Manitoba Club snubbed him, while other Winnipeggers even jeered him in the street. Nor was Ferguson exempt; local worthies who had asked him to explain the *Free Press*'s position at an Empire Club luncheon hissed him off the stage.[60] Despite the antagonistic reaction, however, Dafoe and Ferguson never flinched. The *Free Press* had hit hard on a matter of principle and would continue to do so because Dafoe knew events would confirm their stand – and win back readers.[61] To his credit, Victor Sifton was prepared to back him and absorb the losses.

The *Free Press* was the only major Canadian newspaper to denounce the Munich settlement categorically. Moreover, with fourteen editorials and numerous articles dealing with the crisis between 3 and 29 September its coverage had been almost twice as extensive as that in any other paper. The Montreal *Gazette* and the Toronto *Telegram* and *Globe and Mail* with their predictable jingo-imperialist posturing excepted, other leading English-language dailies were at least mildly supportive of King and Chamberlain. French-language dailies, being universally opposed to involvement in any conflicts that were none of Canada's business, strongly endorsed the government's stated position of 'no commitments.' Another war, after all, had especially traumatic implications for Quebec, as the title of *Le Devoir*'s 29 September editorial – 'L'intervention, c'est la conscription' – spelled out all too clearly.[62]

In the immediate aftermath of Munich, Dafoe was not sure how the *Free Press* should proceed. He suggested a few general points that Ferguson might pursue and was anxious that the paper at least refute the outrageous contention being bandied about in some quarters that collective security would make war inevitable. Ferguson felt they had taken a strong line so far; why not sit back for a time and let Canadians digest the full implications of Munich?[63] It was a sensible strategy and the paper adopted it.

Two years in London had left Dexter fed up with the life of a foreign correspondent, and Sifton's promise that he would be home by Christmas raised his morale considerably. He spent his last weeks putting together a dozen articles for Ferguson detailing the course of the Munich Crisis. The series impressed Dafoe, not in the least, as he candidly admitted, 'because [they] confirm me in my own conclusions.'[64] Needless to say, a reader of even modest intelligence would have had no difficulty distinguishing between the forces of good (collective security) and evil (isolationism and appeasement) in Dexter's final drafts.

Within months, as Dafoe and Ferguson had confidently predicted, events exposed the Munich 'peace' as a sham. During the winter of 1938–9, most Canadians were coming to accept that another European war involving Great Britain was all but inevitable. One small measure of changing attitudes was the reception Dexter received during a month-long speaking tour sponsored by the CIIA (and paid for by Victor Sifton) which took him to every major city from Montreal to Vancouver during the early weeks of 1939. While a warm response from institute members was hardly surprising, Dexter was taken aback by the serious attitude that greeted him when he delivered to several Canadian Club and businessmen's luncheons his pessimistic message on the looming Nazi threat.[65] Another example of the changed mood was the King government's acceleration of an admittedly still modest rearmament program. Other than that concession, however, it continued to hold to its twin policies of 'no commitments' and 'parliament will decide' more tightly than ever. Unlike the *Free Press*, which on this issue could and did speak for itself and the consequences be damned, Mackenzie King bore the responsibility of holding the country and his party together; he felt, probably correctly, that he had little room for manoeuvre in either instance. Years later the Liberal leader still grumbled over how much easier it had seemed to govern the country from Winnipeg than from Ottawa.[66] The problem for the prime minister and his colleagues, of course, was that while a growing majority of Canadians now saw war as inevitable, there was anything but unanimity over just what the extent of Canada's involvement should be. So while King's public statements left less and less doubt that Ottawa should stand by Britain's side in any war with Nazi Germany, he remained considerably more vague when it came to spelling out precisely what that participation would entail.

On 15 March, 1939 Germany repudiated the Munich accord and marched into what remained of Czechoslovakia. For the *Free Press,* this was complete vindication; as Dave Rogers, editor of the Sifton-owned *Regina Leader-Post,* reminded his cabinet minister brother, Norman, they had been 'dead right all the way through' and now everyone knew it.[67] With pointed sarcasm, Ferguson entitled his commentary 'Lies and Optimism: A Record of Nazi Lies and British Belief in Them Since the Munich Pact.'[68] It was difficult to find any Canadian who believed in appeasement now, but Ferguson was not above pricking a few memories – and consciences. 'There were quarters where it was appreciated that isolationism, in the 20th century interdependent world, was a myth without foundation in reality, but they were voices crying out in the wilderness,' he pointedly observed, and 'today we face the consequences of [these] follies.'[69]

During the remaining few months of peace, as the democratic countries scrambled in *sauve qui peut* fashion to build alliances and rearm, the temptation to gloat must have been overwhelming, but Ferguson agreed with Victor Sifton that the *Free Press* should avoid 'antagoniz[ing] hopelessly the dummkopfs who are now groping towards the idea that Neville [Chamberlain] had been wrong right through.'[70] Among these, in the *Free Press* view, were Mackenzie King, his cabinet, and the nest of anti-League isolationists at External Affairs led by Skelton and Loring Christie, whose supposed sinister influence on the prime minister had infuriated the *Free Press* crowd for years.[71] Still, even the paper's moderate tone was too much for some of the 'dummkopfs.' In the House of Commons, Mackenzie King took a swipe at 'those who are continually asserting that war ... is only postponed'; in what was clearly a thinly disguised attempt to rebut the *Free Press,* he offered that 'it must have taken a good deal of confidence in one's powers of guessing the future to be sufficiently certain of what might happen in 1940 to have been ready to plunge the world into war in 1938.'[72]

For Dafoe, the League and collective security had involved basic principles; there could be no backing away from their defence regardless of any short-term embarrassment, financial or otherwise, to him or the paper. The future, of course, confirmed his stand and, with it, his position as something of a prophet and patron saint among postwar internationalists. Nevertheless, although a model of journalistic technique, the campaign conducted by

Dafoe, Ferguson, and Dexter was, practically speaking, a futile exercise. Only a minority of their readers had been prepared to listen to their arguments, and on this issue their editorial influence had been almost nil; the exercise only illustrated the limited influence of any newspaper in shaping hardened public opinion. Throughout, there had been an element of naïveté in Dafoe's position, as Ferguson later claimed to have grasped. It lay in Dafoe's chronic overestimation of the capacity of nations, large and small, to act responsibly towards one another, and in particular the influence the weak could realistically expect to exert over the strong. This was precisely King's and Skelton's criticism of Dafoe.[73] And while Dafoe's position that Canada, like New Zealand, could have taken a principled stand did carry a certain logic, it also ignored the considerations of national unity that the Canadian government had to weigh.

During the late 1930s nationalist critics of both neutralist and collective security convictions created a great deal of noise. In intellectual circles, international affairs, even in its most technical aspects, was a constant topic of debate. Most Canadians, however, only wanted peace and to be left alone, and they cared little about what was said. In the aftermath of Munich, when appeasement became discredited and war inevitable, the public overwhelmingly opted for the comfort of the British tie and prepared for the worst. At least Dafoe, Ferguson, Dexter, and Victor Sifton, driven by their shared conviction that the *Free Press* had a mission to keep the idea of civilized international behaviour and collective security embodied in the League of Nations alive in Canada, had a public forum in which to promote their views – and a prominent one at that. Moreover, thanks to the close relationship Dexter had forged with Pearson, a development that was to prove a harbinger of things to come, the *Free Press* had been able to mount the strongest possible campaign – though, even with this advantage, not strong enough. Yet among the intellectual and opinion-making circles to which Dafoe, Sifton, and the others were consciously appealing, not to mention its mass of ordinary readers, the newspaper's solitary stands during the 1930s as self-appointed national conscience ultimately enhanced its prestige and made it a more effective proponent of collective security and internationalism in general during and after the war. Unfortunately, the 'Munich triumph,' by inflating the *Free Press's* sense of its own importance, also saddled it with a tradition its publishers and Dafoe's successors found harder to sustain. The implications of that problem, however, lay a decade or more in the future.

'When I make a talk these days, I find heads wagging assent when I turn to collective security,' Ferguson wrote Clifford Sifton with evident satisfaction only three months after the outbreak of the war. Unfortunately, 'the bill of goods has been sold too late.'[74] It had certainly not been for lack of trying by the *Free Press*. Moreover, in light of postwar Canadian attitudes, his verdict was also premature.

2

'The number one saboteur in Canada'

The *Financial Post* and Rearmament

As a loyal ally of private enterprise, the *Financial Post* had traditionally viewed Ottawa with deep suspicion. Its self-appointed duty was to impress upon government the virtues of 'business efficiency' and to check 'partisan excesses.' Just as war transformed the business-government relationship, so too it would necessitate a transformation in the outlook of the *Financial Post* and its publishers. That would not mean an abdication of its traditional responsibilities. As its aggressive and oftentimes bitter two-and-a-half-year campaign as watchdog over the government's role first in rearmament and then in the mobilization of the war economy would clearly indicate, the *Post* would ensure that errant government policies and administration would not go unquestioned.

The *Financial Post,* a weekly aimed at branch bank managers, had been launched in January 1907. As with most other Maclean Publishing ventures, the *Post* would be shaped by Colonel Maclean's able protégé and the company's driving force during the interwar years, Horace Talmage Hunter. Excessiveley cautious and pretty much of a plodder intellectually, Hunter liked to see himself as a master architect drafting basic principles and long-range plans although in practice he exercised tight control over even the most mundane administrative matters. Moreover, his style of management was very paternalistic. While loyalty and competence were both highly valued, the latter could be sacrificed if need be to ensure the former. Working one's way up through the ranks was the company ideal, but in practice the key to advancement lay in becoming attached to a company favourite – with the predictable result that senior management became clogged with devoted mediocrities.

On the editorial side, Hunter laced his rhetoric with references to 'sound business' and 'sound government,' though it was never clear precisely what these terms meant except that they were a reflection of his unshakeable faith in the superiority of free enterprise. Translated into practice with the *Financial Post* they meant the paper would adopt a strong pro-business stance on all issues involving the business community – in other words, on all issues – and support the political party most attentive to that community's larger interests as defined by Hunter and his lieutenants.[1]

Foremost among these lieutenants was Floyd Sherman Chalmers. Raised in poverty by his grandparents, Chalmers's unhappy childhood left him with a yearning to belong that he never overcame. Graduating from high school in Toronto in 1917 with the marks but not the money for university, he had turned to journalism. From the first day Chalmers was hooked, though his budding career was soon interrupted by the war. He was lucky, however, and his military experience was confined to a year in England trying to master the intricacies of the tank. The postwar depression which greeted him after demobilization left little chance of his resuming work on a daily and, when the *Post* offered him a job as a combination reporter and advertising salesman at $30 a week, he took it.

Chalmers was a hard worker, ambitious, and a born salesman, qualities that Hunter, who was roundly dissatisfied with the *Post,* quickly noticed. Before long, it was clear that Chalmers was being groomed for the editorship, a position he finally claimed in 1925. His private assessment of the paper was that its tone was too combative and that it wasted too much ink on trivialities and tilting at windmills.[2] The fact that it had been a consistent money-maker for the company was due more to the weakness of the paper's competitors than its own strengths. Now Chalmers would have an opportunity to put his ideas into practice.

The new editor was a competent manager and a shrewd businessman. Despite pretensions to the contrary, Chalmers never showed more than an ordinary (some would say very ordinary) talent for the journalistic side of his work. His real strength was a knack for sensing that talent in others and harnessing it. As for his commitment to Maclean Publishing, that was total: Chalmers became the quintessential company man in an organization where that quality was valued very highly indeed. By the mid 1930s circulation was moving steadily ahead of competitors, and the improvement in the overall quality of the paper was apparent even to long-time critics like J.W. Dafoe.[3] Editorial judgments had become far more rational and, with respect to the two main parties, relatively nonpartisan, too. Meanwhile the news reporting, despite a small staff and a smaller budget, was also quite solid. If the *Financial Post* still soldiered loyally on behalf of the interests of the heavyweights of Canadian business and finance, it was no longer the unquestioning mouthpiece of past years.

A feature article in the 1 September 1938 issue of the *Post*'s sister publication, *Maclean's,* entitled 'Canada's Armament Mystery,' accused the Department of National Defence of shady dealings in the awarding of munitions contracts. The article, though written by Colonel George Drew, a well-known Ontario Conservative, was based entirely on the investigations of the magazine's managing editor, Arthur Irwin. It focused on a contract for Bren light machine guns recently awarded without tender to a company with solid connections to the Liberal party. Even at this late stage, rearmament remained a deeply divisive issue among Canadians. For the King government, which as Dafoe wryly observed, 'didn't know the Bren gun was loaded,'⁴ the ensuing scandal was acutely embarrassing.

To Hunter and the other leading lights of Maclean Publishing management, the application of 'sound business practices' to public administration was an article of faith and alerting Canadians to transgressions a clear duty.⁵ Reinforcing this principle was the bitterness they shared with many Canadian businessmen over the laggard pace of Ottawa's rearmament program. This tardiness had not only left the country virtually defenceless but denied depression-ravaged Canadian industry the considerable economic benefits that would have followed. Here was an opportunity to champion an issue in which the interests of the nation and not just of private enterprise were clearly at stake.

Immediately after Drew's article appeared, the *Financial Post,* which in Chalmers's absence (somewhat ironically he was touring Germany on an official press junket) was being edited in effect by Hunter himself, demanded an independent inquiry into all the allegations. Shaken and anxious to deflect criticism, the Mackenzie King government was only too eager to comply.⁶ When the resultant Davis Royal Commission began its hearings on 26 September it was quickly apparent that the government had shrewdly decided to defend itself by focusing on the motives of Maclean Publishing and, in particular, the Drew connection. Of leading Tories, only Arthur Meighen was more bitterly disliked by Liberals.⁷

Judge Davis's inquiry lasted two months and, although his report vindicated Maclean Publishing's role in the scandal, it also stopped short of accusing the Department of National Defence, as the *Financial Post* had come close to doing, of favouritism and patronage so blatant as to border on outright corruption. To dilute the impact of the judge's findings, Senator Norman Lambert, one of the abler Liberal 'backroomers,' took the precaution of distributing an advance 'summary' to the press which conveniently toned down the judge's more damaging criticisms of National

Defence practices.[8] A day before the final report was tabled, the prime minister attempted to spike critics' guns by pledging his government to implement its chief recommendation: the establishment of a defence purchasing board to oversee all military contracting.

Not surprisingly, the government's deft countermoves and the less than overwhelming support of the rest of the Canadian press for the *Post*'s stand that Ian Mackenzie, the minister of national defence, and his deputy, General Léo Laflèche, be fired quickly deflated the initial euphoria that had swept the weekly. Nevertheless, after some consultation, Hunter decided the paper would continue hammering away at the larger issue of government procurement practices, confident that the 'facts' must eventually arouse public indignation. Rather than accusations of corruption, it was attacks on 'inefficiency,' 'incompetence,' 'waste,' and the supposed chronic dearth in the Department of National Defence of 'men of integrity and the ordinary business ability ... required for the efficient management of any organization' that would set the tone of this follow-up campaign.[9]

At the first of a series of editorial conferences in March 1939 to work out a plan in detail, Irwin pointed to the reforms they had already achieved – namely, the the establishment of the Defence Purchasing Board and the appointment of more able staff to the Department of National Defence – and the tax dollars they would save. Ken Wilson, Chalmers's astute editorial lieutenant, sensed that the public felt the rearmament program's inadequacies had been pretty much addressed and that further press criticism was uncalled for. Indeed, it might even scare off future British war orders. To reinforce his case, he pointed to the increasingly angry tone of letters from the business community, letters that were more critical of the *Financial Post* than the government. If these grumblings solidified into outright resentment, advertising losses could cripple the company's lucrative trade papers. Wilson had been right: the government had outflanked the *Financial Post* by shifting the public's attention from the question of method to concrete result, namely rearmament, and by the spring of 1939 most English Canadians favoured rearmament – the faster the better. Few now cared, as Irwin had wryly pointed out, whether the source of supply was 'a thug or a parson.' As for trying to oust cabinet lightweights like Mackenzie, this might simply whet the public's appetite for bigger change. What if the government itself fell? Given the sad disarray in Conservative ranks, Hunter, Chalmers, Irwin, and Wilson found that a sobering thought.

The question was not whether incompetence and waste had been completely rooted out in Ottawa – no one at the *Post* believed that for a minute – but rather how to raise this issue most effectively in the paper's editorial and news columns. Backed by Irwin, Wilson argued for investigating other aspects of defence contracting, particularly the workings of the Defence Purchasing Board, where they were bound to uncover hard evidence of new scandals which would make it 'easier ... to build up in the minds of our readers the realization of the importance of the job we set out to do.'[10] Hunter embraced the plan enthusiastically and in early June detailed Irwin to carry out the investigation full time.[11] In the meantime, they would have to be patient, for breaking any stories prematurely would serve only to provide the government with an opening to discredit the process.

It was summer before the *Financial Post* again began firing editorial salvoes at the government.[12] The first had hardly landed before Canada was at war, a turn of events *Post* staffers immediately recognized was bound to divert attention from the government's shortcomings by encouraging a 'let's-get-on-with-it' attitude among the press and the public alike. Indeed, for a time, even the Conservatives seemed to have lost their taste for the issue. Chalmers frankly admitted that readers might perceive any further criticism as an anti-government vendetta. More importantly, there was now also the question of public confidence to consider and, indeed, government emissaries did approach Chalmers counselling caution on just these grounds.[13] Having weighed these same factors, Irwin, Hunter, and Napier Moore, the editor of *Maclean's,* responded with an amazing scheme: the company would secretly inform the prime minister that there would be no further exposés if the government dropped Mackenzie and launched a thorough overhaul of his department. Neither Hunter nor anyone else seems to have considered that the ploy, no matter how well intentioned, was nothing more than a dubious form political blackmail. At the last minute, however, Hunter, fearing the wily King would demand to see their proof and then use it to muzzle the *Post* and root out its sources, got cold feet and the offer was never extended. In the end, all that came from this round of soul-searching was a decision that the investigations and exposés would continue. As Chalmers put it, the war simply heightened the urgency of cleaning up the mess.[14]

In the months since the Bren gun affair had erupted, Mackenzie King had frequently considered sacking Ian Mackenzie. Though likeable enough and certainly a loyal party man, Mackenzie was no administrator; unfortunately, his private life also fell short of the standards usually looked for in ministers of the crown, at least by King. Now, thanks to the *Financial Post*'s persistent attacks, he was clearly becoming a heavy liability to the government.[15] Finally, on 19 September 1939, King shifted him to the politically harmless portfolio of Pensions and National Health. The *Post* welcomed the news, not in the least because it gave the paper a pretext to set about dropping the Bren gun issue without losing face. The new head of National

Defence was Norman Rogers, one of the cabinet's brightest minds and a
personal favourite of the prime minister. At Maclean Publishing, however,
Rogers's appointment was greeted with little enthusiasm. Hunter off-hand-
edly dismissed him as 'the type of university professor who is lacking in
knowledge of business,' while Chalmers's verdict was a hardly reassuring
'honest but weak.'[16]

Meanwhile, Ottawa was rife with rumours that the paper had accumulated explosive evidence of undue profit-taking in defence contracts.[17] For
the past six months, Irwin had been travelling across the country in a gru-
elling schedule of eighteen-hour days probing for fresh scandals, and plenty had come to light. His first leads, which had come from General A.G.L.
McNaughton, convinced both Irwin and his superiors that there must be a
lot more skeletons to uncover. During the ensuing weeks, many individuals, both inside and outside the government, had cooperated when approached, and some had actually sought him out to tell their story. His
informants were a diverse crew, from McNaughton to C.G. Power, the acting minister during Rogers's frequent absences, and Toronto businessman
and financier E.P. Taylor. Irwin's diligence now enabled the *Financial Post*
to expose a succession of contracting scams.[18] Most of them were leftovers
from the Mackenzie-Laflèche era and involved the time-honoured fields of
patronage – real estate and construction. Certainly there was nothing on the
scale of his revelations about the Bren gun contract a year earlier. Nevertheless, the allegations were serious enough and, judging from the boost
they gave *Post* circulation, the public were alarmed.[19] While an embarrassed
government initially restrained itself from commenting publicly in order to
avoid giving the reports any credibility, steps were promptly initiated to
ensure that each accusation was thoroughly investigated.[20] The results, it is
worth noting, quickly found their way to Wilson and confirmed every detail
of the newspaper's allegations.

When Conservative MPs began citing the *Financial Post* stories chapter
and verse, however, the government counter-attacked. Walter Thompson,
the chief press censor, telephoned Chalmers to ask why the paper continued to publish accounts which were obviously so damaging to public confidence, and which he had suggested to Irwin two months earlier should
cease. Thompson tried to be conciliatory and, while he stopped short of
ordering the *Post* to desist, he left no doubt that he thought this penalty appropriate. Thompson concluded their conversation by suggesting a meeting with Rogers, which he could arrange. Chalmers felt such a get-together
with the minister was pointless; only talking to King directly would do any
good. Reality dictated otherwise, however; as Thompson was quick to point
out, 'King saw no one' and Rogers it would have to be.[21]

This meeting was, to say the least, strained. Rogers first tried to persuade Chalmers to tone down the paper's attacks by assuring him that the department had been cleaned up and by reminding him that the press had a responsibility in wartime to forgo some rights of criticism for the sake of national unity. In principle, Chalmers agreed with this argument, but when the harried minister lectured Chalmers that running down *Post* allegations was now absorbing many of the department's best men virtually full time, Chalmers's sympathy evaporated. As far as he could see, the government had consistently and stubbornly refused to admit any wrongdoing and had repeatedly failed to reform unless pushed hard. Under the circumstances, the *Financial Post* felt it had an overriding public responsibility to expose the mess Irwin had uncovered and let the public judge. In truth, neither side had much sympathy for the other's position. Chalmers concluded that Rogers was honest and able, but blinded by his Liberal partisanship. For their part, the minister and his senior staff were more convinced than ever that the actions of the *Financial Post* were politically motivated. Rebuffed, the usually mild-mannered Rogers publicly rebuked the *Post* for 'deliberately misleading' Canadians; Chalmers responded with a series of sternly worded editorials dismissing these accusations and once again demanding more efficient government administration.[22]

The Liberals' surprise election call in January 1940 placed the *Financial Post* in a quandary: How could it continue to publish damaging criticism of the government's record without appearing partisan, at any rate to the Liberals and their sympathizers? No amount of discussion at editorial conferences seemed to produce a consensus on whether to desist temporarily. Even if in Hunter's considered opinion neither party deserved to be elected,[23] someone did have to win, and the fact that an 'independent organization such as The Financial Post [had] to do the digging and find out what is going on "behind the scenes"' hardly recommended the Conservatives in his eyes. The sad truth was, as he well knew, that when a prominent Conservative journalist had privately suggested that the party carry out its own investigations, no money could be found in party coffers. Certainly Hunter never took seriously Conservative leader Robert Manion's call for a cabinet drawing on the best men from all parties as well as able outsiders – his 'Best Brains' proposal. Indeed, he considered any sort of all-party government extremely dangerous, undoubtedly out of fear that it would fatally weaken the two-party system and open the door to radical, anti-business parties. In the end, despite deep reservations about Mackenzie King's supposed lack of enthusiasm for the war, Hunter and the *Financial Post* concluded that the country's best hope was a re-elected Liberal government stiffened 'with good, courageous, practical business leadership.'[24] During the last few weeks of the campaign the paper also resumed publication of Irwin's well-documented accounts of bungling and corruption. But as scandals went, the latest revelations were small fry.[25] Interestingly, they no longer carried Irwin's byline, an indication perhaps that Chalmers, ambitious and deeply involved in company politics, was now determined his paper would garner all the credit.

The re-election of the Liberals on 27 March 1940 caused no great disappointment in the editorial offices of the *Financial Post*. Yet the size of their mandate did raise two serious questions: Was it credible to continue attacking the government's preparedness record? Would the Liberals now feel any need to heed the *Post*'s advice? In a post-election scoop, Wilson reported that the much maligned War Supply Board (the successor to the earlier Defence Purchasing Board) was about to be reorganized into a full ministry, probably under the cabinet's resident business genius, C.D. Howe. Here, at least, was reason to hope that a 'strong business approach' to running the war economy was in the offing. Not surprisingly, when the new Department of Munitions and Supply materialized only a few weeks later, the *Post* welcomed the announcement enthusiastically.[26] The honeymoon was brief, however, for the paper was soon denouncing Howe's failure to utilize 'the cream of Canada's industrial brains.' What was needed, the *Post* argued, was an industrial czar with complete authority to direct the key work of the new department – procurement – along 'strong business lines,'[27] leaving Howe to handle overall policy-making and, of course, the thankless political responsibility of publicly defending the department's record.

The shift to attacks on the efficiency (though not the honesty) of the Department of Munitions and Supply was significant. Irwin had done his job very well – so well, in fact, that even relatively petty contracting scandals seemed to be occurring less frequently. Furthermore, while their exposure may have continued to occupy a disproportionate amount of the time of overworked ministers, these revelations seemed to have neglible impact on public opinion. More significantly, at least partly in response to the Bren gun affair and subsequent stories in *Maclean's* and the *Financial Post*, the government had rooted out most of the patronage from the defence sector.[28] Yet so suspicious were the *Post* staff that even when this result was corroborated by trusted informants, they had a hard time seeing, let alone acknowledging, that they had already achieved one of their principal objectives – a non-partisan war effort. This hesitation explains their surprise and disappointment when they found themselves reproached, sometimes vehemently, by a growing segment of the business community. What good was the *Post* doing by rehashing old mistakes? The government had already cleared them up or was in the process of doing so, and the performance of the war economy was now favourable by any standard. Furthermore, it seemed that many of the businessmen-bureaucrats Howe and the Wartime Prices and Trade Board had recruited shared the sentiments of their friends in the private sector. Finally, there were ominous signs of an advertiser backlash.[29]

Concurrently, however, the *Financial Post* was receiving far less flattering appraisals of the performance of the new Department of Munitions and Supply. For instance, R.K. Vaughan, the former head of the Defence Purchasing Board and one of Irwin's principal informants on the earlier stories, told Wilson that the situation in Ottawa was chaotic and crying out for competent people to be put in charge. Wallace Campbell, a Ford executive who, until his recent resignation, had been chairman of the War Supply Board, was another of the disgruntled businessman-bureaucrats who had similarly unburdened himself.[30] Wilson had an open mind when it came to the government's capacity to run things and he certainly displayed sound judgment on most matters. But even he had heard this litany often enough to conclude that 'an entirely business administration' of war production was needed to prevent a disaster.[31]

The simple fact is that Howe was trying to assemble, almost overnight, the largest organization the country had ever seen and the shakedown was inevitably proving painful. Many of the problems being encountered had the same source: the failure of Howe's personality and those of his businessmen-administrators to mesh. The very epitome of the engineer, Howe was a doer, not a thinker, and he bragged about the distinction. As the master of ad hoc improvisations, he was not concerned with peacetime procedures and costs. 'If we lose the war,' he liked to say, 'nothing will matter ... [and] if we win ... the cost will have been of no consequence and will have been forgotten.'[32] Of course he was right. What Howe frequently failed to take into account was businessmen's deeply ingrained suspicion of government interference in their operations. After all, 'government efficiency' was for most of them a contradiction in terms. Nor were patience and consideration of personal sensibilities Howe's longsuits. His self-proclaimed status as the only essential factor in the Canadian war equation reflected his enormous ego and talent in at best equal proportions and led him to be disdainful of political colleagues, bureaucrats, and businessmen alike.

Certainly Howe left few men unmoved, sparking admiring loyalty and brooding animosity, often in the same individuals. Unfortunately for the smooth functioning of Munitions and Supply, his was not the only overdeveloped ego involved. Another belonged to H.R. MacMillan, a wealthy British Columbia industrialist whom Howe had recruited as one of his principal lieutenants. A confrontation between the two was inevitable. Only the ground was in question, and that turned out to be aircraft production.

Canada's prewar aviation industry had been hardpressed to produce even one hundred aircraft a year, most of them copies of out-of-date designs. Now, chiefly to meet the needs of the British Commonwealth Air Training Plan, the same industry was being asked to turn out thousands of modern types. Predictably, the problems of converting the industry to a war footing were enormous. To speed things up, Howe had established a crown corporation, Federal Aircraft in Montreal. A feud promptly broke out between Howe's appointee as director-general of aircraft production, Ralph Bell, and Federal's abrasive manager (and well-known Howe crony), Ray Lawson. For business as well as ideological reasons, the privately owned Canadian aircraft manufacturers were intent on strangling the infant state-run aeronautical enterprise in its cradle and to that end gladly joined in Bell's anti-Lawson scheming.

This, in turn, attracted the attention of MacMillan, a passionate free enterpriser and an avowed Tory who harboured the gravest doubts about the government in general and the Department of Munitions and Supply in particular. Bluntly put, MacMillan saw a Liberal hack behind every filing cabinet at Howe's department and he dismissed the minister's purported administrative genius as a joke. Indeed, he had hardly arrived in Ottawa before he began fulminating openly at dinner parties and the like, proclaiming that he would either take Howe's job or go home, 'leaving a mess well exposed at the Government's doorstep.'[33] During the late autumn he regaled Chalmers with accounts of the complete disorganization within the Howe empire; in typically straightforward fashion he bluntly asked the *Financial Post* editor just what he was going to do with the information.[34] Thanks to the tireless efforts of Wilson, Irwin, and Grant Dexter, the *Winnipeg Free Press* Ottawa correspondent who doubled as a *Post* stringer, Chalmers already knew the whole story. He just did not feel the time was right to make use of it.

Chalmers's strategy was to publicize the aircraft muddle as a surefire way of forcing Howe's hand and making him clean up the 'mess' in his department once and for all. The opening salvo was a front-page article in the 16 November 1940 issue of the *Financial Post* calling yet again for the appointment of a 'war chief' to oversee production. The paper quoted MacMillan by name, and a host of other 'top business executives' serving in Ottawa joined in anonymously.[35]

Although it was not yet public knowledge, the cabinet had just handed MacMillan the chairmanship of the Wartime Requirements Board, which had been set up to impose production priorities and a semblance of financial accountability on Munitions and Supply – in effect to rein Howe in. While MacMillan clearly had the necessary brains and experience, his ego, low boiling point, and political unreliability made his choice a calculated gamble.[36] From the *Post*'s perspective, MacMillan's new job was a long overdue step that carried the added bonus of giving him, and by association their revelations, increased credibility.

In the 14 December 1940 issue, Chalmers accused Howe of stupidity for leaving experienced business managers to struggle on 'with no more authority than office boys.' He concluded with a statement that must have warmed the hearts of MacMillan and all Howe's other unhappy players: 'Production of the munitions of war is an industrial job and it should be entrusted to industrialists.' This lecture was followed by a succession of front-page articles on the 'aircraft crisis,' featuring inflammatory headlines and making liberal use of quotations from unnamed industry experts, one of whom was Ralph Bell.[37] Howe tapped MacMillan as the principal leak and ordered him to keep his mouth shut. He could have saved his breath, for MacMillan was hardly the sort to be called to heel by a mere politician. In fact, however, Howe was wrong; MacMillan had certainly spoken to *Post* representatives, but on this occasion at least he had not been their principal source. The ranks of those, both inside and outside the Department of Munitions and Supply, who wondered whether Howe's results would ever match his rhetoric were growing every day, and many were eager to air their doubts to the *Financial Post* via the Dexter and Wilson pipelines.[38] Matters were obviously getting out of hand, and if Munitions and Supply were to blow up in the government's face, a first-class political crisis was assured.

In February 1941, with Howe temporarily in Britain, MacMillan and his assistant, Harry Carmichael, conducted a personal investigation of the aircraft production woes which confirmed their worst suspicions. When Howe returned, they threatened to resign if he did not adopt their recommendations immediately, and then promptly leaked them to the *Financial Post* through Irwin, whom Hunter had earlier recommended to Carmichael as 'absolutely reliable and very discreet.'[39] It was inexcusable behaviour for public servants, but then neither MacMillan nor Carmichael (nor a great many other dollar-a-year men) felt they should have to comply with the ordinary rules.

The *Financial Post* published the material with great fanfare. After all, it reinforced the long-standing *Post* argument that Howe was the major obstacle blocking efficient administration at Munitions and Supply.[40] Publication had not been a straightforward matter, however; like all newspapers, the *Financial Post* was subject to both official (and unofficial) press censorship. Clearly the paper was dealing with very sensitive material, and there was always the possibility (as there had been at all stages of the *Post*'s campaign) that the paper, its staff, or its sources might face prosecution under the War Measures Act.[41] Like most editors and publishers, however, Chalmers and Hunter considered that in all but the most extenuating circumstances press censorship and especially self-censorship was prejudicial to the efficient prosecution of the war.

The MacMillan-Carmichael power play says as much about their political naïveté as anything else. To be sure, Howe was not especially popular among his cabinet colleagues, but there was no danger he would be sacrificed to a bunch of 'Tory tycoons,' as Mackenzie King acidly dismissed them.[42] Most Liberals considered the whole brouhaha a sort of thinly veiled businessmen's *coup d'état* aimed at foisting 'national government' upon them less than a year after the electorate had overwhelmingly rejected it.

MacMillan followed through with his resignation, but almost as quickly was persuaded to stay on. That task fell to a diverse coalition including Howe, who was prepared to keep MacMillan 'if he could stop talking and stabbing people ... in the back,' as well as Clifford Clark, the deputy minister of finance, and Graham Towers, governor of the Bank of Canada. Towers saw MacMillan as someone, and perhaps the only one, strong enough to rein in Howe's spending spree.[43]

To deal with the political storm, Howe launched a counter-attack in the House of Commons in which he vigorously defended his department and in particular its aircraft production record. The Conservatives were determined to cripple Howe during this debate and, as usual, were forced to rely heavily on *Financial Post* reports for their ammunition. When Richard Bell, Conservative House leader R.B. Hansen's secretary, went further and asked Chalmers directly for more inside information, Chalmers strenuously protested that his paper did not want to become too closely associated in the public mind with politically partisan attacks. Nevertheless, the Conservatives needed to look no further than the nearest newsstand for weekly inspiration in their ongoing battle with the minister of munitions and supply. Chalmers even went so far as to reprint in full, without any comment, a particularly scathing (and self-serving) indictment of Federal Aircraft – and indirectly of Howe – put together by the private aircraft manufacturers, as if the accusations were a statement of unquestioned facts.[44]

While the *Post* was acting from conviction, it is easy to see how some would have seen their criticism as a vendetta against Howe. After all, Howe and the *Post* had been sparring almost continuously since early 1939 when it had fallen to him to defend the Bren gun contract in Parliament. Finally, on 26 February 1941, at the height of the aircraft debate in the House of Commons, Howe lashed out at his tormentor. There had been, he said indignantly, 'vicious editorials in the papers based not on fact but on hearsay, street rumours, private conversations with somebody ... [which reflected] a feeling in the press that any rumour about the Department of Munitions and Supply is worthy of publication ... [and] the leader in that has been the Financial Post.' With the undivided attention of the House and press gallery now assured, Howe bluntly offered that 'the number one saboteur in Canada since the beginning of the war is the Financial Post of Toronto.'[45] It was a dramatic performance, one of Howe's best, and, as Irwin strongly suspected, the ploy of a skilled politician under heavy attack who was intent on shifting the public's attention away from his beleaguered department. If so, it was certainly successful.

Hunter, Chalmers, and most of the others at the *Post* took Howe's attack at face value, however, and felt complimented. At long last their criticisms might be achieving results. Chalmers had actually had some forewarning of Howe's intentions and time to prepare a sanctimonious response. It was the same old *Post* refrain – the need for 'a non-political, fulltime general manager to direct the organization of production' – and basically an only slightly altered version of MacMillan's proposals.[46] MacMillan and those who thought like him had been right in concluding that Howe's unorthodox managerial techniques were causing a lot of the problems. But by ignoring the constitutional tradition of parliamentary accountability, the 'production czar' solution was fundamentally flawed, a point not lost on more thoughtful press observers like Dafoe.

Within a few weeks, the crisis had begun to subside. The *Financial Post* paused to fire a few parting shots at Howe, then quietly abandoned the issue. An appointment as director-general of shipbuilding placated MacMillan, who, despite muttered threats about returning to Vancouver, desperately wanted to remain at the centre of power. Carmichael, meanwhile, took over as director-general of aircraft production and, under his direction, the management group whom Grant Dexter had sarcastically labelled 'as pretty a band of cutthroats and pirates as ever sat around a table' finally began pulling together.[47] Before long, Canadian factories were turning out a flood of trainers and some combat planes as well and, by 1944, aircraft manufacturing was generally recognized as one of the great wartime production success stories.

In the aftermath of Howe's 'number one saboteur' charge, the English-language press rallied to the *Post*'s defence with a flurry of pious freedom-of-the-press editorials. For more dispassionate observers like Dafoe, however, the incident revealed once again the government's frustrating unwillingness to accept even constructive criticism. As Hunter moaned, 'we have failed to get over to [them] the fact that we are trying to help them.' Remedy the problems and 'we would be only too glad to get back of them in a most enthusiastic way.'[48] But the government was under a terrific strain and this, if it did not excuse its irascibility, at least goes some way towards explaining it.

Although the response of rival publishers had been heartening, reader support was considerably less enthusiastic. Allegations impugning the company's motives – that it was 'Tory from the toes up' or out to destroy Munitions and Supply in order to reopen munitions contracting to its war-profiteering friends – did not sway many, but in the heated political atmosphere even such wild accusations were not being dismissed out of hand.[49] A more widely heard criticism admitted that the *Financial Post* had done a lot of good earlier, but those businessmen who voiced this view now believed that the paper's continual hammering at Howe and his department's direction of war production was damaging public confidence in the war effort. Furthermore, Howe's reforms, especially the fact he had assembled a competent business team to run Munitions and Supply, were being ignored by the paper. In other words, things were fundamentally different now and the *Post*'s coverage should reflect as much.[50] It has to be remembered that Howe had made great strides in winning over the business community. After the lean Depression years, industry was booming, thanks largely to the spending orgy of the Department of Munitions and Supply, and not surprisingly Howe was now getting most of the credit. By the summer of 1941, then, there was not only considerably less to criticize in the nation's war production program but considerably less interest in hearing what criticisms there were – a fact the Conservative party was beginning to absorb.[51]

This realization must have influenced the *Financial Post,* but there was another factor that almost certainly entered into their considerations, too. Chiefly through Ken Wilson, the *Post* was developing close ties with senior economic bureaucrats, contacts that enabled the latter to influence the paper's editorial and news coverage in subtle but increasingly persuasive ways. As early as the spring of 1940, Towers had tried to impress upon Chalmers the influence the *Post* exercised over businessmen, and consequently its special wartime responsibilities not to arouse too many uncertainties among its readers. Towers had pointedly suggested that sometimes the national interest might even overshadow the paper's responsibility to those readers. Since it rarely dawned on Chalmers (or anyone else at the *Financial Post*) that the two were different, he was quite taken aback by Towers's observation.[52] Exactly how much hinting of this sort occurred the following spring is not recorded, but any would have reinforced the case already being made by businessmen inside and outside government service that enough was enough.

Moreover, the final chapter of the *Post*'s Munitions and Supply campaign, by focusing almost exclusively on alleged shortcomings in Howe which increasingly did not match the facts, had become so personalized and hence so apparently partisan that it was endangering the company's cherished image of political neutrality. If the attacks continued, Mackenzie King would not have been the only one to conclude that the *Post* represented 'the interests that have been after me from the start.'[53] It was certainly disconcerting for Hunter, a 'Liberal with reservations,' to find his prized weekly lumped in with blatantly pro-Tory and anti-King press organs such as the Montreal *Gazette* and the Toronto *Telegram*.

At Maclean Publishing, the Bren gun exposé and its follow-up campaign enhanced the career of virtually everyone involved. Chalmers was promoted to executive vice-president in 1942. Wilson had been groomed to take over from him but his losing battle with ulcers forced a change in plans. Instead, that plum went to Ronald McEachern while Wilson, in what turned out to be a brilliant stroke, was appointed the paper's first full-time Ottawa correspondent. Meanwhile, Irwin, whose investigative reporting had so dazzled Hunter, was named managing editor of *Maclean's,* an appointment that made him editor in all but name.

Looking back over the previous two and a half years, the *Financial Post* could point to a considerable legacy of achievement. Their objective had consistently been 'to establish a businesslike, economical system of defence purchasing' and, as Chalmers correctly pointed out in January 1941, 'a great deal of progress has been made toward these objectives.' Moreover, he was right when he said that 'had Canada entered the war with no more competent defence buying organization than existed [in 1938] ... the confusion, waste, inefficiency and graft would have been colossal.' As it was, 'those who exposed [the Bren gun] contract, and the system that made it possible, may look upon that achievement with some pride.'[54]

Nevertheless, there was widespread frustration at the paper with the lack of acclaim the *Post* received for its public-spirited efforts, and Hunter's disclaimer that public approval was incidental had a hollow ring indeed.[55] A year later, he gave vent to some of those feelings, chiding one of his senior advertising executives who had had the temerity to suggest that the *Post* had been over-critical of Ottawa's direction in the past:

We must always keep in mind we are not putting out ... [the] Financial Post to please the people or to make them feel good. We must at all times endeavour to give them the real situation and to give them information and comment which at the time may not be palatable, but in the course of time events will demonstrate that we were right ... I have no regrets at all for the articles we ran commencing with the [Bren gun] contract and which was followed up by

details regarding a number of other [suspicious] contracts ... [and] only wish
we had the staff to follow up this work and dig up further examples of party
patronage, waste and extravagance.

Still, Hunter's conclusion seems to reveal a certain soul-searching over how
the *Post* had handled the rearmament story: 'It is important, of course, to ...
explain our position as thoroughly as possible so as to convince reasonable people that we are carrying on such [a] campaign in a matter of public
interest.'[56]

The *Financial Post*'s efforts to replace Howe as de facto production chief
were wrong and, to say the least, naïve. In retrospect, Howe's unorthodox
management style did not prove a significant impediment to and perhaps
accelerated the full mobilization of the nation's industrial war effort, a reality the *Financial Post* eventually, if grudgingly, acknowledged.[57] But even
as sensible and informed (not to mention politically sympathetic) an observer as Grant Dexter grossly overestimated Howe's responsibility for the early
tribulations of Munitions and Supply.[58] Based on the evidence available to
the *Post* at the time from some of the country's ablest businessmen and civil
servants, Howe did seem to be the major problem. That its editor and publisher would unquestioningly accept the criticisms of leading capitalists like
MacMillan, Bell, and Carmichael was, of course, thoroughly predictable.
Ultimately, it was the Liberal government's success in managing the mobilization of the wartime economy which led the principals at the *Post* to
reassess their position, but Howe's achievement was a lot more obvious in
1943 and 1944 than it had been during the bleak winter of 1940–1.

The political crisis sparked by the leaks of MacMillan and others to the
Financial Post served only to weaken its case.[59] But the fact that the campaign against administrative disorganization in Munitions and Supply ended
with a whimper should not detract from the *Post*'s significant earlier role in
alerting public opinion, and particularly business opinion, to the danger of
inefficiency, incompetence, and corruption in the war effort. During the
twelve months following the original Bren gun contract exposé, its well-
documented and relentless campaign never permitted those in the government who were less than enthusiastic about reforming the system to
consolidate their opposition. Simply put, the *Post*'s reputation within the
business and financial community was such that the government had to
address the issue. Conversely, Irwin, for one, had felt all along that the
paper's efforts must have considerably strengthened the hand of those government members, civil servants, and businessmen who were determined
to avoid any repetition of the scandals and ineptitude that had plagued
munitions production in the country during the Great War.[60] Certainly

Chalmers was not exaggerating when he proudly boasted that the reforms undertaken in response to the criticism of the *Financial Post* had saved Canadians hundreds of millions of dollars between 1939 and 1945.[61] This task fell to the *Post* in large part because the parliamentary opposition was too weak to assume a responsibility that properly belonged to it, and because, for the most part, other publications did not have the resources, credibility, or determination to take up the challenge. Certainly, in this instance, where the interests of business at large legitimately did coincide with the national interest, the *Financial Post* had performed a vital public service.

3

'Some considerable influence
on politics and political action'

The *Winnipeg Free Press* and Conscription

When Canadians found themselves at war for the second time in a generation, J.W. Dafoe was in Ottawa, completing the final drafts of the report of the Royal Commission on Dominion-Provincial Relations. A telephone call from Grant Dexter, the *Free Press*'s parliamentary correspondent, brought the news. Despite the sunny skies and balmy temperatures of that 3 September, it was a day for sombre reflection. Dafoe, whose warnings of the approaching storm had gone largely unheeded, drew no comfort from being proven right in the end. Writing to George Ferguson that evening, he outlined the implications of the new situation for the *Free Press*:

> Of course, the coming of the war will change the [approach to] the editorial page. Your perplexities as to policy and timing of its announcement will largely disappear; unless something is done that we simply cannot stand our business will be to go along with the government and help them out in every possible way by explanations, intelligent publicity and so forth.[1]

Short of military defeat, it was the resurrection of conscription, the issue that had tortured the country during the last eighteen months of the Great War, which caused Dafoe the most anxiety. It was not that he, or for that matter George Ferguson, Grant Dexter, or Victor Sifton, did not accept the basic fairness and efficiency of conscription. They did. Nor was it that they lacked commitment to Canada's all-out participation in the war. Their nationalism alone dictated that the country should do everything it could to defeat Germany. Rather, the hard lessons of 1917–18, when he had been one of conscription's most vociferous advocates, had convinced Dafoe that only the gravest military circumstances could possibly justify sending any but Canadian volunteers abroad. What Dafoe recognized, and it was crucial to his perception of the issue, was that the success of the country's *overall* war effort depended on maintaining a nationwide unity of purpose or, put less delicately, on inducing French-speaking Quebeckers to particpate in Canada's war effort with considerably more enthusiasm than they had displayed during the last conflict. No one at the *Free Press*, Dafoe included, possessed more than the vaguest comprehension of, let alone sympathy for, the sentiments of French Canadians, but all understood that these feelings had to be factored into the national equation.[2]

Perhaps the momentum for compulsory overseas service would ultimately prove irresistible, but national disunity could still be avoided as long as the government could show that conscription was irrefutably necessary. Under such circumstances, the majority would and should have its way, and the minority would go along without having to be bludgeoned. Dafoe intended to use the *Free Press* to achieve two ends: he would shape the crystallization of public opinion to guarantee the broadest possible consensus when and if the day of reckoning dawned and he would ensure that it did not dawn prematurely. Attempting to 'manage' the conscription issue would entail influencing public opinion, both for its own sake and the effect it might have on the government. The difficulty, as Dafoe recognized, was 'to be able to read the problems as they [began] to form and to decide upon [and] advocate [the] solutions in these early stages when public opinion [was] malleable and when you [could] be effective.'[3] In what was likely to be an emotional and partisan issue, that would be no mean feat.

Six months earlier, both the Liberal and Conservative parties had committed themselves publicly to an all-volunteer army if war came. Although broadly endorsing their intent, the *Free Press* had wondered aloud whether 'any good purpose can be served by making the engagement absolute.'[4] Would English Canada demand a large expeditionary force with its inevitable appetite for reinforcements? Previous experience hinted strongly that it would. And while the Liberals, dependent as they were on the French-speaking and 'foreign' vote, had little choice but to remain sensitive to anti-conscription sentiments, it was questionable whether the fractious Conservatives, particularly the 'hard' Tory element epitomized by Arthur Meighen and the Toronto-Montreal 'interests,' would refrain from pursuing a course both conviction and political advantage recommended.[5]

Certainly, Dafoe felt the Conservatives were likely to stir up trouble, and Ferguson needed no prodding. Talk of conscription, the *Free Press* promptly announced at the outbreak of the war, was 'premature' and, while there eventually 'might be need [for it],' that day was 'still in the distant future.'

Preserving national unity was everyone's first priority, and those who would raise this issue now, he hinted darkly, were 'ill-intentioned, captious, and mischievous.'[6]

The first months of the so-called phony war passed uneventfully in Canada and the talk in Ottawa was of 'limited liabilities' rather than endless manpower commitments. For those English Canadians who feared conscription, the steady flow of Quebec enlistments and the surprising ease with which the Quebec Liberals, with some crucial help from their federal colleagues, had vanquished Premier Maurice Duplessis seemed to augur well. Unfortunately, few in English Canada, the *Free Press* included, understood that Quebeckers had taken the federal government's anti-conscriptionist pledges seriously and that there was no sympathy among them for a fight to the last man or dollar.[7] Among Dexter's professional contacts were several Quebec Liberal party organizers, but he relied overwhelmingly on the province's anglophone cabinet minister, the irrepressible and astute 'Chubby' Power, who could usually be counted on for a sober assessment of the political scene in his home province. Dexter had no better than a nodding acquaintance with any of his French-speaking colleagues in the press gallery and, more to the point, he had absorbed all the prejudices about French-speaking Canada which left the Anglo-Saxon Protestants of his generation so comfortably reassured. The simple truth was that Dexter cared little about Quebec, except as it affected the electoral fortunes of the federal Liberal party. Apart from relying on Dexter, Dafoe and Ferguson listened mostly to their friends among current or former members of the CIIA's Montreal chapter, particularly the rising Liberal lawyer Brooke Claxton, businessman Raleigh Parkin, and educator Terrence MacDermot; in practice, however, their interest in Quebec was just as narrowly political as Dexter's. After setting out their position in the first few wartime issues of the *Free Press,* Dafoe and Ferguson were more than happy to leave conscription alone. Privately, they and Dexter had considerable misgivings about the competence of King's government, but what was the alternative?[8] Publicly, the *Free Press* braintrust found little to criticize. Calls for an election to cure the 'weakness' in Ottawa they repeatedly dismissed out of hand, so when the prime minister dissolved parliament on 23 January 1940 and called an election for March, the paper was caught completely off-guard. As Ferguson later wryly noted, 'you could hear a very long way from Winnipeg the squeal of tires taking a sharp corner.'[9]

When the *Free Press* promptly endorsed the government, the newspaper's critics had a field day. Here again was proof that the paper was the Liberal party organ-grinder's trained monkey, and well trained at that. Dafoe never denied his personal sympathies for Canadian Liberalism or the *Free*

Press's broad editorial support for the same. But he adamantly rejected the label 'partisan' – and with good reason. For some years now he had pretty much been able to set his own editorial course, and that course – independent Liberalism – was more than a convenient turn of phrase. In Dafoe's view, an 'independent' newspaper was simply one that formed its own opinions. There was no contradiction, then, in the *Free Press* maintaining a friendly but detached relationship with the political party most sympathetic to the newspaper's views. Given the intellectual tradition of the *Free Press* and the political alternatives, that party was the Liberals. Or as Dafoe rather more colourfully put it when pressed: There were sons of bitches in both parties but 'I can't help coming to the conclusion that there are more sons of bitches in the Tory Party.'[10] In particular, he had concluded that Mackenzie King, for all his obvious flaws, was essential to the maintenance of a vigorous, unified Canadian war effort because he alone could preserve the preconditions of national unity – holding together the Liberal party and keeping the Tory imperialists at bay.

During the war years, Dafoe's position as editorial policy-maker bordered on the absolute. His immense prestige meant he had virtually ceased being subject to the restraints under which editors ordinarily laboured – namely, publishers. This status was buttressed by his own considerable vanity and by the universal respect, bordering on hero worship, in which *Free Press* staff from Ferguson and Dexter down to the humblest copy boy held him. Victor Sifton had been thoroughly overwhelmed, indeed, intimidated, by 'the Chief's' force of character and he seldom deviated from Dafoean orthodoxy. Brother Clifford, a permanent absentee who possessed neither Victor's drive nor his ability, was only too content to leave the business side to Victor and the editorial functions to Dafoe and Ferguson.[11] Of course, with Ferguson and Dexter, and with Bruce Hutchison, after his association with the paper began in 1942, there were regular and frank exchanges on the Free Press's editorial posture. Otherwise, only the advice of Edgar Tarr, a pillar of the CIIA and a longtime friend of Dafoe, Ferguson, and Dexter, carried real influence. Ultimately, everything destined for the editorial page passed through Dafoe's or Ferguson's hands and bore their imprint. It was a paternalistic operation, to be sure, but one which enabled the paper to maintain an intellectual coherence and which worked very effectively.

If the editorial offices were a Dafoe-Ferguson monopoly, then the Ottawa bureau was Dexter's. Whenever Dafoe came east, Liberals and officialdom alike received him almost as a head of state, but by the war, worsening health made it increasingly difficult for him to leave Winnipeg. This debility tied Ferguson, who had an aversion to visiting Ottawa anyway, even more firmly to his desk. Although the *Free Press* Ottawa bureau would increase to five persons by 1943, the arrival of four newcomers had little impact on Dexter's position. He remained Dafoe's Ottawa editor, personal emissary, and one-man intelligence-gathering operation while the others toiled as auxiliaries. If the story was 'political,' which is to say if it was deemed important, it automatically became Dexter's responsibility.[12]

The *Free Press* was fortunate to have someone with Dexter's experience and reporting talents in Ottawa. The rapidly expanding needs of wartime administration brought a tremendous influx of university-trained recruits into the senior ranks of the civil service, especially at the Departments of Finance and External Affairs and at the Bank of Canada. Hundreds more, most of them straight from managers' offices and boardrooms, were brought in by C.D. Howe to staff his sprawling empire at Munitions and Supply. Increasingly, it was these men, the experts, who made the real news, and not the members of parliament. For press gallery reporters, this posed an entirely new set of problems, and many were not up to the challenge. Listening to droning speeches in the House or searching out longtime civil service and political cronies in the capital's various watering holes in quest of the elusive 'scoop' remained the predictable routine of too many gallery regulars. While Dexter was also a veteran of the Hill, he was quick to adapt to and exploit the rapidly changing journalistic environment of wartime Ottawa.

Dexter loved his beat and applied himself with a diligence unequalled among his peers. Especially when it came to researching a story, his thoroughness became legendary. Though by nature a loner, shy, and inhibited, he was among the most amiable of men and succeeded in developing close friendships with many of the most important political and bureaucratic figures of the day. The Dexters lived in picturesque Rockcliffe Park, already by the early 1940s emerging as Ottawa's government enclave. Alice Dexter's deserved reputation as one of the city's finer cooks and most entertaining hostesses was confirmed at their frequent dinner parties. The oppressive heat and humidity of Ottawa Valley summers merely shifted the site of these convivial get-togethers to their cottage in the nearby Gatineau. Through the wide circle of friends they attracted, the couple became a fixture of wartime Ottawa's blossoming social life, and Dexter himself one of the handful of journalists who could claim such acceptance.[13]

Getting the news in wartime Ottawa meant tapping two distinct sources. One was traditional enough: political contacts. As Dafoe's resident envoy, Dexter possessed a permanent entrée into the inner circles of the Liberal party. The fact that the *Free Press* could not be automatically counted upon, yet was known to be sympathetic, meant the Liberals had to cultivate Dafoe, and, as the most convenient channel between the two, Dexter became invaluable to both sides.¹⁴ Dexter got along well with just about everyone in the Liberal establishment. Among his closest contacts were cabinet ministers Tom Crerar (a fellow Manitoban), 'Chubby' Power, J.L. Ralston, and James Ilsley. Norman Lambert, the party's chief organizer and a Manitoban by adoption, had strong ties to the *Free Press*. Promising newcomers like Brooke Claxton, Douglas Abbott, and Angus Macdonald succumbed to the Dexter charm, too.

The other crucial source of information was a group who were almost all newcomers to Ottawa: the mandarins-in-the-making and the other wartime bureaucrats. While the *Free Press* obviously did not exert the same political attraction for these men, Dexter could still rely on human nature. All of them had stories to tell, and a great many, being unused to (or uninterested in) the political aspects of the civil service game, were unusually naïve and loose-lipped. Of course, it was not all naïveté and candour. The desire to promote one's own policy or defeat another's was both understandable and inevitable, while frustration with the intractable workings of government procedure, especially under wartime conditions, was an almost universal complaint of civil servants, whether newcomers or not. Dexter could be very useful as the conscious or at times unwitting participant in resolving these behind-the-scenes struggles. On other occasions, informants simply wanted Dafoe to scent the wind. Regardless of the circumstances, Dexter was known to be willing to listen. Although he typically began every interrogation with a disarming 'I'm not an expert but ...' he was certainly much brighter and far better informed than the usual reporter they encountered. The fact that he was also a storehouse of all sorts of delicious political gossip which he was not averse to sharing for a price certainly helped loosen many tongues around Ottawa.¹⁵

For Dexter and the handful of other journalists of his stature in wartime Ottawa, the 'just between you and me' confidences exchanged with friends over lunch, whether at the Rideau Club or Château Laurier, in an office or living room, or on a downtown street corner were not considered leaks. Instead they were manifestations of a responsible, civilized relationship between journalists, civil servants, and Liberal politicians based largely on trust and mutual respect. And of course with each exchange, another piece of Dexter's puzzle fell into place.

Dexter was quite literally the poor, largely self-educated boy made good and he never lost the sense of awe over his good fortune as he wandered through the corridors of power. He especially liked to encourage the belief that he had a special relationship with the ultimate Ottawa source, Mackenzie King, a harmless enough exercise in self-flattery but certainly a delusion. In fact King, who rarely forgot press slights no matter how trivial, distrusted newspapermen as a group. Nonetheless, his personal liking for Dexter and undoubted respect for his political insights, together with the *Free Press* cachet, earned Dafoe's 'minor satellite' fairly regular invitations to Laurier House and Kingsmere.[16] In the end it hardly mattered whether Dexter could peer directly into the byzantine workings of King's mind or not. So numerous and well-placed were his sources both within and outside the government that usually there was not much the prime minister could have told Dexter he did not already at least strongly suspect.[17]

Regardless of how or why he received it, Dexter's precious intelligence was distilled and quickly sent on to Dafoe and Ferguson. Knowing full well that, as Dafoe put it, 'things are never so bad, and never so good as Dexter says they are,' both men were by now skilled at distinguishing between the 'factual' as compared to the 'emotional' Dexter.[18] Insiders' accounts of who was advocating what in Ottawa and which course of action seemed the likely winner provided invaluable background for the formulation of the *Free Press*'s editorial strategy and the timing of its ensuing messages to government and public alike. At the same time, it is not clear whether the possession of so much off-the-record information, with its obvious potential for compromising the paper's freedom of action, troubled any of the *Free Press* players. It seems, however, that the practical view prevailed. Dexter himself appears to have been concerned only about preserving the confidentiality of his sources, since trust was both a practical necessity and a matter of honour in the game he played out behind the scenes.[19]

In the early months of 1940, however, it was a national election, and not fear of being compromised by too much inside information, which was the immediate concern of the paper's principals. The *Free Press* justified its support of the government by pointing out that it had ably prosecuted the war so far and that the Liberals were the only party with nationwide support – an honest reflection of Dafoe's and Ferguson's private views and an assessment that many moderate Conservatives appear to have shared.[20] In the established fashion of the paper, the lead editorials took the high road while Dexter, in a series of articles written in his lucid but dry, almost pedantic style, dismantled the Tory platform plank by plank. One subject, however, was noticeable by its absence: the *Free Press* conveniently managed to avoid mentioning conscription at all.

The dimensions of the Liberals' electoral victory in March 1940 exceeded even their most optimistic expectations, and for many Conservatives, who had only grudgingly supported their party's formal stand against conscription, the result was bitter indeed. 'Canada has its "national government,"' the *Free Press* concluded approvingly, but privately Dafoe feared that King and other Liberals would interpret the result as a complete endorsement of their 'no conscription' plank. As the paper quickly pointed out, the mandate the Liberals had received was clearly to 'subordinate everything to winning the war.'[21] The insertion of 'everything' was clearly intended for certain eyes in Ottawa.

Within three months of King's landslide, the stunning defeat of Anglo-French forces on the continent had transformed a still pitifully unprepared Canada into Britain's principal active ally. Nothing more was heard of 'limited liability,' and the government moved quickly to implement the National Resources Mobilization Act, legislation which, among other things, imposed conscription for home defence. This act seemed to steady the nation, and, with it, the broader issue of overseas conscription temporarily receded. But the question was for how long? The Conservative party's drift back to its traditional pro-conscription stance was inevitable. If large numbers of English-speaking Canadians ever began to harbour doubts about the adequacy of the volunteer system to maintain the strength of the country's fighting forces, the call for compulsion would be irresistible.

The *Free Press* was now particularly well-informed on the army's manpower problems because, in the spring of 1940, Victor Sifton had gone to Ottawa at Ralston's request to become master general of ordnance, with a mandate to clean up the administrative chaos in defence procurement. While eager to tackle the job, Sifton was initially worried that the appointment would compromise his paper's editorial freedom – every embarrassing revelation would be attributed to a Sifton leak.[22] In the event, however, his definition of what constituted a leak did not preclude informing Winnipeg of the department's murkier goings-on, or Dafoe and Ferguson from discreetly making use of the information.

Manpower policy remained a muddle well into the war as the competing demands of industry and the armed forces were allowed to expand unchecked. In part this simply reflected the government's fear that establishing a rigorous 'national service' program would revive the conscription debate. Regardless of the underlying reasons, commitments were being made as if the country's manpower reserves were inexhaustible. By the summer of 1941 the main Conservative newspapers were grumbling about a manpower crisis and the 'failure' of voluntary enlistment to raise the 'necessary' troops for overseas service. This line did double duty in creating a 'boom' for the return to active politics of Arthur Meighen, the darling of the ardent conscriptionists.[23] For the *Winnipeg Free Press,* such a campaign aimed at arousing public opinion was fraught with dangers. As Dexter bleakly put it: 'It makes the Quebec situation completely impossible and may well divide the country right down the middle.'[24] Of course, the spectre of Meighen's political resurrection only added to the *Press*'s anxiety. Dexter and Ferguson argued strongly that this latest 'threat' ought to be confronted head on, but Dafoe thought it more prudent for the *Free Press* to continue as the voice of moderation and, one might add, delay.[25]

Privately, however, Dafoe was beginning to have serious doubts – not about the threat posed by Meighen and the Conservatives but about whether King would introduce conscription under any circumstances. So far, the evidence was only circumstantial, but it suggested that the prime minister was attempting to wriggle out of a commitment Dafoe felt had been made to Canadians and, just as important, to him and the *Free Press* personally. It was this commitment that had earned the government the newspaper's staunch support since the outbreak of the war, support its editor felt – and not without justification – had contributed in no small way to a smoothing of the political waters through which the Liberals had had to navigate since the fall of 1939.

When King visited the West in the early summer of 1941, his schedule naturally included discussions with Dafoe and Ferguson. Their exchange of views was predictably frank. Firmly committed to using compulsion in the last resort, Dafoe demanded a pledge from King that he was not in principle opposed to conscription. King said he was not, but at the same time insisted that he would resign rather than lead a conscriptionist ministry.[26] Clearly, this was all the *Free Press* was going to get, and it seems to have been enough for the time being.

The encounter, however, disturbed Ferguson, who despaired that King had lost touch with reality. Ferguson's own sense of the public mood, confided to Dexter, was that conscription had become almost inevitable and it made more sense to face the issue head on than to pretend that it would somehow go away, as both the government and the *Free Press* seemed to be doing. If the paper continued to lie low, surely it ran the risk of 'end[ing] up at the tail-end of the procession with many useful contributions to the debate left unsaid.'[27] But it was Dafoe's views that prevailed.

In contrast to the renewed agitation in the press for overseas conscription, the push to continue expanding the army – the so-called big army debate – was being fought out away from the public gaze. Victor Sifton was only one of several insiders appalled by the army's complete lack of foresight in assessing its manpower requirements. In a stream of memos, he tried to impress upon Ralston that continued expansion of the army would inevitably bring conscription and, in the process, derail the national war effort of which the army was, in Sifton's opinion, far from the most important part.[28] But for Ralston, overwhelmed by his immediate responsibilities and with his own set of priorities for distinguishing between the militarily desirable and the politically feasible, Sifton's arguments seemed too political. For his part, Ferguson was convinced that the 'big army' scheme had to be defeated, and Dexter knew that the senior economic bureaucrats at Finance and the Bank hoped the *Free Press* would 'howl like fiends' in an effort to derail it.[29]

The cabinet debate on the army's proposals, which, if adopted, would amount to almost a doubling of the overseas army's strength, began in September 1941 and dragged on for several months. Within a matter of weeks, but still three months after Ferguson had first pressed for them, *Free Press* editorials began questioning the assumptions of the plan's advocates. Expanding agricultural and industrial production were paramount, the argument went, but even in a purely military context the army's needs had to be balanced against those of the navy and air force. No one questioned that Canada was in the war to the limit, but to measure the nation's contribution by counting bayonets was not just misleading, it was irresponsible.[30] Ferguson and Dafoe had good reason to be alarmed for, via Sifton, they had obtained a copy of a secret report which showed indisputably that the manpower cupboard was bare. Only 600,000 men remained for the armed forces, even if they all volunteered, and half the army's allotment were French-speaking and therefore effectively unassimilable, given the prevailing structure of (and attitudes within) the army. This was reality, not the wishful thinking or conscriptionist logic upon which the army based its grandiose plans.[31]

As the government staggered towards a decision, the *Free Press* accelerated its efforts to refute the premature demands for conscription emanating from 'journalistic amateurs' and 'arm-chair strategists' which were doing 'serious injury to ... national unity.'[32] Yet it was careful to do so in a way that would not be misconstrued by those in Ottawa for whom resistance to conscription appeared to be an end in itself. By late 1941 Dafoe's pessimism was deepening; the time was rapidly approaching, he wrote, when 'there [would] be the devil to pay whatever course [was] followed.'[33]

The outbreak of war in the Pacific on 7 December 1941 dramatically altered everyone's perspective. With Canada facing the real possibility of attacks against its own territory, there was now a potential justification for the overwhelmingly conscript home defence army. At the same time, Canadian conscriptionists were quick to point out that the United States, under circumstances identical to Canada's, already had conscription and did not indulge in the absurdity of separate home and overseas armies.

The 'big army' plan was adopted early in 1942. Despite the misgivings of some ministers, the cabinet had been persuaded of the need largely by the disastrous military situation in the Pacific and by general staff promises, based on the latter's sanguine manpower 'studies,' that they could raise and maintain the additional combat units without conscription. Raise them, yes, but, as Dexter shrewdly recognized, the problem was going to be reinforcements.[34]

Once made public, the army's plans did nothing to dam the rising tide of pro-conscription opinion. The campaign launched 'spontaneously' the previous summer by powerful business interests opposed to the King government lacked neither financial backing nor publicity outlets and was growing more vocal by the day. As always, Dafoe had no qualms about the rightness of conscription, but where was the need in 1942?[35] A gloomy Ferguson despaired that the ranting of the 'jackasses who have been yelling for 40 divisions in Europe' had cost the *Free Press* the breathing spell on which they had all counted and added to his doubts about the wisdom of continuing their low-key editorial approach.[36]

In fact, the super-patriots were now only a small part of the problem. For a great many sincere, moderately minded people, Dafoe lamented, conscription for overseas service had 'become the symbol of their attitude towards the war' and, unfortunately, 'the strength of the position is in its irrationality; there is no way of dealing with it except by removing the symbol.' The government's original pledge of no overseas conscription had been unavoidable – 'the difficulty to-day is how to void the pledge with a minimum of heart-burning and bad feeling.' Dafoe penned these thoughts in a letter to his old friend Tom Crerar. In effect, the letter was Dafoe's conscription manifesto. In it, he acknowledged yet again that 'apart from the considerations [of Quebec opinion] which quite properly have been regarded by the government as restraints upon its complete freedom of action, I know no single argument against conscription that has any weight [and] there are overwhelming arguments on the other side.' His belief that, but for the unpatriotic shenanigans of the 'Toronto mischief-makers' stirring up French-Canadian resistance, the matter of overseas service by NRMA (conscript) troops would have arisen and been resolved 'naturally' was, to say the least, too optimistic. Dafoe desperately wished to do what he could to 'prevent the present difficulty leaving an aftermath that will poison our politics for another twenty-five years.' If this disaster was to be avoided, Quebec's friends must make appeals to the moderate leaders of that province 'to collaborate with the government in devising a way out.' How much influence the *Free Press* could exert in this direction was debatable, but it would make the effort. The cold, hard reality was that 'the pledge to refrain from sending conscripts overseas has to go, not because it practically impedes the Canadian war effort – so far it hasn't – but because public feeling demands it.'[37] Public feeling in English Canada, that is.

Even the cabinet now seemed to be in the grip of the conscription fever.[38]

Several powerful ministers, in particular Ralston, finance minister James Ilsley, and Angus Macdonald, minister of national defence for naval services, had always been uncomfortable supporters of the policy of relying exclusively on voluntary recruitment for overseas service and were now adamant that the time had come, as Dexter put it, to quit dancing around the conscription issue.[39] A few English-speaking ministers still felt that the political dangers associated with conscription far outweighed any military necessity – the *Free Press*'s position – while others did not care as long as a decision was made (Howe), were as strongly opposed to conscription as King (agriculture minister Gardiner), or carried little weight. Naturally, the Quebec bloc, including Power, the minister of national defence for air, was dead set against any change.

Recognizing that continued inaction was a recipe for disaster, Dafoe had been mulling over various strategies to defuse the issue. Seven months after having rejected the idea of a public vote (and warning King to do likewise), he now reluctantly embraced some sort of direct reference to the people. Knowing that Crerar would pass on his views to the prime minister, Dafoe had closed his 12 January letter by stressing that in any plebiscite the government should opt for the least restrictive and divisive course by simply asking voters to relieve it of its 'moral obligation' not to impose conscription. Ferguson, however, remained to be convinced, having concluded that adopting conscription now, despite all its attendant problems, made the most sense.[40] He worried that King, for personal as much as state reasons, intended to postpone a decision indefinitely, with the plebiscite simply being another diversionary ploy. At least Dafoe agreed with him that the newspaper had to become more openly critical of government manpower policy and press for the introduction of effective controls.

Independently, Mackenzie King had also grasped the merits of a plebiscite, and in several stormy cabinet meetings he managed to carry his colleagues with him.[41] The question chosen was simple: Would Canadians release the government from its commitment to limit conscription to the defence of Canadian territory? Pointedly, there was no mention of when, if ever, conscripts would be ordered overseas. In the words of the prime minister's subsequent explanation, it would be 'not necessarily conscription but conscription if necessary.'

Aware that the decision was imminent, the *Free Press* hastily set about preparing its readers for the news. This required a certain nimbleness because the paper had continually insisted that if the military situation ever necessitated full conscription the government already had the constitutional right (not to mention the responsiblity) to renege on its pledge without consulting anyone. The first editorial appeared a week before the rumours of the government's plans crept into the *Free Press*'s news columns. After mildly chiding the government for its 'suspected' course of action, Dafoe pointed out that given the need to achieve 'something of the nature of consent' if Ottawa was to inaugurate a 'change of policy already desirable and likely to become more imperative,' a plebiscite had merit.[42] Succeeding editorials painted the plebiscite's advantages in ever rosier hues. One informed readers that it would give the country the opportunity to resolve the controversy 'without bitterness,' while another reassured them that the prime minister was not on principle opposed to conscription and had proposed the vote as the most effective way of implementing it. Such claims stretched the truth, but in comparison with the incendiary rhetoric of the pro-conscription press they were positively restrained. Finally, on 2 February, shortly after exhorting French Canada to fall in with the rest of the country, Dafoe unleashed his definitive editorial broadside, denouncing the 'fomenters of discord' who were irresponsibly fabricating a crisis in the hope of discrediting the plebiscite, destroying the government, and bringing about their goal of immediate conscription.

Arthur Meighen's stunning defeat by a CCF candidate in a Toronto by-election during the early stages of the plebiscite campaign cheered the self-proclaimed forces of moderation considerably.[43] Yet Meighen's unexpected demise was offset by the plebiscite's bleak prospects in Quebec. Even without the well-organized *non* campaign being waged there by *La Ligue pour la Défense du Canada* and the government's own pathetic efforts to inspire a *oui* vote, the outcome was all too predictable. Still, an overwhelming 'yes' vote from English Canada, besides pressuring King to end his backing and filling, would presumably strengthen the hand of those moderate Quebeckers prepared to see reality. At any rate, this was the sanguine view: conscription with some sort of reconciliation. Nonetheless, Dafoe was not blind to the possibility that a solid *non* from Quebec might lead French Canadians to behave 'intransigently.'[44] If this happened, it would be Quebec's fault since the act of holding the plebiscite was in itself proof of English Canada's good will. As for English Canada, he recognized that rather than burying the conscription bogey, the whole exercise might simply give it added life. Yet it was a risk he was prepared to take. The crucial thing was to make ordinary Canadians realize that a 'yes' vote was the choice for moderates and not just the fire-eaters. In contrast to Dafoe, the prospect of a straight English-French result left Ferguson and Dexter completely depressed.[45]

As the campaign dragged on through February and March, the *Free Press* editorials continued alternately to exhort and plead for a decisive 'yes' vote on 27 April. The paper took great pains to point out that this did not mean immediate conscription but would respresent a symbolic commitment to the national mobilization for total war which every thinking Canadian already supported.[46] Even news columns took on an editorial tone, a tactic the *Free Press* usually strove to avoid and clear evidence that Dafoe, Ferguson, and Dexter were becoming more desperate to get their point across. It was a propaganda campaign, plain and simple, and they made no effort to deny it.

The 27 April result confirmed the worst fears of moderates: an overwhelming 'yes' vote from English Canada and an equally unambiguous *non* from Quebec. From the *Free Press*'s perspective, it was sad that French Canada had demonstrated such a lamentable 'misunderstanding' of the larger issues at stake. Nevertheless, the paper tried to make the best of the outcome by claiming it had vindicated King's policy of consultation and by asserting that the government could now conduct the war as it saw fit, confident that any initiative would command 'instant and overwhelming support.'[47] Dafoe struggled to maintain the fiction that 'the affirmative vote was not directly a vote on conscription ... but an instruction to the Government to let nothing stand in the way' of Canada's war effort. Yet even he had to admit such fine distinctions had probably escaped most 'yes' voters. Obviously the government now had to amend Section 3 of the National Resources Mobilization Act which barred the use of conscripts overseas.[48]

The favourable gloss the *Free Press* put on events in the immediate aftermath of the plebiscite did not match the state of the government, which was 'pretty wobbly.'[49] Despite the prime minister's promise that there would be no conscription now and none in the future without consulting parliament, P.J.A. Cardin, the minister of transport and public works and the senior francophone minister from Quebec, resigned on 11 May, citing the broken 1939 pledge to Quebeckers. More importantly, Ralston, who interpreted the result as a call for immediate conscription and saw no good reason to hesitate in enacting it, was threatening to follow suit. Ilsley and Macdonald stuck by their Nova Scotia colleague out of loyalty and a shared antipathy for King. Both men also felt that if and when overseas conscription became necessary, an order-in-council ought to be sufficient rather than King's promised parliamentary debate, but this the prime minister adamantly refused to concede.[50]

Dafoe was deeply troubled by Dexter's reports, confirmed by Crerar, the Niagara of cabinet leaks, that the government was badly split. During the past two-and-a-half years, King's performance had earned the grudging respect of Dafoe and Ferguson, but now they felt he was playing a dangerous political game by appearing to imply to his wavering French-speaking supporters that they would have another chance to block conscription in parliament.[51] For both men, bill 80 (the removal of section 3) meant conscription was definitely decided upon; all that remained was to implement it when it proved necessary. As far as the *Free Press* braintrust could see, Quebeckers no longer had a grievance. Anyway, Quebec had nothing to gain by wrecking the Liberal government. As long as the bulk of the army sat in England, cries for immediate conscription from Tory militants merely played into Liberal hands. Objectively, the government was actually in a strong position, but it had to cease acting so indecisively.[52]

Through Dexter, several ministers including Macdonald and Crerar sought Dafoe's advice on how to break the deadlock. Dafoe wired Macdonald that 'compromise' on the interpretation of bill 80 was justified if it assured the possibility of conscription later and prevented a breakup of the government; there was no justification for 'precipitate action' while a solution was still being sought. Macdonald took the advice to heart and decided that holding a limited parliamentary debate or vote of confidence before sending the NRMA men abroad was not grounds for resignation. He would stay on 'until the real showdown came.'[53]

Even for the *Free Press,* perched on the extreme conciliatory wing of English-Canadian opinion, patience with French Canadians had just about evaporated during the heat of the recent months. To its credit, the paper at least made some effort editorially to understand Quebec opinion and interpret it to an English-Canadian audience that was uninterested and unsympathetic at the best of times. Still, hardening attitudes on Carlton Street, and the larger body of opinion it represented, did not bode well if the conscription issue flared up again. Ferguson's sympathy for the militant anti-conscriptionist rump in Quebec was 'presque à bout.' As for French-Canadian complaints about their place in the armed forces and the running of the war effort in general, these grievances, he readily admitted, were real, but little could be done about them now. As he pointed out to a friend, he and Dexter had tried long and hard to do the job of bringing Quebec to its senses and had urged others to do likewise, but 'we might just as well have pissed against the wind.'[54] Quebec, as he now despaired to Dexter, was Canada's 'club foot,' and while 'we may not like our club foot ... it's there and we must adjust our minds to it and our policies as well.'[55] Ever the pessimist, Ferguson feared that the plebiscite exercise had merely delayed the confrontation. But Dafoe remained guardedly optimistic even when confronted with Quebec's pervasive sense of betrayal over the plebiscite and its simmering bitterness over the smug attitude of Anglo Canadians that 'Canada and the war are our show, being run according to our ideas, with the French tagging along behind.'[56] While fearful of the *nationalistes,* he also felt that if it was made clear to this faction that they found no sympathy in English Canada – not an especially tall order – Quebec would accept the will of the majority when the time came. What the country would now

get, he fervently hoped, was an end to the seemingly interminable squab-
bling.

During the crisis, King had lamented in his diary that Ralston 'does not
see the political aspect, using that word in its best sense, at all.'[57] Dafoe recognized that calls for conscription in 1941 and 1942 had been, as one press
gallery reporter aptly described it, 'an artificially stimulated crisis in
advance of its time.'[58] Thus, Dafoe had charted the editorial course of the
Winnipeg Free Press accordingly, using as his beacon not Liberal sympathies
but the national interest as he discerned it. Considering how close the government had come to disaster, the resolution of the crisis was satisfactory
enough to the *Free Press*. The government would survive, largely because
the alternatives, especially the prospect of life after King, were more
unpalatable to the participants.[59] Certainly the passage of bill 80 seemed to
have decided the conscription issue once and for all. If conscription came,
there would be a formal if perfunctory parliamentary debate, then the conscripts would be sent overseas by order-in-council. It was a policy designed
to soften the inevitable blow to Quebec and, in that respect, it had Dafoe's
full agreement.[60] Nevertheless, as he mulled over the outcome, Dexter concluded that King would have national unity, if possible with conscription,
and not the other way round.[61] Given that he, Dafoe, Ferguson, and Sifton
would support conscription if it ever proved necessary – if possible with
national unity but if need be without it – the possibility of open conflict
between the *Free Press* and Mackenzie King remained.

After the summer of 1942, conscription rapidly faded from view as an
issue in English Canada. This suited the *Free Press,* and not just because a
divisive issue had apparently been laid to rest. While endearing it to the
Liberal party, the paper's strong support of the government's actions had
damaged its credibility with many readers, or certainly that is what its principals feared. Dafoe was determined to rectify this lapse in confidence by
focusing on issues where the 'independence' of the *Free Press*'s stance would
be more obvious.[62]

The conscription crisis of 1942 was Dafoe's last great editorial battle. His
death on 9 January 1944 was a major loss to the *Winnipeg Free Press,* Canadian journalism, and the Liberal government.[63] Dafoe had assumed (and
hoped) that George Ferguson, whom he had groomed for two decades,
would succeed him as editor, but Victor Sifton wanted none of that. With
'the Chief' gone, he was bent on controlling the editorial side along with
the rest of the newspaper, and a strong editor obviously did not fit into these
plans. What emerged instead was an ill-defined and unwieldly arrangement
that installed Ferguson, Dexter, and Bruce Hutchison as co-editors, with
Sifton overseeing the lot.

William Bruce Hutchison was born on 5 June 1901 in Prescott, Ontario, but the family had moved to British Columbia when he was an infant, finally settling in Victoria. In the spring of 1918, while still in high school and on the look-out for interesting part-time work, Hutchison was approached by the editor of the *Victoria Times* with the offer of a temporary job covering sport. Hutchison's flair for reporting and writing, combined with a talent for cartooning, made him a useful addition to the staff of a small daily. The job became permanent and plans for university were indefinitely postponed. Step by step, Hutchison worked his way up the reportorial ladder, finally earning a stint at the provincial legislature where his appetite for politics was firmly whetted. In 1928, after spending a year in the press gallery at Ottawa, Hutchison moved on to the Tory *Vancouver Province* as their chief political reporter, no mean challenge for a confirmed Grit. All the while, he had continued to build a solid reputation as a freelance writer by turning out pieces for leading Canadian and American magazines. Finally, in 1938, Hutchison was appointed editor of the *Vancouver Sun*. Despite that daily's solidly Liberal leanings, an interfering publisher made his editorial job almost unbearable. Thus, when Dafoe and Victor Sifton began courting his services, he was more than willing to listen. For a couple of years he contributed informally to the *Free Press* editorial page, but in early 1944, shortly after Dafoe's death, the link was made official.[64]

Hutchison was shy, smoked but rarely drank, and had a 'perpetually rumpled look,' but he could write beautiful prose – so beautiful, Floyd Chalmers quipped, that it sometimes obscured his point. He also had a disarming way of ingratiating himself with sources. During forays to Ottawa, he had already built an extensive network of contacts within the Liberal party and the civil service, and in both circles he was viewed as a journalistic 'comer.'[65] Still, the *Free Press* connection proved an invaluable asset both in opening doors and in expanding his readership among influential Canadians.[66]

Despite his appointment as associate editor under the new Sifton scheme, Hutchison refused to budge from Vancouver Island for more than a few weeks at a time; Dexter, too, refused to move to Winnipeg permanently. That left Ferguson with most of the day-to-day editorial responsibilities but without the necessary authority.[67] Everyone tried to carry on as if Dafoe was still there, and the *Free Press*'s editorial philosophy hardly changed at all. Still, it remained to be seen how Sifton and his editorial triumvirate would handle a major crisis or what influence the newspaper would be able to exert in Dafoe's absence.

By the spring of 1944 conscription had become such an uncontentious issue that many Liberals had even lost their political fear of it. Casualties in Italy and in the air war over Germany, while heavy, were manageable.

With the threat of a Japanese invasion of Canada completely removed, the *raison d'être* for a conscript home defence army, the much maligned 'zombies,' had vanished. Indeed, in English Canada the 'zombies' hung around the neck of the government 'like a bag of cement'[68] and, as far as the *Free Press* was concerned, the less said about them the better. When Burt Richardson, the number two in the Ottawa bureau, matter-of-factly suggested in a draft manpower piece that labour shortages would eventually force the country to face the question of the draftees – and what to do with them – Hutchison was horrified. What on earth was the point of 'anticipat[ing] now what may be a hell of a thing which we find great difficulty in defending?'[69] The truth was that Victor Sifton had concluded months earlier that the home defence units were a waste of men and money and, consequently, should have been sent to Europe long before. For Ferguson, Hutchison and Dexter, it was now a daily struggle merely to keep him on side.[70]

Within weeks of the Normandy invasion on 6 June 1944, virtually all remaining units of the Canadian army were engaged in heavy fighting. Dexter's 1942 prediction that there would be great difficulties reinforcing the army if it was allowed to grow too big was being put to the test and it was not long before the conscriptionist pot began to simmer once again. But when even the minister of national defence professed satisfaction with the recruiting situation, talk of a crisis really did seem to carry a sense of unreality. Dexter, who knew from labour department sources that the so-called reinforcement shortfall existed 'only in the minds of the [Officers'] Mess and the Tory party,' was anxious to rebut the rumours in print.[71] Ferguson was worried, too, but he was even more concerned with what he saw as the growing editorial disarray at the *Free Press*.[72] Effective editorial planning meant that Hutchison and Dexter had to take on more editorial responsibility – and that obviously meant spending more time in Winnipeg. Despite Ferguson's concerns, nothing changed; he lacked the authority to impose his ideas, and Victor Sifton had no interest in strengthening Ferguson's hand.

The second conscription storm broke without warning in mid September with shocking revelations in the Toronto press which were quickly picked up nationally. According to Major Conn Smythe, a well-known Toronto sports entrepreneur and ardent Tory recently invalided home from Europe, the army's reinforcement situation was now so desperate that rifle companies in France and Italy were having to make do with virtually untrained replacements while wounded men were being rushed back to their units as soon as they were fit. If true, the allegations were a scandal, not to mention political dynamite. Ralston set off for Europe on a hurried investigation and returned convinced that somehow, despite months of reports from his staff to the contrary, the army had indeed run out of trained infantrymen.[73] It was to cope with precisely this situation that parliament had passed bill 80 two years earlier. On 19 October a haggard Ralston presented his case for immediate conscription to the Cabinet War Committee and five days later at a full cabinet meeting. Understandably, the thought that they would have to face conscription again at this late date, with the war nearly over and certainly won, appalled King and his supporters. No lover of the military, he felt that the army chiefs had confused means with ends. To Mackenzie King, 'conscription if necessary' had meant necessary to win the war, not necessary to keep the army up to strength. But such arguments, whatever their larger merit, made no impact whatsoever on Ralston. Since 1942 he had considered the 'zombies' a potential reserve for the regulars, and now it was the government's duty to send them to the front lines.[74] There was little room for compromise here, and the government and country soon found themselves in the throes of a full-blown political crisis.

Unlike most Canadian dailies, the *Winnipeg Free Press* held back from reporting the swirling rumours of cabinet turmoil. The first news accounts, without comment, appeared in the paper only on 27 October, with an editorial three days later simply calling for the public to be given the facts. On 1 November, Ralston 'resigned'[75] from the cabinet, to be replaced by General Andrew McNaughton, the only senior officer on record as unequivocally supporting the voluntary recruiting system. King gave McNaughton the futile assignment of trying to pry the necessary thousands of reinforcements voluntarily from among the ranks of the remaining NRMA troops, the very men who had stubbornly resisted all previous efforts to induce (or coerce) them to 'go active.'

The *Free Press* expressed mock surprise at these developments even though Dexter and Hutchison, both of whom fortuitously happened to be in Ottawa as the crisis broke, had known what was brewing for several days. Obviously, it was hardly possible to ignore the resignation of the defence minister, but the paper calmly responded by urging that McNaughton be given enough time to assess the situation properly. Until then, the *Free Press* was suspending judgment. A series of bland editorials 'that appeared to say something but really said nothing' followed.[76] On one point, however, there was no room for qualifications. 'What is needed, and needed now,' Ferguson sternly noted, with an obvious eye on the East Block, 'is confirmation by the prime minister of his past declarations that he will apply bill 80 if necessary.'[77] In fact, this statement was aimed as much at Victor Sifton, who had been only reluctantly persuaded to go along with Ferguson's low-key editorial strategy, as at Mackenzie King.

The indefatigable Dexter and Hutchison scurried about Ottawa like a pair

of ferrets, ready to listen to anyone who wanted to talk. Ottawa, being well
stocked with conscriptionists and King-haters, literally bubbled over with
rumours and gossip. Both reporters were in almost constant touch with the
leading figures of the conscriptionist camp, including Macdonald, Ilsley,
and Crerar (a recent convert) as well as Senator Norman Lambert, Bill Ben-
nett (Howe's assistant), and John Connolly (Macdonald's), frequently sitting in on their late-night strategy sessions at Crerar's Clemow Avenue
residence. But they were also in contact with the less numerous anti-conscriptionists, including Power and a bevy of faceless civil servants and
political aides, among them Norman Robertson, Arnold Heeney, and Jack
Pickersgill.[78]

The political temperature rose sharply on 12 November when Ralston
presented his side of the controversy to the House of Commons. According to the ex-minister, the shortage of trained infantry reinforcements was
real and could be remedied quickly only by tapping the home defence units.
The government, he asserted in his most damning criticism, was not committed to taking this action. Ralston was widely respected in English Canada;
there were reports of movie audiences spontaneously cheering the appearance of his picture during newsreels. Thus, the effect of his statements on
public opinion was electric, with the publisher of the *Free Press* a prime
example. On 13 November, opinion polling indicated that 57 per cent of
Canadians, and close to 80 per cent of anglophones, favoured dispatching
conscripts to Europe.[79] Even Dexter, despite long-standing reservations
about Ralston's ministerial abilities, admired his principled stand.[80]

The best efforts of Ferguson, Hutchison, and Edgar Tarr could barely
contain Sifton. Tempers flared; he accused his editors of leaving the *Free
Press*'s editorial policy in confusion and discredit, and backed down only
when Hutchison threatened to quit. Ferguson, too, had always supported
conscription. He had been prepared to give the government every opportunity, but now, with the case apparently incontrovertible, King seemed to
be trying to weasel out of his commitments. After everything the *Free Press*
had done, Ferguson took that as a personal affront. Furthermore, it seemed
to him that English-Canadian opinion was so inflamed that reneging on the
clear intent of bill 80 had become a worse threat to national unity than any
anger Quebeckers might feel.[81] Clearly the *Winnipeg Free Press* could no
longer avoid calling for conscription; their conditions had been met.

Nonetheless, the newspaper did not launch an unrestrained assault on
either the government or King himself. Ferguson calmly called on Ottawa
to act promptly to remedy the reinforcement shortages using whatever
means proved most effective. But unless success was guaranteed, the volunteer effort should be discontinued by the end of November. 'So far as this

newspaper is concerned Mr. King and his Government are committed,' the *Free Press* reminded waverers in Ottawa.[82] Of course, this meant conscription, and everyone knew it.

The cabinet crisis peaked immediately prior to the reconvening of parliament on 22 November. Despite diametrically opposed views, both cabinet factions, and the few remaining undecideds, were desperately searching for some way to keep the Liberal ship of state from foundering. It was clear that there would have to be some sort of conscription or the cabinet would shatter. The *Free Press* understood this dilemma, and indeed, through Hutchison, was even receiving memos directly from King while simultaneously using Crerar to press its own views on the prime minister.[83]

At the proverbial stroke of midnight, King undertook a complete *volte face*. First, he took the precaution of ensuring that Dexter and the publishers of two other key Liberal-leaning dailies, the *Toronto Star* and the *Montreal Star*, had been informed of the imminent change.[84] Then he told his cabinet colleagues that McNaughton had found the volunteer system wanting after all, and hence the government would send 16,000 conscripts overseas forthwith. Later, King's explanations for his change of heart would run from fear of an army revolt (which Dexter charitably dismissed as a symptom of the prime minister's war exhaustion) to the loss of support of all the Liberals' English-language newspapers and, most credible of all, the threatened resignation of cabinet heavyweights like Howe and Ilsley.

King's formal announcement of conscription came too late to stop a Ferguson editorial sharply questioning the prime minister's interpretation of the commitments implicit in Bill 80. It was sufficiently harsh that Dexter later felt moved to apologize privately.[85] The following day, however, a much relieved *Free Press* rallied to the government's defence. Victor Sifton, who only days earlier had been poised to order his reluctant editors to demand the government's hide, defended King's course and his newspaper's support of it in the light of cold reality: 'it is a fact that the pledge was honored, however unwillingly ... It seems to me that it is wise for us to accept the situation with as good grace as possible now that we have achieved the principal objective. The alternatives are not very satisfactory.'[86] The *Free Press* then buried the issue with all the haste it could muster, a decision which, judging by the comment in other dailies, accurately reflected English-Canadian opinion.

The *Free Press*'s performance had once again earned considerable praise from its admirers for moderation, objectivity, and foresight. Initially, the paper had downplayed the crisis, suspicious that it was a Tory creature without any real foundation. But once it became clear from private and public sources that English-Canadian opinion would be satisfied only with sending at least some of the conscripts overseas, that the Liberal government's survival was at stake, and that the newspaper's own credibility was threatened, the *Free Press* declared for conscription with a clear conscience. Yet even then the newspaper took pains to distinguish between a wrong-headed government policy and the government itself.

The *Free Press* saw itself as an educator of public opinion. On conscription, it had attempted to moderate that opinion or, to use the military metaphor, to carry out a delaying action against its premature adoption. The danger, as the paper correctly perceived, was not that diehard anti-conscriptionists and isolationists would frustrate the will of the majority but that the rabid conscriptionists would gain the upper hand and inflame otherwise moderate public opinion, making the issue a test of patriotism as it had become in 1917.

But Dafoe also saw another role for the paper. 'As you know,' he wrote to an academic friend in the United States during the height of the 1942 crisis, 'the Free Press is pretty widely read by public men ... and men of affairs; and thus exercises some considerable influence on policies and political action.'[87] While the paper consistently overrated its own influence, it did have a sizeable following among the country's administrative, business, and political elite and in particular within the highest Liberal party circles. This influence it exerted subtly to strengthen voices of moderation inside and outside government ranks and to prevent the anti-conscriptionists, notably King himself, from blocking conscription altogether. It is hard not to believe, as Ferguson later argued, that the accumulated effect was significant.[88]

Save for a few noteworthy exceptions, the *Winnipeg Free Press* solidly endorsed the King government throughout the war years. This apparent closeness was due to a combination of factors: the editors' and publishers' conception of their wartime responsibilities, their deep-rooted political sentiments, and their own objectives – preserving national unity and keeping the Tories out of power as much as keeping the Grits in. It was an approach following naturally from Dafoe's rejection of adversarialism as an acceptable framework for press-government relations. Practically speaking, he believed that 'influence on policies and political action' required a newspaper to establish and maintain a functioning, civilized relationship with any government such as Mackenzie King's with which it was in basic sympathy. As for the Liberals, they were, especially after 1942, in no position to ignore their journalistic friends, and the *Free Press* was the one commanding the most editorial respect from politically independent English-speaking Canadians.

The consistent policy of the *Winnipeg Free Press* throughout the war had been, to parrot King's slogan, 'not necessarily conscription, but conscription if necessary.' Overseas conscription, unless its proponents could prove it to be absolutely necessary in either the military or the broadest political sense, could not be justified because its adoption under any other circumstances would dangerously undermine national unity and, with it, the national war effort. Of course, from the perspective of the *Free Press*, 'national unity' implied a consideration of the attitudes of both English- and French-speaking Canadians, though it ultimately depended on the will of the majority being respected.

During the 1942 crisis, the *Free Press* was able to play a significant role both in moderating the public debate and in influencing the government. Timing, the slow evolution of events, and the relative flexibility of English-Canadian public opinion assisted the editors greatly. Dafoe's immense personal prestige was also significant. Ferguson, Hutchison, and Dexter were not so fortunate in the autumn of 1944 when the second crisis erupted and English-Canadian opinion soon hardened, with the result that the newspaper was able to exercise only limited influence on the public debate. In contrast, its influence on the government's decision to invoke bill 80, while hardly pivotal, was still very real.

Influence, of course, is difficult to measure. Suffice to say that the subtraction of the *Free Press*'s reasoned editorial approach from the national debate which surrounded the conscription question would hardly have contributed to a more successful resolution of the country's dilemma. Governments are typically judged on the extent to which they achieve their objectives, though it is recognized that independent factors can contribute measurably to any success. If one applies the same standard to newspapers, the *Winnipeg Free Press* went a considerable distance towards achieving its ends. When overseas conscription was 'necessary,' when its continued avoidance threatened national unity from the point of view of the English-Canadian majority, it was implemented. But it was not implemented in such a way as to alienate irreparably the minority who remained strongly opposed. In essence, that had been the objective of the newspaper and the men who directed it from the outset.

4

'In detail and with complete accuracy'

Ken Wilson and the
Making of an Authoritative Voice

After six years of war, no aspect of the Canadian state had been more profoundly or permanently transformed than the traditional role of government and the shape of its relationship with the business and financial community. As the country's leading business newspaper, the *Financial Post* had been in the forefront in chronicling these changes. While the paper remained formally suspicious of the political side of government, its impression of the highly competent bureaucratic elite on whose shoulders the Liberal government seemed to perch so reassuringly had grown increasingly favourable. During the early stages of the conflict, of course, the *Financial Post* had been outspokenly critical of the Liberals' management of the economic side of the national war effort. But once it had become apparent that Ottawa was acting with both competence and foresight, the *Post* had settled comfortably into the preferred wartime role of cheerleader and spokesman.

When peace returned in 1945, the 'Government party' and its confident senior civil service, by building upon the successful and mutually beneficial wartime axis forged with private business and financial interests, were clearly determined to continue exercising a central role in the management of the economy. For its part, the *Financial Post* encountered little difficulty in supporting Ottawa's broad objectives. No clearer evidence could be wanted of the pervasiveness of the consensus on the key socio-economic questions which characterized business-government relations during these years.

The appointment of Ken Wilson as the *Financial Post*'s full-time Ottawa editor in 1941 and of Ronald McEachern as its editor the following year greatly facilitated the paper's integration into this business-government relationship. McEachern's abilities as a writer and reporter were impressive and, when coupled with a broad understanding of business and financial affairs and keen powers of analysis, made him a far superior editor to Chalmers. While Wilson's career was cut short by a fatal air crash in 1952, during his eleven-year tenure in Ottawa he established himself as one of the outstanding journalists covering the national scene; in the realm of economic affairs, in particular, he was unequalled. So strong were the bonds of mutual respect and intellectual compatibility between Wilson and the civil service elite and their political masters that by the postwar years, he had become almost indistinguishable from them. Under the circumstances, it was hardly surprising that the *Post* emerged as a sort of official spokesman on economic matters, a development that enhanced its usefulness as a link between the federal government and its business constituency.

McEachern held a doctorate in history from the University of Toronto and was an accomplished organist as well. Unfortunately, he was also a difficult personality. When dealing with the captains of industry, McEachern oozed charm and could drink with the best with them, and he quickly won their confidence. But in the editorial offices of the *Financial Post* there was little evidence of personal warmth; he was a tyrant who treated everyone, and not the least management, with thinly veiled contempt. Nevertheless, his refusal to brook interference on the editorial side, combined with the fact that he drove himself as hard as or harder than any of his staff, earned him grudging respect. Management tolerated McEachern because of his loyalty to the company and his solidly pro-business leanings, and because his talents were indispensable to the *Post*'s success. The bottom line, after all, was profitability, and under McEachern's innovative direction the paper's profitability, prestige, and circulation, which nearly doubled within ten years of his appointment as editor, all soared.[1]

Ken Wilson, five years McEachern's senior, was a happy contrast to his editor, combining all the latter's strengths as a journalist with an endearing personality. Born in Yorkshire, he had come to Canada as a six-year-old with his family in 1906. They lived in Toronto before settling in Brantford, but Wilson's father, a civil engineer, had little success finding steady employment in either city. The impact on the family's standard of living was predictable. Nevertheless his mother was determined that her son – there were two other children; a daughter and a retarded son – would have every opportunity to better himself. When the youngster won a place in the prestigious University of Toronto Schools, she managed, by stretching her meagre allowance and taking in boarders, to pay the fees.

It was always intended that Wilson go to university and in 1922 he enrolled at Victoria College, where he decided to major in commerce and finance. Yet his interests were catholic. Political science and poetry were two of his favourites, and history also held a special fascination, sparked in part by a young lecturer who befriended him, the future diplomat Hume Wrong. Like McEachern, Wilson would have happily seized the opportunity to pursue an academic career, but the expense of graduate school was prohibitive. As it was, even with a scholarship his undergraduate years had been a constant financial struggle. Always on the lookout for part-time work, his jobs had run the gamut from door-to-door knife sharpener to restaurant doorman. During the Christmas break in his third year, Wilson sold *Financial Post* subscriptions and copies of the paper's *Business Yearbook* – so successfully, in fact, that he was taken on the following two summers to sell *Post* advertising in the Maritimes.[2]

When Wilson graduated with a Bachelor of Commerce degree in 1926, he was elected life-president of his class, a distinction that spoke highly of both his academic achievements and his social contribution to university life. The *Financial Post* promptly hired him as a junior reporter and his talents quickly blossomed. During the next fifteen years Wilson served as editor of virtually every department at the paper and became, in effect, Chalmers's lieutenant. The two hit it off from the start, undoubtedly sharing the mutual respect of self-made men. Chalmers certainly recognized his colleague's flair for journalism and groomed him as his eventual successor as editor. Wilson, for his part, never lost his respect and affection for Chalmers.

Unfortunately, as Wilson's career prospered, his health steadily deteriorated. The pressure of deskbound editorial work wore him down, in the process seriously aggravating an ulcer problem that dated back to his university days. He had a wife and two children and the added financial responsibility of caring for his brother and parents, and mounting medical bills only added to the strain. In 1939, when doctors removed two-thirds of his stomach, it was clear he would have to find a less stressful job.

Maclean publications had always relied on stringers to cover developments in Ottawa, but as the capital's importance as a news centre grew the use of part-timers, even when they were of Dexter's quality, was proving an increasingly unsatisfactory arrangement for both the *Financial Post* and *Maclean's*. It did not take long for Chalmers, Hunter, and *Maclean's* editor Napier Moore to recognize that in resolving the Wilson situation there might also be a simple solution to the problem of inadequate coverage from Ottawa. The *Post* would offer Wilson the position of full-time Ottawa correspondent and, with an eye to minimizing his disappointment, he would be promised a free hand in developing the position and the byline 'Ottawa editor.'

When Wilson took up his new post in July 1941 he was sharing the experience of hundreds of business executives and academics whose lives were also being disrupted by moves to Ottawa to staff wartime boards and departments. At first, he had difficulty summoning much enthusiasm for his new job. Fortunately, however, the company was able to find him a house in the Glebe, a comfortable residential district on the city's south side, which at least made it possible for his family to join him. After a year in Ottawa, he was still bothered by losing his chance to be *Post* editor, but he admitted that the move had been for the best.[3]

Establishing professional and personal roots in a new environment, especially one as chaotic as wartime Ottawa, was no mean challenge for any reporter. George Ferguson likened the place to a giant maw, pulling in all that came near and swallowing it up in a murky bureaucratic swamp. Yet Wilson found Ottawa to be a reporter's paradise, compact, remarkably open, and bubbling with news – in sum, 'a very friendly and satisfactory city to anyone who will take the trouble to understand and study the individual problems and events that are being enacted [there].'[4]

By temperament, Wilson was a friendly man, not boisterous but outgoing in a quiet, unassuming way. He successfully managed the difficult task of being an unpretentious intellectual and his boyish enthusiasm, wry wit, and generous spirit seemed to leave a lasting and favourable impression on virtually everyone he met. Such personal qualities certainly helped him get established, but Wilson had other advantages, too. While strictly speaking a 'new man' in the press gallery, he was already well acquainted with many of the businessmen who were streaming into Ottawa to work for the Department of Munitions and Supply and the Wartime Prices and Trade Board; he was also on a first-name basis with a number of the economists who had been recruited into the bureaucracy from the private sector. During his time with the *Financial Post,* he had made numerous trips across the country, familiarizing himself with the problems of business, banking, and insurance. These old contacts trusted him and were now well placed to direct valuable information his way.[5] Moreover, having visited Ottawa frequently since 1939, Wilson knew and was known by most cabinet ministers, and was on particularly good terms with Howe and Ilsley. The same could be said for an even more valuable group: their deputy and assistant deputy ministers and key advisers, as well as the chairmen and principal staffers from the permanent civil service who ran many of the specialized boards and bureaus of the wartime bureaucracy. It was these men, most of them university-trained economists with the deputy minister of finance, Dr Clifford Clark, and the governor of the Bank of Canada, Graham Towers, at their centre, who 'constituted the inner spring of the governmental mechanism' in the vital area of wartime economic policy.[6]

Wilson cultivated these men on the social as well as the professional level. Indeed, one of the most notable developments of wartime Ottawa was that these distinctions, at least for a few select journalists, were becoming blurred. The capital was frightfully overcrowded and, especially for new-comers from larger centres like Montreal, Toronto, Winnipeg, and Van-couver, lacking in many of the social amenities. Save for periodic forays to Montreal, there was often little alternative to improvising one's own entertainments. Hosting dinner parties and organizing literary, dancing, or dining clubs were pursued with a passion, and Ruth and Ken Wilson were avid participants. Together with the Dexters, with whom they became close friends, they developed one of Ottawa's more wide-ranging and lively social circles. Skiing was a particular Wilson passion and he took advan-tage of the seemingly interminable winters to introduce many a neophyte to the slopes in the nearby Gatineau.

As promised, Chalmers allowed Wilson complete leeway to develop the Ottawa job as he saw fit. There were frequent telephoned instructions from McEachern, and periodically (certainly too often for Wilson's taste) he had to travel to Toronto for editorial consultation, but, all in all, there was remarkably little overt direction.[7] Because he did not represent a daily, Wil-son was permitted to become only an associate member of the press gallery; he rarely chose to work out of their cramped quarters anyway, preferring to use his home as an office. It was more practical, more confidential, and cer-tainly less constraining. Although Wilson put in long hours, he was still able to avoid the structured schedules of editorial work he had detested in Toron-to. Sundays he tried to keep free for church activities and relaxation with family and friends, and until his workload became too great he always tried to squeeze in time for volunteer work with local Cub and Scout troops. All in all, it was a busy, productive, and balanced life.

The tenor of the *Financial Post*'s wartime reporting was changing dur-ing the winter of 1941–2. Satisfied at last that Howe was restructuring his sprawling empire at Munitions and Supply along the 'sound, businesslike lines' it had been advocating, the paper increasingly supported government war policies in its news columns and editorials. There were still revelations of muddling, frequently unearthed by Wilson himself, and the *Post* was always prepared to publicize the cases of businessmen recruited by Ottawa as wartime administrators who had become exasperated with some policy or other and resigned in frustration or to air their complaints. More often than not, however, Wilson's reports as well as his and McEachern's edito-rials were plainly intended to strengthen the hand of the senior civil service experts against some ill-considered government policy change or wrong-headed opposition by businessmen.[8] The willingness of the highest-ranking officials like Wartime Prices and Trade Board chairman Donald Gordon to confide in Wilson, in sharp contrast to their reticence during the early stages of the war, was a tribute to his and McEachern's ability to inspire confidence. It was also a consequence of the growing recognition on the part of such officials that both men were only too ready to help keep the business and financial community informed and on side. A satisfied Wilson merely noted that he found 'the greatest eagerness on the part of the dollar-a-year men, the civil servants, and our parliamentarians to get their story correctly understood and interpreted in The Post.'⁹ All this, of course, was in keeping with Wilson's and McEachern's assessment of the *Post*'s wartime role. As the McEachern incessantly reminded his staff, every story they covered was a war story. He accepted that businessmen had to be educated to accept the financial restrictions and general regimentation the war necessitated, since significant opposition on their part obviously would undermine or even wreck any economic policy Ottawa pursued. Given the newspaper's increasingly authoritative position, a standing the government was helping to create by providing its Ottawa man with a succession of scoops, the *Financial Post*'s role in this education process was potentially quite helpful.

As long as the war continued, the *Financial Post* would concern itself primarily with the contribution of Canadian business and finance to the national effort. Nevertheless, by 1943, the *Post,* like the government and business, had begun to consider the inevitable transition to peacetime conditions. To carry the country through the postwar reconstruction period, the bureaucratic planners were committed to a continuation of the expansionary economic and fiscal measures adopted so successfully during the war. Income redistribution would play an important role, especially in carrying public opinion, but overall policy was still geared to creating employment and new national wealth by strengthening private enterprise.¹⁰

For the progressively minded element in the business community epitomized by men such as J.S. McLean of Canada Packers, the bureaucracy's plans were workable only if his fellow businessmen would 'lift their sights' beyond prewar thinking and methods.¹¹ Most businessmen, however, were at best lukewarm and had to be won over. The great majority believed that planning and controls had no place in a peacetime free-market economy. There was also pervasive suspicion that the Liberals, hypnotized by the advice of their academic experts, were bent on imposing every sort of utopian socialistic scheme. Two factors, however, worked in the government's favour. One was negative – business's fear of unadulterated socialism in the form of the CCF. But the other was positive – the leading role in reconstruction allotted to C.D. Howe. Literally hundreds of middle- and upper-level managers had worked with 'CD,' and even for those who had not, his feats masterminding war production were the stuff of business legend. Moreover, many of the younger men respected the expertise of the economic wizards toiling for Clark and Towers and, based on their personal wartime experience, were more ready than their seniors to accept that the sort of government intervention proposed by the Liberals really was in the best interests of business.[12]

Although ardent free enterprisers who were anything but comfortable with Ottawa's 'overdose of planning and ... regimented economy,' Hunter and Chalmers were pragmatic enough to recognize that until the CCF threat receded, M.J. Coldwell's brand of socialism was a distinctly greater danger to Canadian business and finance than Mackenzie King's.[13] In contrast, Wilson had no difficulty reconciling his free-enterprise convictions with what he considered to be the responsible degree of economic planning advocated by a government which he knew was sympathetic to business interests. It was not simply a question of Wilson being more open-minded; his intimate knowledge of the economic mandarins bred a familiarity with the men and their ideas and a respect for the competence and pragmatism of both.[14] While anything but radical, McEachern had spent part of the Depression driving a taxi and he, too, felt little nostalgia for traditional laissez-faire nostrums. Given the alternatives, he was willing to try the new Liberal-bureaucratic order – indeed, sometimes too willing to suit his employers.[15] Thus, while critical of some of that order's more obvious social welfare aspects, the *Financial Post* offered modest support for family allowances as a national income measure. It also hailed the bureaucracy's definitive reconstruction blueprint, the White Paper on Employment and Income released in April 1945, as a *magna carta* for postwar Canadian capitalism; in all, McEachern observed, the plan would guarantee 'the maintenance and increasing efficiency of the free enterprise system' and prove socialism unnecessary.[16]

All the government's elaborate postwar plans to save Canadian capitalism from itself hinged on the maintenance of an expanding economy. Conditions abroad during the immediate postwar period, however, threatened to wreck their best efforts to achieve this goal. As the government and, more particularly, the senior echelons of the civil service wrestled with the critical problems of international currency stability and multilateral trade, the need to carry domestic business and financial opinion behind new and sometimes difficult measures was obvious. Given the close relationship which had developed between the bureaucrats and the *Post* during the latter part of the war, it was natural that they should turn to Ken Wilson for assistance.

Ottawa's economic mandarins had always been committed supporters of economic multilateralism, the trade framework Washington was now so enthusiastically promoting. Trade was widely recognized in Ottawa as a key component of the country's postwar economic well-being.[17] In this regard, the priorities were international measures to ensure currency convertibility (particularly of sterling to U.S. dollars) and the drastic reduction of tariffs and other impediments to freer trade. It was assumed, however, that making the multilateral trading world a concrete reality would inevitably entail some significant structural and philosophical changes for Canadians and, not the least, for Canadian businessmen. The imperial preference system, for instance, which still exerted a strong emotional and, for some, practical attraction, might well have to be abandoned or at least significantly modified. In an Ottawa press corps staffed by generalists, Wilson was one of the few who possessed a sufficient grounding in economics to grasp the implications of what the mandarins were advocating when they explained it to him; just as important, he had the facility to simplify it for others, not the least his colleagues in the gallery, whom he often briefed in turn. Certainly the power of the ideas the mandarins were bandying about impressed him. Wilson, after all, was a committed free trader, and he was intellectually sympathetic to progressive economic concepts including Keynesianism.[18] Part of the attraction was clearly a blend of the emotional and a larger intellectual vision. The sheer scale of the multilateralists' postwar plans and their enthusiastic promotion of the cause swept him away just as it did them. In the end, internationalism and patriotism combined with economic pragmatism to bring him down firmly on the side of the new order.

During the last year of the war, Wilson's byline appeared over trade-related articles in the *Post* with increasing frequency. He focused on three themes: the joint commitment of Canada and the United States to work towards a multilateral world; Britain's suspected lack of commitment and very real economic weakness (the two were obviously linked) as obstacles to this goal; and the linkage between postwar Canadian prosperity and the adoption of the multilateralists' agenda. Subtly, as his columns hinted at the results of high-level negotiations and outlined the intricacies of the issues as they bore on Canada, Wilson was helping to transmit to the Canadian business community the economic realities as viewed from the East Block and the Bank of Canada.[19]

When planning for the postwar period, Canadian officials had seriously underestimated both the extent and the duration of the economic difficulties Britain would face. The economic mandarins, of course, were preoccupied with Canada's own economic problems and there was perhaps not enough understanding of the British position. Be that as it may, it was not long after the end of hostilities before Ottawa began showing signs of frustration with the failure of events on the other side of the Atlantic to match their expectations. Privy to their concerns, Wilson shifted his attention during the winter of 1945-6 to the deteriorating state of Anglo-Canadian economic relations. In a mix of bylined and unsigned reports, he outlined the trade and financial problems in stark terms, accusing the British of self-serving tactics and warning his readers to forget sentiment and face reality when contemplating Britain's role in Canada's economic future.[20] The *Post*'s stridently nationalistic and largely realistic tone was clearly intended to stir support, particularly among manufacturers, for a tough stand in defence of Canadian interests. Practically speaking, this meant following the policy leads of the Department of Finance and the Bank of Canada. When weeks of difficult and often less than amicable negotiations finally produced a $1.25 billion loan intended to enable Britain to finance its Canadian imports, the *Financial Post* endorsed it as 'a straight business deal to help put our largest export customer on her feet.'[21] The fact that the *Post* was able to break the story a full week before finance minister Ilsley's official announcement was an indication of just how closely Wilson had been taken into the confidence of Ilsley's subordinates.

Unfortunately, the British loan was only a symptom of a much larger and more critical problem confronting Ottawa. Throughout 1946 it became increasingly clear that the hoped-for economic recovery of Britain and Western Europe on which the revival of a larger and more balanced Canadian trade and ultimately the viability of the multilateralist vision itself depended simply was not taking place. The levels of trade generated – much of it either straight barter arrangements or financed by Canadian credits – were adequate to give the country a positive overall trade balance. But the overall balance was only part of the story. The release of pent-up business and consumer demand in Canada had caused imports from the United States to soar at the same time that Canadian exports to that country were declining. The result was a heavy drain on the country's reserves of American dollars. Normally, trade surpluses with Britain and Europe would have compensated for this imbalance, but owing to worsening shortages of u.s. dollars in Britain and Europe, Canada was increasingly unable to earn sufficient American dollars from her trade with the rest of the world to cover the shortfall in her trade with the United States. Thus, unless Canada could figure out a way to earn more American dollars in Europe, or significantly reduce her mounting trade imbalance with the United States, or preferably a combination of both, the country's massive reserves of American dollars accumulated during the war would soon evaporate.[22] Without a substantial

U.S. dollar reserve, a majority of the economic braintrust in Ottawa feared that Canada's transition to peacetime prosperity would prove much more difficult. The economic implications were obvious, and so were the political. But while the 'dollar problem' was easy enough to indentify, solving it was another matter altogether.[23] Ottawa's hopes were firmly tied to far-reaching American proposals for trade liberalization, which Washington was determined to bring before a world trade conference in 1947. To encourage discussion of (and presumably win converts to) these proposals, especially within the business and financial community, officials in External Affairs had already given drafts to several 'strategically placed individuals.' The lone journalist among them was Wilson, who, they were pleased to report, had 'agreed to the suggestion to do what he can to stimulate interest by printing a summary of the draft Charter and frequent comment in his paper.'[24]

Early in 1947 Wilson had begun pressing McEachern and Chalmers to send one of the *Post*'s own reporters to cover the upcoming International Conference on Trade at Geneva. Although the Geneva proceedings were being described as merely the preliminaries to talks planned for Havana in 1948, Wilson argued perceptively that the outcome of the former, and particularly the fate of sweeping American proposals on multilateral trade, was likely to fix the pattern of postwar trade irreversibly. The implications of such discussions for a major trading nation like Canada, as he pointed out, were obvious. In the end, Wilson's arguments carried the day and, not surprisingly, he was tabbed as the obvious choice to attend.[25] Before setting off for London, where Commonwealth representatives were to meet to hammer out some sort of joint trade position, he wrote a strongly worded attack on the business community's complacent assumption that Canada could continue financing its European trade with dollar credits more or less indefinitely. It was a dose of hard truth for the country's exporters, and one the mandarins were eager to administer.[26]

Wilson's reports from London pressed home the vital importance to Canada of the approaching trade parley at Geneva, the likely position of the government on a range of trade-related issues, and particularly the significance of the Commonwealth's eventual stand on the tricky preference question. Ottawa, he noted, recognized the crucial importance of the existing Commonwealth preference system to some manufacturers and many primary producers, especially farmers. But it was a widely held view among the government's senior economic advisers that the Americans, who considered such arrangements a form of trade 'discrimination,' would not permit Commonwealth preferences to continue, at least in their current form. In that light, Canada's only viable option was to use them as leverage in negotiating meaningful reductions in American tariffs. As Wilson stressed, the danger to Canada was not an end to preferences as such, but rather a British attempt either to hang on stubbornly to them – perhaps sabotaging multilateralism in the process – or, as the more cynical among the mandarins feared, to pitch them overboard in order to strike their own deal with Washington, leaving Canada in the lurch. Such was the level of suspicion – one might almost say paranoia – in Ottawa about British intentions, and particularly the British commitment to multilateralism. A hard-hitting editorial by McEachern made it abundantly clear that on this issue the positions of the government and the *Financial Post* were one and the same. 'The blunt truth is that Canada's economy was never more vulnerable to world conditions,' he warned businessmen. While the preference system could not simply be tossed aside, 'most Canadians will hope that the time has arrived for trading [it] in on something bigger and better.'[27]

Although it is clear that Wilson was being briefed at least in part by senior Canadian civil servants, his independent interpretation of developments and the timing of their publication sometimes caused consternation among his sources. This was particularly true of his report that British officials had surprised (to put it mildly) their Canadian opposite numbers by proposing to raise intra-Commonwealth tariffs as a way of deflecting American criticism of the preference system and of maintaining it along with prevailing British tariff rates more or less intact. Washington was bound to see such thinly veiled protectionism as a complete departure from the spirit of multilateral trade. In the event, the Canadian fears proved groundless; by August 1947 the Americans had accepted British arguments that temporary 'departures' from the multilateralist straight-and-narrow should be permitted for governments wrestling with severe balance-of-payments problems, but this was of course not known in Ottawa earlier in the year.[28] Moreover, the implications of the aforementioned British plan for Commonwealth-bound exports of Canadian manufactures (the *raison d'être*, it must be remembered, for much of the country's branch-plant manufacturing industry) were bound to be harmful. As Wilson reported it, Canada had been strongly opposed to the whole idea. Pearson, the undersecretary of state for external affairs, who somehow caught wind of the gist of Wilson's article prior to its publication, was alarmed at the potential political fallout from the release of such senstive information and hurriedly cabled Canadian trade negotiators for clarification. Wilson's report, of course, had been correct, as far as it went. The Canadian delegation had strongly objected to the British proposal, which they considered both dangerous and foolish, but in addition they had exacted assurances that it would not be raised at Geneva without prior consultation. Either Wilson had lingering doubts about

British intentions and reliability – doubts quietly shared by quite a few senior Canadian officials – or he simply had not been fully informed. Regardless, Pearson was promptly told about the British promise. Still, such was Wilson's credibility in Ottawa, fed by the widespread conviction that he was kept 'in the know' by government officials, that nervous ministers needed reassuring by their deputies and steps were promptly taken to ensure that a fuller explanation appeared in his newspaper.[29]

Being the only Canadian business reporter in attendance, and one already on friendly terms with the prinicipal officials sent to press the Canadian position, guaranteed Wilson special consideration from the delegation at Geneva. The latter included Dana Wilgress, the recently appointed ambassador to Switzerland and the government's senior authority on trade policy, and Sydney Pierce, the chief of the Economics Division at External Affairs and in all likelihood a key source for earlier Wilson stories from London on trade matters.[30] R.S. Milliken, Ford of Canada's export manager and an interested observer, was also a longtime Wilson confidant. Apart from any other considerations, the inevitable socializing of fellow countrymen far from home undoubtedly served to deepen the ties between Wilson and the others.[31] Wilson intently followed the opening stages of the conference, a series of official 'professions of faith' on the future of world trade which 'as a Press Gallery observer,' he confided to McEachern,'I have found ... less platitudinous than I had expected.' No one was completely frank, but the statements invariably contained at least a thread of truth, an indication, he suspected, of the likely national positions when the real negotiations commenced away from the prying eyes of the world press. Apart from 'the magnificence and color of [the] Swiss wonderland,' Wilgress in particular impressed him, as did the head of the British delegation, the brilliant if humourless Sir Stafford Cripps.[32]

Once the conference proper began, Wilson's inside contacts were all the more valuable to the *Post* and its readers. The paper sought to play up his special status, even running a series of photographs showing Wilson and members of the Canadian delegation convivially taking in the sights like so many tourists. Relying on a mix of leaks from the Canadian delegation and his own investigations – Wilson, for example, was the lone foreign newspaperman invited to a select briefing by Will Clayton, the American undersecretary of state for economic affairs and head of the u.s. delegation – he laid bare during the next few weeks the conference's main developments in a steady stream of *Financial Post* reports, most of them Canadian exclusives, as well as in cbc radio commentaries. Copies of the former, it is worth noting, were regularly supplied to the Canadian delegation by Ottawa.[33] The obstacles to agreement at Geneva were formidable and there was unrelieved pessimism in much of the reporting from the conference almost until the end of its deliberations in the fall. Yet Wilson's copy retained a positive tone, a reflection of his boundless enthusiasm for a multilateral trading world and his hunch that some sort of an agreement must, and therefore would, be reached.

In mid May 1947 Wilson left Geneva for London, where, with a little help from his friends, he was able to piece together a full account of the dollar crisis threatening Europe's economic revival. His front-page account reached *Post* readers shortly before a high-level British delegation arrived at Ottawa to discuss mutual economic problems. For some months officials in both the Bank of Canada and the Department of Finance had been anxiously watching the steady decline in the country's reserves of u.s. dollars and privately warning the cabinet of the serious economic implications if the pattern was not reversed. However, the need to prevent 'unrelieved pessimism' in the business and financial community had led the newly appointed finance minister, Douglas Abbott, to downplay the seriousness of the situation.[34] Wilson's revelations in the *Financial Post*'s 17 May issue brought Britain's dollar crisis, and with it Canada's, into the open. The following week's edition devoted the entire feature section to a detailed analysis, with Wilson painting a bleak but broadly accurate picture of catastrophic American dollar shortages strangling trade and threatening the imminent collapse of economic multilateralism on which so many Canadian hopes were pinned. Britain's desperate hope, he concluded, was to convince Washington to prime the international economy with a massive infusion of dollars, and to that end the British government would apply what pressure it could, directly and through Canada's good offices.

Developments now followed rapidly. Urged on by several of his mandarin friends, Wilson won McEachern's approval to mount a sort of journalistic 'royal commission' into ways of resolving Canada's dollar woes. Pearson, one of the idea's enthusiasts, frankly confided to Wilson that such a series from an independent source and ghosted by experts in the civil service would provide the cabinet with the sound advice many of the undersecretary's colleagues in the bureaucracy felt it badly needed. In the event, Wilson wrote the articles himself, supplementing his own extensive knowledge of the problem with the insights of Dr William Mackintosh, one of the most senior economic mandarins until his recent resignation, and those of several other leading economists.[35]

At the end of May 1947, just days before Secretary of State General George C. Marshall first publicly broached the idea of a European economic recovery plan financed by the United States, Wilson commented on the rumours of such an initiative swirling about Ottawa, its implications for

Canada, and the government's eagerness to participate, especially if it meant sharing directly in the u.s. dollar windfall.[36] McEachern was quick to urge them on. Without such American aid there would be no European recovery, and without a revitalized European trade, he ominously warned his readers, 'Canadian industry is finished.'[37] The latter assessment exaggerated Canada's predicament, to be sure, but the paper's admirers in Ottawa were not disappointed by the apocalyptic tone.

By mid June a *Financial Post* campaign boosting the so-called Marshall Plan was in full swing. While President Truman was in Ottawa to discuss European recovery, Wilson indulged in what he called some 'intelligent speculation' on the substance of the talks. Obviously Canada favoured as bold a plan as possible, one that would permit Europeans to spend some of their dollars 'off shore' in Canada. As Wilson undoubtedly knew, Ottawa was desperately banking on Washington's agreement on the latter provision – a sort of new Hyde Park arrangement, as he likened it.[38] With so much riding on the Marshall Plan and a favourable outcome at Geneva, Ottawa was understandably trying to avoid taking any unilateral action to combat Canada's own worsening dollar drain. McEachern, having just returned from a fact-finding trip of his own to Washington, was sympathetic to the American predicament as was Wilson. Both men were aware that the isolationist wing in the Congress was powerful and eagerly casting about for any excuse to scuttle both Truman administration initiatives. At the least, controls aimed at significantly reducing American imports were bound to cut Canada out of any Marshall Plan largesse. Thus, while the daily press played up rumours throughout June and July that some combination of controls, devaluation, gold subsidies, and the like was imminent, the *Financial Post* calmly assured its readers that despite the growing gravity of the situation, no independent Canadian action was planned in the near term.[39]

By the middle of August 1947 Britain was in the throes of a financial crisis. Under the terms of a large recovery loan negotiated earlier with Washington, London had been required to implement the convertibility of sterling into dollars a month earlier. In a world desperately short of dollars but with a surfeit of pounds, the result was predictable and, for the Exchequer's slender dollar reserves, catastrophic. The convertibility experiment was short-lived, the British understandably concluding they should not martyr themselves for the world's economic problems.

In light of this latest crisis, however, Towers was now advising the government in the strongest terms that steps to protect Canada's own reserves of American dollars could not be put off past the fall. This advice came even though there was not yet unanimity within those elements of the bureaucracy most directly involved – the Bank, the Department of Finance, and External Affairs – as to what measures the government should employ.[40] 'Faced with much more difficult and unpleasant alternatives' – import restrictions and currency controls – Wilson duly reported that the government was considering the possibility of seeking a large American loan. In fact, as Wilson wrote, there had still been no cabinet discussion of the dollar crisis (senior ministers would only be briefed by Clark the following week), an omission Wilson noted pointedly in the same article.[41]

Privately, he now found the government's outward calm disturbing. He worried they had decided to make a virtue of inaction. From the *Financial Post*'s position, the situation had altered dramatically during the past few months. Given the dimensions of the economic crisis detailed in its pages, it was irresponsible for the government to continue searching for easy solutions. From now on economic, not political, considerations had to be given priority. There was no justification for the government's failure to be 'more frank and informative about Canada's dollar plight and ... the steps that are being taken to meet [the situation].'[42]

At the same time that senior economic advisers were pressing the cabinet to take those 'much more difficult and unpleasant alternatives,' another serious difficulty demanded their attention. Throughout the summer, and culminating during the convertibility crisis when a high-level British delegation had been in Washington pressing for emergency American assistance, pronouncements by officials in the Attlee government had left the strong impression that Canada, by demanding partial payment for its exports to the United Kingdom in u.s. dollars, had cold-bloodedly weakened British finances. This criticism, combined with London's frequent references to the imminent imposition of austerity measures which promised drastic reductions in some British imports from Canada, created a potentially serious public relations problem for Ottawa at the very time it was trying to steady the Canadian business community's nerves and create a domestic consensus on the country's own difficulties. Understandably, Canadian officials were furious that their British opposite numbers were misrepresenting as little better than extortion what in fact was Canada's generosity. After all, only in June, when the extraordinarily rapid rate of British drawing on the Canadian loan threatened Canada's already precarious position, had Ottawa quietly demanded that no more than 50 per cent of future imports be financed from those credits, with the rest in American dollars.[43] Clark and his colleagues were determined that Canadians (and Americans) know the truth, and Wilson readily cooperated by publicizing their side of the dispute.[44]

This crisis had hardly passed when a new one loomed, sparked by British determination to wring concessions from Canada on the 50:50 payment arrangement. Britain, of course, now found itself in an impossible financial situation and frankly had no choice but to conserve its limited reserves of American dollars however it could to meet essential imports. The Canadians, with serious problems of their own, had little inclination to sympathize. The seriousness with which Ottawa viewed this latest dispute was confirmed by the dispatch of a delegation headed by Finance Minister Abbott to London in early September 1947, ostensibly to attend a meeting of the International Monetary Fund but in fact intended to resolve this latest Anglo-Canadian 'misunderstanding.' Clark, who was especially bitter over recent British behaviour, warned R.B. Bryce, one of his senior officials who was serving as Abbott's principal counsel during the talks, that 'however you may be influenced by sympathy for the British position, it is quite clear no sympathy can be wasted in that quarter.'[45] Finance officials, who were adamant that there be no changes in the arrangements previously agreed to, were conscious that they had 'to consider not only the attitude to be taken in our discussions with the U.K., but also subsequent public discussions of this matter. In other words, we obviously have a case to make to our own people as well.'[46]

Once again, Wilson delivered a sympathetic and calming assessment of the Canadian position, stressing Ottawa's generosity and downplaying the impact of British austerity on Canadian exports, the two points Ottawa particularly wanted conveyed. Predictably, the ensuing discussions brought some very frank exchanges. In the end, Abbott revealed that the imposition of import controls in Canada was now only a matter of the proper timing so as to avoid compromising the Geneva trade talks and minimizing adverse reaction in the United States. This admission finally convinced the British that Canada's dollar woes were indeed serious and that she could expect no more extraordinary sacrifices by her wartime ally.[47]

Throughout the previous months, the access Wilson enjoyed to the inner sanctums of the civil service was crucial to his coverage of developments and the maintenance of the *Post*'s position as an authoritative voice. A private luncheon he had arranged with Clark at the Rideau Club a few days before Abbott left for London clearly illustrates how he operated. Wilson's relations with the Department of Finance were excellent. Clark disliked being pestered by reporters and found most of them dull. His well-deserved reputation for discussing every question in economic technicalities and carefully avoiding any comments that could remotely be construed as 'political' ensured that all but a few gallery members avoided him. But Wilson's understanding of economics allowed him to follow most of Clark's tedious explanations, and straight politics was seldom his primary interest anyway. The two men liked each other and Clark invariably found time for the *Financial Post*'s man whenever he requested it. Wilson, for his part, did not abuse the privilege. As usual, on this occasion Clark 'was reluctant to say anything that might be construed as indicating what government policy might or might not be,' Wilson later reported to McEachern. 'However, I outlined the differences of opinion we were studying and he discussed the points with growing freedom.'[48]

The differences of opinion Wilson was investigating were plans to deal with the now critical drain on Canada's reserves of u.s. dollars. Howe, his principal cabinet confidant, was trying to reassure the *Post* that things were not as black as they seemed, although the minister felt considerably more gloomy when discussing the situation with old political friends. The government needed time to work out a solution behind the scenes, Howe admitted, and Wilson and his paper could help immeasurably by refraining from rocking the boat a little longer.[49] Briefings by Towers, Pearson, Gordon, Max Mackenzie (Howe's deputy minister), and others, however, told a different story – one of growing frustration within the bureaucracy over Abbott's foot-dragging.

Senior Canadian officials had decided some weeks earlier that the time had come to alert the Truman administration to Canada's worsening predicament, but the initial response from the Treasury and State departments was not reassuring. In mid September, Clark personally led a delegation to Washington to drive home to the Americans the drastic choices Canada would soon face and the helpful actions the United States might undertake 'to influence our choice of alternatives.'[50] The meetings, however, left him more pessimistic than ever. Ambassador Hume Wrong had warned Clark that 'in order to make our position thoroughly understood in this country and also in some measure in Canada we shall have to do two things; first, a full and emphatic exposure of the facts will have to be issued and repeated through several channels; secondly, restrictions will have to be imposed which will make a lot of people squeal both at the consuming end in Canada and at the producing end in the United States.'[51] After a week in Washington and New York butting his head against the proverbial wall, Clark could only agree, although he still felt that immediate action, with its potential for damaging the Geneva process and off-shore Marshall Plan provisions, was too risky.

While Canadian diplomats in Washington and cooperative State Department officials set about using their well-developed contacts in the American press to create a sympathetic climate for Canada's predicament, the mandarins seemed to have plans for Wilson, too. Although the documentary evidence does not confirm whether they had arrived at this decision consciously or whether, given the nature of past relations with him, it just seemed the natural thing to do, in late September an excited Wilson informed McEachern that he had been shown a confidential memorandum setting out in detail the policy recommendations hammered out by the Department of Finance and the Bank of Canada.[52] In fact, a secret memo of just the sort Wilson described and which was then circulating within the finance department did bear a strong resemblance to the detailed accounts now appearing under his byline in the pages of the *Financial Post*. With rumours of an imminent devaluation threatening to unravel Abbott's efforts to maintain calm, Wilson had argued with his sources that their information should be used to steady the public mood. At least business would then be able to plan for the devil it knew. Unknown to Wilson, his argument would merely have reinforced the bureaucracy's own convictions that some publicity might be useful both in educating Americans and Canadians alike and in pushing the Liberals to take action. Certainly it is highly unlikely that Wilson would have published a précis of such sensitive material without having a strong sense that this was his sources' intention.

The 27 September issue of the *Financial Post* outlined the bureaucratic proposals soon to be put before the cabinet 'in detail and with complete accuracy,' as Wilson later boasted.[53] There would be no devaluation of the Canadian dollar; their correspondent had that 'on very high authority,' an understatement to say the least. Instead, Ottawa would move to impose a variety of short- and long-term measures to staunch the outflow of American dollars, everything from import embargoes and substitution for U.S. goods and services to higher excise taxes, travel restrictions, and exchange controls. At the same time, Ottawa would seek a substantial loan from Washington for emergency use and confidence-building while the other measures took effect. But these plans, Wilson cautioned, would remain nothing more than a blueprint until subjected to the 'political eye' of the cabinet. As colleague Blair Fraser put it, in getting past that obstacle 'the brainstrust [would have] a tremendous selling job on its hands.'[54] There were considerable risks involved whatever the cabinet chose, and in fact Wilson was not totally unsympathetic to their predicament. Nevertheless, the tone and content of his report left no doubt that he was convinced the government would have to act soon. While there were hopes in some quarters, he acknowledged, that a favourable outcome to the Marshall Plan and international trade negotiations might provide the government with the way out it desperately wanted, the facts of the country's rapidly worsening monthly trade balances were 'piling up [an] imperious argument for drastic and immediate action.'[55]

Two weeks later, Wilson, having returned from Washington where he had met with various American and Canadian officials to discuss the status of the Marshall Plan, Canadian borrowing prospects, and related matters, moderated his tone slightly by admitting that the government faced a difficult choice between all-out import controls and hedging bets on the possible timely arrival of Marshall Plan aid. Until the u.s. policy picture was clearer, Ottawa, he felt, would find some way to avoid full-blown austerity and the bureaucratic controls, rising prices, and political unpopularity such a program would entail. Nevertheless, he reiterated that 'something must be done and done very quickly,' precisely the advice Abbott was receiving from his most senior advisers.[56] When the following week Wilson noted in a lead article headlined 'Muddle Still Reigns on Dollar Dilemma' that Abbott's return from London had not sparked the expected decision-taking, the Conservative opposition quickly seized this evidence of Liberal irresponsibility to launch their own attack on 'Liberal inaction.'

In fact, a special committee of cabinet, chaired by the finance minister, was intently considering a program of action which everyone seemed to recognize could not be put off for much longer, and the cabinet as a whole was briefed at length by Towers, Clark, and several of their officials on 24 October.[57] Meanwhile, negotiations between Ottawa and Washington were entering their critical final stages. Clark, Towers, and their advisers were unanimously of the opinion that Washington had to be shocked into helping Canada find a minimally disruptive exit from its balance-of-trade problems. With that in mind, two dollar-conservation programs had been drawn up, one unabashedly discriminatory towards the United States (the so-called A plan) and the other (B plan) one that would at least attempt to avoid the appearance of discrimination. In effect, the strategy was to intimidate the Americans with the former while promising to implement the more palatable B plan if they adopted appropriate measures to assist Canada. Chief among these was the provision for off-shore purchases under the European Recovery Program, as the Marshall Plan was to be officially called. Of course, no one was under any illusions that convincing the Truman administration of Canada's special needs was one thing and convincing the Congress quite another.[58]

At the end of October, another Canadian delegation, this time including both Clark and Towers, trekked to Washington under the public cover that these talks were merely consultations on the general world economic situation. Pointing out that Canada's u.s. dollar reserves had declined an alarming 15 per cent in the five weeks since their last talks, and now amounted to slightly less than half the figure at the beginning of the year,[59] the Canadians stressed that either the A or the B plan would have to be introduced by the middle of November at the latest. As Clark later noted, the almost uninterrupted litany of 'banned,' 'prohibited,' 'discriminatory,' 'cut-off,' and 'drastically reduced' sprinkled through the A plan seemed at last to have the desired shock effect. Nonetheless, the chastened Americans protested vigorously that the deadline threatened to have serious repercussions in the Congress and urged the Canadians to wait until early 1948, when both the Geneva agreements and the European Recovery Program should be in place. Clark and Towers, however, were adamant – Canada had no more manoeuvring room – and while the delegation returned to Ottawa with little in the way of concrete pledges, they were now much more confident that the administration was prepared to press hard to meet Canada's special needs.[60]

Early November brought another success for the A plan, when difficult negotiations to obtain a $500 million loan from the U.S. Import-Export Bank were successfully concluded. As well, there was welcome news from Geneva that, despite a last-minute scare that the conference might break up over Anglo-American differences on the Commonwealth preferences issue, a General Agreement on Tariffs and Trade had been reached.[61] While the Geneva meetings had produced much less than the multilateralist millennium hoped for at the end of the war, the results for Canada, thanks to skilful negotiation and some luck, were quite favourable. A month earlier, Wilson had informed *Post* readers that success at Geneva now seemed certain and that details of the new tariff regulations would be announced on or about 18 November, to come into effect on 1 January 1948. The date was perhaps no more than an educated guess – on 18 November the follow-on trade conference at Havana was scheduled to open – but it was in fact the date chosen as cabinet ministers were officially notified three days after Wilson's article appeared. The *Financial Post*'s GATT scoop was especially sweet for Wilson and McEachern as the *Montreal Gazette,* the mouthpiece of the Montreal business community, had been confidently predicting that the Geneva talks had collapsed.[62]

Wilson was confident that the government would move on the more publicly unpopular parts of the dollar-conservation program once the Geneva result was officially known. It made political sense, after all, to sweeten the bad news with some good, which was precisely the government's thinking. In the 8 November issue of the *Post,* Wilson reported that the early reconvening of parliament set for 5 December would not deal with matters arising out of Geneva, as the prime minister asserted and Abbott and others in the cabinet were dutifully repeating, but rather with the legislative backing necessary for some of the more drastic measures the government intended to use in solving the dollar crisis. Ottawa's ploy, he suggested, 'fits precisely into the sort of pattern that has been emerging here in recent weeks [in which] the government is apparently eager and determined to show that its main purpose and convictions centre around the principles of expansionist multilateral trade.' Measures along these lines combined with GATT and further trade liberalization still to be negotiated between Ottawa and Washington, would form the centrepiece of the government's sales job. When combined with the now expected benefits from the Marshall Plan and an American loan, they would enable Ottawa to water down the painful emergency program of selected restrictions, embargoes, quotas, and tax increases designed to produce a drastic short-term reduction in the cost of U.S. imports. The tone and content of the article, and especially its spelling out of the general details of the supposedly secret dollar-conservation program, infuriated King, or so Wilson was later told. The prime minister's mood cannot have been helped by a McEachern editorial in the same issue which disparaged King's own failure to show any leadership while praising Abbott for his courage in finally speaking out clearly and bluntly about the dollar crisis before a recent meeting of manufacturers in Montreal. But what might have been an embarrassing situation for Wilson and the *Post* was quickly defused by Abbott who dismissed the story as the inevitable result of good reporting.[63] The finance minister's defence was hardly surprising; some of Wilson's stories had come directly from his office and, after the valuable service Wilson had rendered over the past few months, it was hardly in the government's interest to harass him.

The following week, Wilson, like his mandarin sources, breathed a sigh of relief over news that the much-hoped-for off-shore provisions benefiting Canada had been included in the European Recovery Program package being submitted to Congress and seemed likely to win passage. However, this would be no panacea, he warned, and 'in no sense remove[d] the need for quotas, embargoes and other restrictive measures' that would still have to be imposed temporarily, though these would now be much less severe and of shorter duration than feared. For the same issue, Wilson had prepared a lengthy article outlining a broad range of practical steps that could be taken to expand Canadian exports to the United States, suggestions which, like so much of what he had been writing, were markedly similar to ones that had been discussed within the Department of Finance during the preceding weeks.[64]

On 17 November, the prime minister, who was in London for the royal wedding, publicly announced the successful conclusion of the Geneva negotiations. Immediately following this radio address, Abbott took to the airwaves to explain the details of the government's dollar-conservation program, a program that differed in no essential way from the one outlined by Wilson a little over a week earlier. During the weeks preceding these public statements, officials in Ottawa and at the embassy in Washington had been deeply concerned with having them properly explained to both Americans and Canadians. 'Giving guidance to the press,' as Wilgress had succinctly stated the problem, thus became a minor industry in both capitals.[65] Understandably, the reception accorded Abbott's speech was deemed particularly crucial and, as such, it was carefully crafted by Louis Rasminsky of the Bank of Canada in consultation with Clark and Donald Gordon, then shown to State Department officials for vetting to avoid any embarrassments in Washington. Canadian reporters were given detailed closed-door briefings the evening of the address, and, the following morning, press conferences were held in both capitals. Events proved that the precautions taken were well worthwhile.

Once Ottawa moved itself to action, the *Financial Post*'s editorial support was never in doubt. McEachern and Wilson had no difficulty with the government's position that temporary trade restrictions were not inconsistent with a long-term commitment to freer trade. Some sections of the business community – for instance, American branch plants and most companies undertaking major expansions – were bound to be unhappy with the import controls, but McEachern urged them to consider the future good of the economy.[66] This wholehearted endorsement, frequently restated over the coming months, was obviously helpful to the government, as were the supportive speeches Wilson made before various business groups across the country.

From the perspective of the *Financial Post*, Wilson's coverage of the two major economic stories of 1947 had been a superb achievement. As Wilson himself reflected with understandable pride, his reports had 'forecast very closely the main lines of government action,' and in the process further enhanced the *Post*'s claim to be *the* authority on Canadian business and financial affairs.[67]

And what of the dollar crisis itself? Considerable difficulties remained to be overcome and, indeed, six months later at a private briefing, Towers would express nothing stronger than 'modest optimism' that the decline in Canada's dollar reserves had been permanently arrested.[68] Nevertheless, the measures announced in November 1947, in conjunction with the benefits which, by the spring of 1948, began to flow Canada's way under the European Recovery Program, would at least reduce the problem to manageable dimensions by the end of that year; thereafter, the situation improved steadily.

During the next four years Wilson's reputation continued to grow. As the *Financial Post*'s unquestioned star and Chalmers's protégé, he enjoyed almost complete freedom of action in his reporting. In this respect, Wilson was fortunate and knew it; while he and McEachern certainly recognized each other's talents, their relationship was strained. Wilson found McEachern's attempts to edit his copy in what he considered petty ways especially irksome and, as much as possible, he avoided direct contact with his editor.[69]

Increasingly, Wilson began to deal with public policy issues in the broadest sense, breaking completely from the restraints of straight business reporting. His columns consistently offered general support for the Liberals' economic and fiscal policies, with criticisms typically focusing on policy details, not guiding principles. As a consequence, he came to be seen in a growing number of eyes as a Liberal sympathizer, an allegation he casually shrugged off although it offended his sense of professionalism. More to the point, such an accusation missed the mark; while Wilson in his private moments was almost assuredly an independent Liberal, the principal basis of his support was an unshakeable confidence in the mandarinate's competence and vision. Certainly nothing aroused his ire more quickly than gratuitous slights to the bureaucracy or its 'fancy ideas.'[70] Furthermore, as his coverage of the Geneva trade talks and dollar crisis had clearly revealed, his extensive contacts within the government were essential if his reporting was to be informed. After all, Wilson saw himself as a 'reporter' whose role was to raise issues and foreshadow policy, preferably in advance of his peers, and then interpret these ideas in light of the facts, not opinion. To do this, background was essential. In most instances, such clarifications were given for just that purpose, background rather than attribution. Yet the understanding between reporter and source was such that this rarely had to be stated. When it came to publication, Wilson used his judgment. Naturally, personal and professional considerations usually though not always ensured that his source's wishes were respected. Ultimately, in keeping with the responsible, civilized tone that characterized his relationship with the civil service, the most powerful check was self-imposed. Wilson felt he had a responsibility to his readers. to be properly informed and to his mandarin friends to explain the workings of their policies correctly.[71] Retaining the confidence of the policy-makers, and hence access to the facts, was essential if he and his newspaper were going to carry out their self-appointed mandate successfully. As for the Liberal party, its outstanding virtue in his eyes was its willingness to give the bureaucracy its head.

Wilson's chief contribution to the transformation of national affairs reporting away from the traditional parliament-centred approach was his concern with the details of the formulation and workings of policy. Since these tasks were increasingly the preserve of the civil service, it is not surprising that he developed close professional relationships with only a handful of politicians. All of these men, save for Pearson (whom he had known as a mandarin), held economically important portfolios: Ilsley and Abbott in Finance, Claxton in National Defence, and Howe in his various cabinet incarnations. In contrast, his contacts within the bureaucracy included virtually everyone of importance in the Departments of Finance, Trade and Commerce, Reconstruction, and External Affairs as well as in the Bank of Canada, Privy Council Office, and Prime Minister's Office – in other words, the heart of the postwar mandarinate.

Press relations were extraordinarily informal during this period; neither Finance nor the Bank bothered to set up formal press bureaus before the early 1950s. Abbott, with a knack for handling newspapermen that came close to matching Pearson's calculated affability, reaped considerable dividends from his casual, personal approach and was on very good terms with Wilson. Arranging interviews with Clark and his senior advisers was also straightforward, although what the curious reporter learned, or whether he was asked back, was another matter. In contrast, Graham Towers had little use for most reporters and was always cautious even with those few who were in favour, preferring to confine his interviews to the correction of their misunderstandings of Bank policy. Fortunately, Towers's attitude was not rigidly copied by all his senior officials. Moreover, when circumstances dictated, even the governor of the Bank of Canada could be more accessible and forthright, especially to a journalist of Wilson's calibre.[72] As for External Affairs, most of Canada's diplomats, starting with Pearson, had a well-developed sense of the valuable ways in which the press could be helpful. Wilson held a privileged position and was able to make the most of the largely ad hoc arragements that prevailed in Ottawa at this time. In the case of the Department of Finance, for example, monthly meetings with the minister usually sufficed, but his sessions with Clark and other senior aides took place much more frequently. In the case of the Bank of Canada, Wilson's visits became a weekly ritual.[73]

Invariably, Wilson received inside information at these sessions, and his own style as a reporter had much to do with it. To begin with, he was a thorough researcher who made certain he was fully briefed for any interview, a quality that naturally impressed his sources. Usually, he would ask for clarification or guidance on only one or two points, with the implication that he planned to pursue the story elsewhere. Finally, he had become especially convincing at conveying the impression that he knew considerably more than he really did, a ploy intended to make his sources talk more freely.

Most importantly, Finance and the Bank continued to find it useful to keep Wilson's readers properly informed. Stories had a way of getting out, and the government's intentions might as well be presented accurately. As long as one respected the mandarins' sensibilities about impartiality and confidentiality, private briefings and what amounted to ghost-writing on technical topics of an economic nature could be arranged for a select group of journalists, of whom Wilson was the leading member and foremost beneficiary.[74] The reasons are simple: quite apart from his connection with the *Financial Post*, he was widely viewed as the most able, discreet, and intellectually sympathetic vehicle the press gallery offered for this purpose. And the more authoritative and hence credible he became to his readers, the more useful, too, in quashing rumours or touting plans still in the formulation stage or even in prodding reluctant cabinets.

On occasion, situations arose when Wilson's eagerness for an exclusive story or unwillingness to play along strained the relationship. And there were instances when his revelations embarrassed the government politically, although, since both men liked to play the watch-dog role, these leaks bothered Wilson little and McEachern still less.[75] Liberal politicians tended to be pragmatic about such indiscretions, but not so the obsessively secretive Towers, who, by the late 1940s, had concluded that Wilson was no longer sufficiently reliable to be shown the most sensitive material.[76] In practice, however, Towers's officials irregularly enforced his edict and it was only a minor inconvenience at worst. Wilson's relations with the Department of Finance, with its well-deserved reputation during Clark's tenure for the artful use of 'selective disclosures,' had always been warmer and more productive anyway.

As valuable as Wilson's bureaucratic contacts were, he was always more than simply an Ottawa man. While admiring the mandarins and sympathizing with their vision of Canada, his roots remained firmly planted in the business community and he spent a great deal of time assiduously cultivating contacts there. Industrialist Gordon Cockshutt, president of the Canadian Manufacturers Association during the immediate postwar years and a leading industrialist, was a particularly close friend. Wilson also served as an adviser to the Canada–United States Committee of the Canadian Chamber of Commerce and the Chamber of Commerce of the United States, an important lobbying group on both sides of the border. Through his friendship with J.D. Gibson, chief economist of the Bank of Nova Scotia, he was invited on several occasions to participate with prominent private-sector economists and businessmen in informal discussions of economic and public policy matters. As Wilson's star rose, Maclean-Hunter itself arranged get-togethers with select groups of executives where their man in Ottawa could dazzle with his insider's knowledge. Just as valuably, Wilson used these occasions to learn what businessmen were thinking about current public questions.[77] Of course, if intimate government contacts heightened his credibility with the latter group, the reverse was also true. In addition to a heavy schedule of such face-to-face encounters, management encouraged Wilson to accept as many of the frequent opportunities to speak at business functions as he could and generally to become involved in any organization or activity that brought him into contact with important business and financial figures. These contacts enhanced not only his profile, but, in the process, the profile of the *Financial Post* as well.[78]

Finally, Wilson gained great advantages from his close working and personal relationship with C.D. Howe. As minister of reconstruction and, later, through the joint portfolios of Trade and Commerce and Defence Production, Howe continued in the postwar years his wartime role as the link between business and government. Along with Abbott and St Laurent, he ensured that the climate in postwar Ottawa remained decidedly sympathetic to business's interests. A centre of power bringing together the political, bureaucratic, and corporate elites coalesced around Howe's departments, ensuring that, as sociologist John Porter would later observe, "'Howe's boys" enjoyed a position somewhere between influence and power that was as significant as that enjoyed by the "boys" of Finance, [the Bank of Canada] and External Affairs.'[79] As an enthusiast for Canadian economic development on a grand scale, Wilson naturally admired Howe. Like him, Wilson also felt frustrated by the myopia, inertia, and smug self-satisfaction that both felt all too often characterized their country's business and financial communities during this period. Moreover, both men were unabashedly pro-American. In Wilson's case, this was a long-standing sympathy which had been strengthened considerably in both the practical and the emotional sense by contacts with business and government during and after the war, and which translated into an enthusiasm for closer economic ties with the United States.[80] For a great many rising middle-level executives, men who as yet did not merit the special treatment Howe accorded his millionaire lieutenants in the country's corporate boardrooms, Wilson's weekly synopses in the *Financial Post* were the principal source of inside information. This suited Howe, as did the opportunities to use Wilson as a policy-stalking horse, and he treated him accordingly; one senior bureaucrat quipped only partly in jest that, thanks to Howe, Wilson might as well have 'lived under the cabinet table.'[81]

As an 'informed source,' the *Financial Post* was clearly perceived within the government as being a useful platform from which to speak to a particularly important constituency.[82] For its part, Maclean-Hunter management felt that by facilitating dialogue between business and government the paper exercised a great deal of clout, especially editorially. It was a comfortable illusion that most of the *Post*'s senior employees, including Wilson (though not McEachern), shared.[83] What cannot be overestimated is the degree of acceptance Wilson earned in the senior levels of the civil service and in the business and financial community. First and foremost this position enabled him to observe and relate the dominant role being played by the economic mandarins in shaping postwar Canada. Wilson's reports, buttressed by their briefings, illustrated the extent to which the boundary between the exercise of influence and actual power had blurred until, as in the case of the management of the dollar crisis, it had become imperceptible.[84] These intimate contacts were based on mutual interest, to be sure, but also on considerable respect and goodwill. By the late 1940s, they established Wilson as one of *the* journalistic authorities in English-speaking Canada, a state of affairs his editor readily acknowledged was central to such prestige, success, and influence as the *Financial Post* enjoyed.[85]

'We believe that as people are educated along sound lines,' Horace Hunter piously lectured his editors in 1946, 'they will support the right type of government and legislation.'[86] Educating people along 'sound lines' was precisely what Wilson and the *Financial Post* had attempted to do in 1947, and with some success, although the principal beneficiary was probably the Liberal government's reputation. In an era of responsible, civilized journalism and a pervasive government-business consensus in which it seemed natural to believe that the government was on the right course, being authoritative and being independent were not deemed to be incompatible. For Ken Wilson and the *Financial Post,* competent explanation had become the primary objective, and partnership, not adversarialism, the preferred arrangement.

5

'A uniquely Canadian force'

Blair Fraser and *Maclean's*

During the postwar decade, the determination of Maclean-Hunter Publishing to entrench the *Financial Post* as the leading source of news and opinion for the Canadian business and financial community was matched by its ambitions for the company's other flagship publication, *Maclean's* magazine. Targeting the rapidly expanding middle class, Maclean-Hunter officials and editorial staff were intent on producing a glossy, readable, mass-circulation magazine that would be unabashedly Canadian in content and outlook, or, as Ralph Allen, editor of *Maclean's* during the 1950s put it, 'a magazine that Canadians will read *and* respect.'[1] Not everyone agreed with the distinctive bourgeois brand of pan-Canadian nationalism *Maclean's* espoused during the late 1940s and 1950s, or that the magazine was the vital national institution it confidently claimed to be. Yet in a largely pre-television era, when only CBC radio could be said to share its goal of raising the national consciousness of English-speaking Canadians on a nationwide basis, the impact of *Maclean's* was considerable.

Maclean's was a journalists' magazine, and none of the talented writers employed on its staff made a greater contribution to its success in presenting Canada and the world to Canadian readers than Blair Fraser. Indeed, for a generation of Canadians, *Maclean's* and Blair Fraser became all but synonymous. Whether through his regular 'Backstage at Ottawa' column or his many feature articles, the urbane, intellectual Fraser's role was to provide his readers with an insider's glimpse of national politics. What emerged, however, was a thoughtful analysis of national affairs. This, coupled with the fact that alone among print journalists he reached a national audience, firmly established Fraser as a columnist-commentator in the mould of a

Walter Lippmann or a James Reston. In the era of so-called responsible, civilized journalism, Fraser became its epitome.

Maclean's magazine first appeared under that name in 1911, offering an
uninspiring collection of excerpts from American magazines, second-rate
fiction, and 'puff' pieces on the business and political cronies of its name-
sake. By the mid 1920s, however, Horace Hunter began to transform the
magazine into a thoroughly Canadian publication.² That meant assembling
a better staff, and, with the good fortune that often seemed to smile on his
personnel decisions, he managed in 1925 to acquire the services of a talented young Toronto newspaperman, William Arthur Irwin.

Born in Ayr, Ontario, on 27 May 1898, Irwin was the eldest son of the
Rev. A.J. Irwin, a Methodist minister of radical views. Of necessity, the
Irwin children were raised in a frugal style, but one that also nurtured a
respect for intellectual values and dissenting opinion. When the Rev. Irwin
accepted a teaching position at Winnipeg's Wesley College, the youngster
accompanied his family to the booming and boisterous Manitoba capital.
After completing his schooling in Winnipeg, he enrolled in university, only
to quit after two years to enlist in the CEF. Irwin ended up in the artillery,
in fact serving in the same battery as Brooke Claxton, the prominent Liberal cabinet minister of the 1940s and 1950s, and fought his way across
northern France in the climactic battles of the last year of the war. Like so
many of his comrades in the CEF, Grant Dexter and George Ferguson
included, he emerged from the experience a passionate nationalist with a
healthy suspicion of the Anglo-imperialist mentality. After being demobi-
lized, he resumed his studies, graduating in 1921 from the University of
Toronto's Victoria College with a BA in political science and a strong interest
in journalism. Irwin found work with the *Mail and Empire,* then switched
to the *Globe.* In 1925 he was sent to Ottawa for a taste of parliamentary
reporting, a sure sign he was marked for promotion. However, the stint in
Ottawa turned out to be a disillusioning experience. Politics were and
remained a passion, but the general calibre of reporter he encountered in the
press gallery was distinctly disappointing. After a few months on the Hill,
Irwin returned to Toronto to work as an editorial writer. Within a matter of
weeks, however, he had resigned over *Globe* publisher George Jaffray's
refusal to endorse the Mackenzie King government's low-tariff policies.³

In 1926, a year after Irwin had come to *Maclean's,* Hunter decided the
time was ripe for an editorial shakeup. But he considered the twenty-eight-
year-old Irwin too young and, one suspects, potentially too independently
minded for the job. Instead, the editorship went to Henry Napier Moore, a
transplanted Englishman whose anglophilia, snobbery, loyalty, and general aversion to unconventional ideas or opinions – rather than any hidden

editorial talents – made him irresistible to Hunter and Maclean.[4] From the outset, Hunter recognized that Irwin, not Moore, was the competent journalist. In a move that bore all the signs of Hunter's byzantine management style, an arrangement soon evolved under which Moore retained the title of editor while Irwin, as associate editor, was encouraged to assume more of the responsibility for shaping the magazine's development.

With a minuscule budget and only a three-man staff (including Moore), Irwin faced the formidable challenge of having to Canadianize both Moore and *Maclean's* and, at the same time, upgrade the overall quality of the newsstand product. His promotion from associate to managing editor in 1942 made Irwin editor in all but name, answerable only to Floyd Chalmers, whose own relations with Moore were chilly. Finally, in 1945, Irwin's appointment as editor was formalized.[5]

To understand Irwin's Canadianism is to understand the postwar role he envisaged for *Maclean's*. Irwin shared the vision of that group of young English-Canadian intellectuals for whom the Great War and the Great Depression were formative adult experiences and who constituted, to use historian Douglas Owram's apt phrase, the 'government generation.' Their first allegiance was to Canada, a North American nation, and not some vague imperial entity. Like them, Irwin believed passionately that his country must possess an independent voice in the world, and that Canada's future was bounded only by the timidity and lack of vision of Canadians – unfortunate qualities they were determined to banish from the country's character. Furthermore, Canadians, as a middle-aged Irwin would phrase it, must be made to act along 'broad national lines.'[6] While some of Irwin's contemporaries eventually chose politics, the civil service, academe, or even business as the careers that would enable them to translate their national vision into reality, others like Dexter, Ferguson, and Irwin chose journalism.[7] By the 1930s Irwin's intentions were no less ambitious than to make over *Maclean's* into a dynamic, indeed, indispensable, nationalizing force.

The character of a publication, as Irwin never tired of explaining, was shaped by the editorial line, not the bottom line. With that in mind, he set out to assemble a first-rate team of writers and correspondents. Previous magazine experience was unimportant; few Canadians had any and, anyway, Irwin himself had started as a newspaperman. What he wanted were bright, ambitious, open-minded young men (and women) with a flair for writing and an affinity for his own brand of Canadianism. The challenge of writing for a national audience was an obvious attraction, and Irwin's own persuasive powers were almost irresistible. In short order he assembled the finest writing staff in the country, including Blair Fraser. At the same time he relentlessly pursued the larger editorial budgets that were an obvious precondition to transforming the magazine. Despite Chalmers's resistance to such 'extravagance,' particularly when it occurred in the guise of salary increases, Irwin managed to increase the funds available for the 'creative' side of the magazine's operations substantially during his tenure as editor.[8] While the editorial resources at *Maclean's* were never lavish, more money meant, for instance, that he could regularly dispatch reporters and feature-writers to cover stories from one end of the country to the other and, when circumstances warranted, even abroad, an unheard of indulgence for any other Canadian magazine and most of the country's newspapers.

Circulation and advertising figures confirmed that readers were responding favourably to the format and content changes in *Maclean's* engineered by Irwin. By 1946 fully 80 per cent of the magazine's content originated in Canada. Four years later, with a circulation of over 400,000 per issue and a total readership estimated at 1.25 million evenly distributed throughout the English-speaking regions of the country, fully one in four university-educated Canadians, and a comparable number of upper middle-income earners, were regular readers. When one considered circulation and advertising revenue alone, *Maclean's* was the country's leading general-interest magazine, and by a considerable margin.[9] While *Maclean's* never made more than insignificant profits, the company, thanks to its enormously profitable trade journals and job-printing business, was in the strongest economic position of any Canadian magazine publisher. That said, higher Canadian production costs and intense competition for advertising revenue and readers from American periodicals (and in particular those with so-called Canadian editions) were a constant source of anxiety. Given the cultural contribution it liked to think it was making in keeping *Maclean's* afloat, a card the company always played to the hilt, Maclean-Hunter began to perceive itself as a virtual martyr to Canadian nationalism.[10] While the Liberals provided little more than sympathy, the constant expectation that real help lay just around the next electoral corner ensured that as long as the Liberals appeared invincible at the polls, Maclean-Hunter was not likely to go out of its way to alienate them.

As publisher, Chalmers viewed *Maclean's* as a business venture, though admittedly of a unique sort, whereas the editorial staff saw it as a creative cultural endeavour. Irwin always enjoyed reminding anyone within earshot that journalism was for journalists, and he left no doubt where he thought this left Chalmers. Singlemindedly dedicated to 'his' magazine and just as protective of 'his' staff, Irwin was quick to challenge any infringement of his editorial prerogatives, usually successfully. For the most part the editorial team he and his successor Ralph Allen built were socially conscious, progressively minded small-l liberals, and, although some were certainly more critical of the status quo than others, the *Maclean's* editorial offices were hardly a hotbed of radicalism. Nevertheless, all dismissed Chalmers as a small-c conservative and a very large-c conformist who identified totally with the company. Chalmers in turn was convinced that the editorial side was 'almost too uninhibited' and needed to be watched 'carefully,' although in practice his 'supervision' seldom got beyond the meddling stage.[11] Serious conflicts were rare because Chalmers usually backed off, and Hunter's vague suspicion that Chalmers was too ambitious for control and hence needed to be watched himself also acted as a check.[12]

A majority of the editorial confrontations which did occur centred on the coverage of business stories. Both Hunter and Chalmers pined for a speedy postwar return to free-enterprise conditions; the 'creeping socialism' of younger Liberals like Brooke Claxton and Paul Martin and their faceless advisers in the bureaucracy alarmed them. Predictably, Hunter and his associates subscribed to the view that the Liberals, for reasons of unadulterated political expediency – after all, workers voted, and there were large numbers of them – were backing trade unionism's seemingly inexorable march across the Canadian business landscape. Chalmers never tired of encouraging his editors to indulge in 'vigorous criticism and controversy,' while at the same time exhorting them to place the full weight of *Maclean's* behind business's 'positive, dynamic Canadianism.'[13] Irwin held to a different view, one based more on his disdain for the business community's smugness and conservatism than on any deeply held critique of the free-enterprise system. As far as he was concerned, *Maclean's* would cover every aspect of Canadian life, the flattering and the not so flattering, and there would be no more 'lean[ing] over backwards in [the] handling of business stories.'[14] Hard-hitting articles like Allen's 'I Left My Wife Crying,' which focused on the 1946 Hamilton Steel strike, and Fraser's 'Strike Town' on the previous year's Ford strike at Windsor as well as 'Who Are the Income Tax Dodgers?' led prominent business friends of Hunter and Chalmers to grumble about the two reporters' 'chronically negative view of business.'[15] Save for generating brief flurries of memos, however, incidents like these had no long-term impact on the operation of the magazine, and the unrepentant Fraser and Allen both remained in the company's good graces.

Tension between the editorial staff and management aside, the postwar decade at *Maclean's* is now considered to have been, creatively speaking, the magazine's 'golden age.' Irwin set high standards, inspired his colleagues, and allowed them to write with minimum constraint. Staff morale and *élan* were high.[16] When Irwin left the magazine in 1949 to head the National Film Board, Ralph Allen was his handpicked successor. A newspaperman, war correspondent, and novelist, the out-going, hard-drinking Allen was, like his predecessor, a no-nonsense guy who was devoted to his staff and kept management at arm's length. If anything, Irwin's former assistant proved a superior writer and editor, and unquestionably possessed more of the common touch in handling colleagues than his taciturn, teetotalling predecessor. Most importantly, Allen was just as passionately committed as Irwin to the use of *Maclean's* as an instrument of nation-building.

Although most of its staff, Irwin and Allen included, overrated the magazine's achievements, *Maclean's* did win high praise among journalists and a large circle of educated English Canadians.[17] Allen proudly declared it 'an editorial force unique in Canada and uniquely Canadian.'[18] Management, however, and not a few on the writing side, held to the exaggerated view that *Maclean's* was an innovative force at or close to the centre of Canadian public life. Nearly everyone took heart from the magazine's critical success – its circulation and especially, as Chalmers put it, its 'circulation quality ... and in the degree of acceptance of *Maclean's* as the great national magazine of Canada.'[19]

Among the many talented journalists who worked at *Maclean's* during the 1940s and 1950s, none was held in higher regard by the magazine's readers than its Ottawa editor, Blair Fraser. Through his regular political commentaries and feature articles on the domestic and international scene, this quiet but passionate nationalist consciously set out to impart to his readers his personal enthusiasm for a dynamic new Canadianism. In the process, Fraser made a unique contribution to raising the national consciousness of a generation of his English-speaking countrymen.

Robert Blair Fraser was born at Sydney, Nova Scotia, on 17 April 1909. His father, who had worked his way up from common labourer to general supervisor of the Dominion Steel and Coal Corporation, was a stern but humane man with whom his oldest son, despite the obvious bonds of respect and affection between them, seems to have had an ambivalent relationship. There was no ambivalence about growing up in Sydney, however; Fraser later admitted that he had disliked the grimy mill town 'even before I knew that there was anywhere else,' and he left for good at the age of sixteen to enrol at Acadia University. There he drifted from interest to interest, graduating in the end with a BA in English but no real prospects. When a high school teaching job opened in Stanstead, Quebec, he tried that, but barely lasted the year. It was a shattering experience for an insecure nineteen year old and it left him with a sense of failure he never completely overcame.[20]

Fraser then moved to Montreal, where he immediately found work as a reporter, first on the *Herald* and then on the *Star*. He chose newspaper work, he later confided self-deprecatingly, because he 'didn't have the imagination to do anything else.'[21] From the start, both journalism and Montreal intoxicated him. Still, marriage in 1931 led Fraser to take a better-paying job in the public-relations department of the Montreal Heat, Light and Power Company. Less than a year later, like thousands of others, he was on the street, a casualty of the onset of hard times. Despite having a wife to support and no job prospects, Fraser was stubbornly determined to stick it out in Montreal and resisted the temptation to return to Sydney. For more than a year he and Jean, like thousands of Montreal couples, endured on hope and the meagre earnings from occasional part-time work. When his father arranged temporary work on the docks watering piles of coal, Fraser walked the miles to and from their Westmount apartment to save the streetcar fare. Finally, in November 1933, he managed to land a proofreader's job at the *Gazette*. The pay was $10 a week, raised to $12 once his employers learned he was married.

For the next decade, the *Montreal Gazette* was Fraser's home. Promotion came rapidly, from proofreader to reporter, city editor, news editor, and finally associate editor and editorial writer. Much of the time he had to work nights and, the newspaper business being what it was, the pay was never very good; despite these obvious disadvantages, he thoroughly enjoyed what he was doing. These were memorable years in other ways, too. The idealist in Fraser's makeup led him to become involved in several of the left-wing circles and causes that abounded in Montreal during the 1930s. In the process, he struck up a friendship with Frank Scott, actively supported the Spanish Republican cause, and, on a more mundane level, joined in an abortive attempt to unionize the *Gazette* editorial staff. These associations reflected neither Marxist nor radical sympathies, but simply a lifelong suspicion of privilege inherited from his father, a fundamental open-mindedness, and a genuine sympathy for the underdog.[22]

Despite his love affair with Montreal and his thorough enjoyment of the writing responsibilities of his job, by the early years of the war he was becoming increasingly disillusioned with his situation. The *Gazette*, after all, was *the* arch-Tory newspaper in Canada, and the likelihood of someone with Fraser's outlook fitting in was slim. Frustrations related to policy differences accumulated, especially over the touchy issue of overseas conscription, a policy he adamantly opposed. He found publisher John Bassett's condescending efforts to influence him on issues like the titles to be reviewed on the book page he edited infuriating.[23] There were options, of course. Fraser had built a solid reputation in newspaper circles and had already turned down attractive offers from both the *Globe and Mail* and *Maclean's* to serve as their parliamentary reporter. Finally, in the autumn of 1943, he accepted that his differences with the *Gazette* were irreconcilable. Irwin approached Fraser again, and this time he needed little persuading. On 1 January 1944 he officially took up his new position as the magazine's Ottawa editor.

The Frasers, now with two sons and a couple of young English children in tow, settled into crowded wartime Ottawa as best they could. Jean was unhappy over leaving Montreal and her teaching job there and never really adapted to Ottawa. At first, despite his father's encouragement to make something of *Maclean's,* Blair, too, was ambivalent.[24] Earlier visits to the capital had left him unimpressed with either the city or the practitioners of its foremost industry. He also worried whether writing for a twice-monthly could compete with the excitement of meeting a daily deadline. Yet as he immersed himself in his new job, his attitude quickly changed. For one thing, he found that the so-called Ottawa atmosphere about which some observers complained bitterly – 'the cynical chit-chat of Rideau Club and Press Gallery and ... drippings of gossipy old men' – was much exaggerated.[25] What deeply impressed him now was the obvious dedication and competence of the men, elected and appointed, who were directing Canada's war effort. Moreover, the city itself was not at all dull; on the contrary, as the centre of wartime action in Canada it was a reporter's dream. There is no doubt the longer lead times imposed by the publication schedule of *Maclean's* made it harder to keep copy current, but even here there was a favourable trade-off since he was able to indulge in more interpretation and analysis. Ken Wilson and Grant Dexter both proved a great help as Fraser struggled to find his legs during those difficult first months in the Ottawa fog. By the war's end, he had completely fallen in love with the much maligned city and its political life, and in that sense he, too, had become an Ottawa man.

Irwin could not have been more pleased with Fraser's work, and even Chalmers agreed that if his editor could 'locate one or two more Blair Frasers' an increase in the editorial budget of *Maclean's* would be fully justified. Fraser's copy, whether for his regular 'Backstage at Ottawa' column or for periodic feature articles, was superb, written in a gracious, fluid style with the touches of subtle wit and rapier-like criticism that came to characterize his writing for *Maclean's.* Comments from some quarters that Fraser overestimated the average reader's intelligence did not bother Irwin at all. Indeed, most of the time he proved to have a real facility for simplifying complexities, or, as one businessman jokingly put it, 'he is able to present [the facts] in a way that we ordinary "dopes" can understand.'[26] Editor and correspondent developed a close relationship, professionally and personally, which carried over into the Allen regime. Both Irwin and Fraser had similar outlooks on most questions and, while they remained in regular contact by telephone and through Fraser's weekly memos, in practice Fraser needed and received little overt direction.[27]

Fraser put a tremendous amount of effort into his columns. A natural pride in the quality of his writing partially explains this diligence, but what he was trying to accomplish in the broader sense had a lot to do with it, too. A 'man with a notebook,' as 'Backstage' was anonymously signed until 1950, was someone who dealt primarily in facts and their explanation. With respect to public affairs, this meant attempting more than a simple outline of what was happening. His goal was to frame events in the larger context of what the government was trying to do and why, who the actors were and the reasons they thought the way they did, and to do it as objectively as he could – precisely what Irwin wanted.[28]

But to do this well and to keep Irwin confidentially informed on government goings-on, which was, after all, the other *raison d'être* for his being in Ottawa, it was essential to obtain the necessary background information. That meant securing ready access to the most knowledgeable sources – and increasingly these were senior civil servants. On principle, Fraser did not even try to establish close relationships with leading political figures. There were only three departures from this rule, but he had known them all before they entered politics: Mike Pearson, still a senior civil servant when the two first met in Ottawa, and Montrealers Brooke Claxton (a fellow CIIA member) and Douglas Abbott. Of course, as all three men became powerful ministers in postwar Liberal cabinets, they represented significant exceptions from his rule. Bureaucrats, however, were another matter; after all, their confidences were essential to his style of reporting. The great majority of the mandarins soon came to admire Fraser both as a journalist and as a man. Like Grant Dexter, he was a wonderful font of political gossip, and he certainly knew more about the 'larger picture' than even most deputy ministers. When it came to publicizing programs, hoisting trial balloons, correcting misunderstandings, or creating a groundswell of support, Fraser, with his flair for simplifying explanations and a national readership (and listenership), was the most useful of all the Ottawa press corps. It helped, of course, that the abler bureaucrats respected his intelligence and appreciated his perceptive understanding of their problems. And, as a reliable player in the responsible, civilized relationship, Fraser could be trusted absolutely to ensure that his civil service informants would be spared the embarrassment of being linked to any surprises in the pages of *Maclean's*.[29]

For his part, Fraser rapidly developed a professional affinity for the mandarins. During more philosophical moments, he characterized the great majority of people, himself included, as merely 'thinkers' and 'watchers.' The remainder, the group he held in highest regard, were the 'doers,' and there was no doubt as to where the mandarins belonged. Fraser was attuned to what they were trying to accomplish; he, too, was an internationalist, believed in the activist state, valued pragmatism, and disparaged doctrinaire solutions. It was a description that neatly fit most of the senior bureaucrats. In his opinion, they were decent, competent, respectable men intent on making their country more humane and dynamic, as indeed they were.[30]

In the still intimate surroundings of postwar Ottawa, Fraser and the mandarins forged social ties that reinforced the goodwill already fostered by their mutual professional respect. Blair Fraser slipped easily and comfortably into the social life of this quintessential government town. The Frasers initially lived in the west end of the city, but by 1952 had moved to the Rockcliffe Park district, home to Ottawa's political and bureaucratic elite. Grant Dexter lived a few doors away, as did the editor of the *Ottawa Journal,* Grattan O'Leary, and these two, along with Ken Wilson and a few others, constituted Ottawa's journalistic elite. Fraser, with one of the most amiable and unpretentious of personalities and a real *joie de vivre* – he was a wonderful storyteller and enthusiastic dancer and singer, and enjoyed his martinis – was readily welcomed into their social circle. Like them, he gained an entrée into the larger social circle of the diplomatic community, cabinet ministers, and senior civil servants to whose dinner and cocktail parties these journalists were invited on a regular basis.[31]

Socially and intellectually sophisticated himself, Fraser was a particular admirer of the mandarins' style: their wry wit, relaxed nature, and subtle manner; in fact, he came to mirror their style in his own life.[32] He was at ease with them over lunch – none of his contemporaries was more adept at working the Rideau Club – at dinner parties, and when he joined them skiing, canoeing, or sailing. Through these activities, he developed a small but intimate circle of friendships that included Pearson, Arnold Heeney, R.B. Bryce, Dr Omand Solandt, Davidson Dunton, Mitchell Sharp, and Gordon Robertson. Not surprisingly, by the 1950s Fraser was very much a part of the Ottawa establishment, though he always resented this allusion. Indeed, no matter how close he became to the civil service at the personal and professional level, and he was immensely proud of his contacts, he never considered himself a government 'insider' and sensed quite correctly that the bureaucrats felt the same way.

Fraser loved his work, but he also recognized the necessity periodically of putting some distance between himself and Ottawa. During his early years with *Maclean's,* he and the family began to vacation at North Hatley in the Eastern Townships and in 1950 he jointly purchased a cottage there with Frank Scott. Days spent swimming or sailing on Lake Massawippi were followed by evenings of stimulating conversation with luminaries drawn from the circle of American and Montreal intellectuals who also summered there. Fraser's restlessness and his need to surmount physical challenges led him to take up canoeing. In the early 1950s he was one of the founding members of the 'Voyageurs,' a group of middle-aged diplomats, civil servants, and businessmen who shared a love of the wilderness and a yearning to discover Canadian life 'beyond the pavement,' to use the words of Dr Tony Lovink, the Netherlands ambassador and another of the group's originals.[33] For Fraser, the expeditions not only served to recharge his spirit but deepened his sense of Canadianism. Canoeing through the Shield came to symbolize Canada, being in an almost mythical way the allegory of a man pitting his strength against nature and at the same time accepting her.

During the immediate postwar years, Chalmers and Irwin wanted *Maclean's* to de-emphasize international affairs and focus instead on domestic stories. They were especially interested in those tying in with 'reconfederation' – the 'new Canadianism' supposedly stimulated by the war. Reconfederation was *the* favoured subject at *Maclean's* during this period, one management had concluded was of more interest to a population tired of reading about the world after six years of war.[34] Despite any reservations Fraser might have had about the shift, the emphasis on events nearer to home still gave him ample opportunity to research and report on interesting developments in national politics. In his writing about these events, no effort was made to hide the perspectives he hoped his readers would share. If anything, such open biases seem to have enhanced his credibility with them. Certainly, readership surveys repeatedly confirmed that his 'Backstage' columns were the most widely read part of the magazine, typically scoring ratings of 75 to 80 per cent.[35] For instance, in 1946 when it appeared that federal-provincial negotiations on taxing powers had become hopelessly deadlocked, thus compromising Ottawa's social welfare initiatives, he castigated those in Ontario who were selfishly prepared to see the central government weakened just because they feared that the CCF might someday win a national election. Fraser knew what the Liberals' proposals, formulated by his civil service friends, would mean for the average Canadian, and he defended Ottawa's position with passion: 'Maybe this fear of government action is well grounded. Maybe the government will do more harm than good with its efforts to combat depression – maybe "balance-wheel" financing is a crackpot idea. But even then I don't think we can take a chance on paralytic government. I don't think the Canadian people would stand for it.'[36]

When he thought it was justified, Fraser had no qualms about being openly critical of the federal government. 'Hovels for Heroes' was a scathing indictment of Ottawa's handling of veterans' housing, and he followed it up in several 'Backstage' columns.[37] The story of the housing scandal, which caused a minor political furore and considerable short-term embarrassment for the Liberals, had in fact been leaked to Fraser by senior employees of the Wartime Housing Corporation who were indignant over the government's handling of the problem and, he suspected, keen to get some action by stirring up public outrage. Quite a number of civil servants were 'boiling' and 'would co-operate' with him, he assured Irwin, and indeed they did.

When it came to confronting the federal government, however, Fraser was more likely to cajole in private and only as a last resort go public. In 1947, for example, he got wind of a scheme hatched by Ian Mackenzie to block the conversion of surplus Department of National Defence buildings in Vancouver into temporary veterans' accommodation so that the land could be sold to a local brewery. The arrangement, smelling of patronage and linked to a minister Maclean-Hunter officials had despised for years, seemed a heaven-sent opportunity to flail the Liberals in print and teach them a lesson. Yet Fraser also knew that government housing authorities, backed by C.D. Howe, intended to invoke their emergency powers to thwart Mackenzie's plans. 'Treat this [story] as completely confidential since now the structures will be converted to housing,' he urged Irwin in a memo. Still, just in case, Fraser had made certain that he would be the first to hear of any stalling, and 'in that case, of course, we might be able to do our own little bit to help move things along.'[38] It was just not his style to criticize 'unconstructively,' especially when, in his mind, there was no reason to doubt that the Liberal government's policies and personalities were fundamentally sound.

There was one subject that invariably provided Fraser with an outlet for both his progressive instincts and his nationalist sympathies: Quebec. Fraser had learned to speak passable French during his Montreal newspaper days – 'police court French,' as he jokingly dismissed it. Moreover, for an English-speaking Canadian, he had always brought a remarkably open-minded approach to a society he tried hard to comprehend. By the time he left Montreal in 1943, he had developed a genuine sympathy for Quebec and the problems and aspirations of Quebeckers. True, he was not blind to what he saw with Anglo-Saxon eyes as French Canada's 'inadequacies,' but he exhibited none of the profound ignorance and condescension which coloured the views of most English-speaking Quebeckers. Fraser was disappointed that even in Ottawa, where he had expected a broader view, his peers, as James Gray of the *Winnipeg Free Press* put it, 'didn't give a damn about Quebec.'[39] With the rarest of exceptions, the same dismissive attitude prevailed among most English-speaking bureaucrats and politicians.

By the admittedly dismal standards of the day, Maclean-Hunter's attitude towards Quebec was also remarkably enlightened. It is no exaggeration to say that most otherwise-informed English Canadians had written off Quebec as hopelessly priest-ridden, backward, corrupt, and probably disloyal, too. For far too many, the province, at best, was seen as a kaleidoscope of images of jolly habitants, quaint villages, Rocket Richard, and maple syrup time. That 'the French' had been able to retain even this modest heritage was a tribute to the generous and patient spirit of the majority. Put bluntly, French-speaking Quebeckers were simply not destined to play a progressive role in Canadian life. Indeed, save for their unfortunate prominence in the Liberal party, they hardly played a role at all.

To Hunter and Chalmers, Quebec was at least part of Canada and, while they understood practically nothing about it, they did recognize that for the country to function one had to accept the fact of Quebec. Bringing Quebec into the mainstream was clearly the only way to forge any unity of national purpose. Hence their sincere willingness to assume the task of educating English-speaking Canadians about their French-speaking fellow citizens and, in the case of bilingual francophones, the reverse as well. Hunter made an annual summer pilgrimage to the posh resort at Murray Bay on Quebec's North Shore, where he could at least keep in touch with the views of well-to-do French Canadians. Once promoted to the vice-presidency of the company, Chalmers, with Hunter's encouragement, began to investigate the feasibility of a French-language edition of *Maclean's,* partly as a commercial venture (*Reader's Digest* published in French), but also so the magazine could more effectively promote its Canadianist views. Unfortunately, during the 1940s and 1950s the economics of such an undertaking were simply not viable.[40]

Irwin did not really understand Quebec either, but his liberal instincts at least predisposed him to approach the subject rationally. In 1944, for instance, a memo circulated to all staff on the subject of 'Maclean's and Quebec' pointedly noted: 'We accept and support the Canadian idea – which is the development of a nation on the basis of two cultures, two languages and two religions. We defend and have consistently defended the legal and moral right of Quebec to preserve those special institutions and customs which are theirs as a matter, not of sufferance, but of right.'[41] This may have been his 'only "special policy" for Quebec,' as he put it, but by the standards of the 1940s it was enlightment itself. Certainly both he and later Allen encouraged Fraser to approach the subject as he saw fit, confident of full editorial backing. Indeed, if anything, Allen was even more enthusiastic than his predecessor about covering Quebec stories. He strongly supported Chalmers's 'le magazine *Maclean*' scheme, and for two years even required all the editorial staff in the Toronto office to take French lessons.[42]

The second feature article written by Fraser for *Maclean's*[43] was a remarkably insightful and balanced story on Maxime Raymond, the onetime Liberal MP who now led the nationalist and anti-conscriptionist Bloc Populaire Canadien and consequently was one of the most detested men in English Canada during the latter stages of the war. 'Until English Canadians ... stop thinking of French Canadian nationalists as in some way criminal and personally evil,' he pointedly observed, 'misunderstandings will be endemic and inevitable in this country.'[44]

That summer, Fraser busied himself with the research for a second article on Quebec, this one to focus on wartime divisions between English and French Canadians. Acting on the urging of a Quebec friend, he had begun to read some of the strongly *nationaliste* writings of the Abbé Groulx to better understand French-speaking Quebec's alienation. Groulx's assertions 'about the destiny of Quebec to be a French Catholic *state* [Fraser's emphasis] in North America' came as a real revelation and, although he did not know exactly what to make of them, he found it hard to put Groulx down. In contrast, the imminent prospect of the Union Nationale's return to power completely depressed him.[45] The resulting article, appropriately entitled 'Crisis in Quebec,' appeared in the 15 August issue of *Maclean's* and much of it clearly bore the imprint of Mason Wade, an American-born professor of Quebec history who suffered few of the 'rose-coloured illusions' of his English-Canadian friends. Fraser had talked to Wade at some length during the preparation of the piece, and Wade had painted a grim picture of what the mass of ordinary Quebeckers were really feeling. In Wade's view, Fraser told Irwin: 'The Quebec situation is absolutely explosive – not in a political sense, but in relation to the war and to ... inter-racial tension [there] generally. [He] says there's enough loose powder lying around and enough people waving matches to set off a blast any time which in his opinion would be worse than 1917. Says he thought he might be an alarmist but has checked with all the soberist heads he knows and his impression is confirmed everywhere. He thinks a number of seemingly trivial things might be enough to set off the firecrackers – things like a silly speech out West, or a new conscription campaign or what not.'[46]

In his article, Fraser seemed to delight in puncturing all the comfortable myths about Quebec so cherished by English Canadians. As far as the Quebecois (sic) were concerned, he pointed out, no plebiscite which carried in English-speaking Canada but was defeated in Quebec (he was referring here to the conscription crisis of 1942) could excuse the federal government from a pledge which the citizens of that province felt had been made exclusively to them. Their views on the war effort, he continued, were held with a sense of grievance, not guilt, and English Canadians would have to recognize and address this fact. Given that within a matter of weeks Canada would once again find itself in the throes of a full-blown conscription crisis, the story's timing was eerie, and its observations, thanks to information from the likes of Wade and Frank Scott as well as Fraser's own open-mindedness, was strikingly accurate. However, as pleased as Fraser was with the job he had done, the article's conclusions flew in the face of Hunter's own ardently pro-conscriptionist views, not to mention his laughably naïve assumptions as to how a reluctant Quebec might be rallied to the flag – quite literally by having a distinctive Canadian national flag to rally around. In the end, however, Hunter was reassured when several of his wealthy French-Canadian acquaintances congratulated him on the fairness of the article and his courage in printing it.[47]

As a Montreal reporter, Fraser had seen the 'Duplessis system,' including the co-opting of the province's English-language press, firsthand, and distance did not soften his outlook. In 1945 he launched a bitter attack on the shake-downs of liquor licensees practised by the Duplessis machine which earned him and *Maclean's* the Union Nationale leader's lasting enmity. Duplessis's attitude was adequately summed up by a calculated outburst in the National Assembly some months later in which he accused Fraser of being 'a liar and a Liberal spy.'[48] But press attacks on Duplessis, while popular sport outside Quebec, only served to enhance his reputation at home. Fraser, however, was not satisfied with taking pot shots at *La forteresse Duplessis* from a safe distance. What set him apart was the attention he paid to the struggling anti-Duplessis opposition within Quebec. While the number of articles he produced were few, a mere three over the next four years, their sophistication far outweighed anything else appearing in the English-Canadian press during the same period. This reflected the quality of the contacts Fraser had cultivated with several respected French-Canadian journalists and other informed, progressively minded Quebeckers, both francophone and anglophone. It was through these sources that he became aware of the reformist currents, clerical and secular, which were stirring below the seemingly tranquil surface of postwar Quebec. Sadly, among his peers, Fraser was almost alone in this regard, for apart from John Bird of Southam's Ottawa bureau, who was fluently bilingual, none of the other leading English-speaking reporters had any contacts at all within the French-speaking community, and it showed all too clearly in their writing.[49]

Fraser first brought his ideas together in a 1947 article entitled 'What Now Jean Baptiste?' The title, like so many others chosen in Toronto for his features, infuriated him, but the article itself carefully examined the changes wrought by the war on Quebec's traditional isolation within Canada. Among the most important, he stressed, was the emergence of a solid and self-aware French-Canadian working class 'beginning to feel that French-Canadian tradition holds no solution to its problems' of low wages, high unemployment, and linguistic discrimination. Another was the fact that the Catholic church's traditional domination, which he hastened to point out had always been exaggerated by English-speaking Protestants, was now being challenged from within by both laymen and clergy. Fraser optimistically saw in the calls for educational reform and the remarkable work of Fr Georges-Henri Lévesque and his followers to establish a non-confessional system of cooperatives and *caisses populaires* further evidence of the strength of a liberal, pan-Canadian movement within the province. He readily admitted that the power of conservatism with its 'spiritual' – that is, nationalist – resources unknown in English-Canadian conservatism seemed permanently entrenched. Yet those determined to breach French Canada's isolation once and for all and make her an integral part of Canada now had one reason for hope: 'a new feeling of the people.' Surely the question was no longer, 'Shall there be change in Quebec?' Fraser presciently if somewhat prematurely concluded, but rather, 'What kind of change will there be?'[50]

By the late 1940s Fraser's reputation in English Canada as an expert on Quebec was well established. His articles were widely read even if the full significance of his analysis was not always appreciated. Within reformist circles in French-speaking Canada his assessments were generally well received. Such individuals tended to see Fraser as an *anglais* liberal whose first allegiance, refreshingly, was to Canada, not Britain, and who could say critical things about Duplessis and correspondingly favourable things about his opponents; similar writing appeared nowhere else in the Quebec press save *Le Devoir*.[51]

Maclean's made scant mention of the Asbestos strike of February–June 1949; it was in good company, for coverage of this watershed labour dispute in the English-Canadian press was abysmal. The fact that the Canadian edition of *Time* magazine ran a sensational anti-Duplessis report on the outbreak of violence between the strikers and the provincial police grated on Fraser and other English-Canadian reporters, too, for it served as an embarrassing reminder that they were never able to criticize the Quebec premier as often or as vigorously as they might have liked.[52] Nevertheless, shortly after the conclusion of the strike – and here one has to bear in mind the extended lead times in effect at *Maclean's,* especially for feature articles – Fraser examined the confrontation's long-term significance for Quebec. The new-found militancy of the Canadian Confederation of Catholic Workers (CTCC) struck him as a 'major triumph for the [liberal] wing of the Roman Catholic Church.' He recognized, however, that the remarkable phenomenon of the church rallying solidly behind the miners had to be seen for what it was: the fear of the majority conservative faction that the strike's failure would have written *finis* to the confessional unions. Certainly there was truth to this. Despite the fact that Fraser had exaggerated the extent of church support for the strikers, future events confirmed his conclusion that the unprecedented action of the church in pitting itself against the Union Nationale was a 'political time bomb of incalculable potency.'[53]

The Asbestos article showed just how well informed Fraser was. On this occasion, apart from tapping his usual sources, he had also sought out Jean Marchand, the secretary-general and driving force of the CTCC. Marchand was a graduate of the controversial Faculty of Social Sciences at Université Laval, which Fraser correctly identified as the 'major source and inspiration of the new spirit among Quebec Roman Catholics.'[54] Fraser had come to see Fr Lévesque, the founder and dean of the faculty, as the epitome of the progressively minded, pan-Canadian nationalist Québécois and he greatly admired him. Lévesque, for his part, respected the *Maclean's* reporter both as a man and as a journalist.[55] Through the Dominican priest, Fraser had in turn met Doris Lussier, his secretary, and Fr Gérard Dion, a professor of industrial relations at Laval and labour activist, both of whom contributed significantly to his understanding of the issues at stake.

Duplessis had never liked the activities of Fr Lévesque and his associates at Laval, but when they sided openly with labour at Asbestos, he was furious. With the wholehearted support of conservative elements in the clergy whom Lévesque and his followers had alienated during their various liberal crusades, Duplessis was now determined to silence the troublesome priest and his faculty.[56] Silencing Fr Lévesque proved a difficult matter, however. For one thing, his appointment in 1949 to the St Laurent government's Royal Commission on National Development in the Arts, Letters and Sciences headed by Vincent Massey had made him something of a national figure. This, and his connections with the Liberal party, assured him a certain measure of protection, but at the same time further damned him in his detractors' eyes.

As pressure mounted to oust Lévesque from Laval, English-Canadian admirers rallied to his defence.[57] It seems likely that Massey, for one, approached Fraser with the suggestion that something might be done, though undoubtedly the idea of generating some publicity through a *Maclean's* article had many sponsors. Privately, Fraser must have harboured doubts about the wisdom of this course. Not only was he *persona non grata* with the Union Nationale and Le Chef, but he was also well aware that, as he had once written, 'the applause of Toronto is ruin in Quebec.'[58] Nevertheless, the risk must have seemed worth running. Obviously, any article would have to be dramatic to make an impact, and fairness and accuracy would be crucial. Thus he consciously avoided talking to the man at the centre of the storm, but made a point of publicly seeking out labour minister Antonio Barette and Monsignor Vandry, the rector of Laval, to make certain he got the points of view of the provincial government and the university and was *known* to have done so.[59] Inevitably, however, he relied heavily on sources among the progressives, who in this instance proved unusually candid.

'The Fight over Father Levesque' appeared in the 1 July 1950 issue of the magazine. It was an emotionally charged piece cast in David and Goliath terms: Fr Lévesque 'idealized by liberal youth as the very symbol of freedom and social progress' versus the clerical conservatives and the Union Nationale. The Duplessis government's threat to cripple Laval financially if the administration did not dismiss this troublesome priest was the immediate issue, as Mgr Vandry had frankly admitted to Fraser. But the current confrontation went far beyond petty politics, as Fraser rightly stressed. Lévesque, a Dominican, was also the victim of powerful church intrigues pitting the Jesuits against his order, and the liberals in general, of whom he was the acknowledged leader, against the far more numerous and powerful conservatives. Partly this bitter struggle was a reaction against the events of 1949, and here Fraser reminded his readers of the suspicious retirement of Archbishop Charbonneau of Montreal, a strong supporter of the Asbestos strikers and long a thorn in the side of the clerical conservatives. Fraser admired Charbonneau's compassion and liberalism, and he made no effort to hide his conviction that the church had meekly succumbed to pressure from Quebec City in dismissing him. Now, with Charbonneau eliminated, Fr Lévesque was the most visible of the remaining liberals among the province's clergy.

'Against Levesque,' Fraser decried, 'are all the men who want Quebec to stay exactly as it is, or still better, as it was 50 years ago': the nationalists obsessed with 'autonomy' and 'isolation,' and the Jesuits and the great majority of the other clergy, most of whom had been openly pro-Vichy during the war. 'For him [were] the men who believe [intellectual and social] change [are] imminent or overdue' and whose patriotism was of the 'all-Canadian' variety. Among the liberally minded, Lévesque had become the very symbol of 'social progress' and 'intellectual liberation.' 'If they get Levesque,' he quoted an unnamed French-speaking journalist, 'it'll be a worse defeat for us than the Charbonneau affair.' Of course, by the time his article appeared, Lévesque might already have been fired, Fraser admitted somewhat melodramatically. But then again, maybe not. What gave Fraser hope? 'A loyal and devoted Catholic [trade unionist] said to me: "If they fire Levesque, too, I really will begin to believe that Duplessis is running

the Church in this province" – That's probably the best of reasons for thinking they won't fire him.'[60]

Precisely that – linking the political domination of the Catholic church to
Fr Lévesque's fate – had been Fraser's strategy.[61] He was counting on neither
party wanting to give credence to this allegation. While the pressure on
Lévesque continued, he managed to retain his teaching position at Laval for
another five years. No one can be certain what role, if any, Fraser's article
actually played in this reprieve, but Lévesque was personally convinced that
Fraser's intervention had been crucial.[62]

Reaction from Quebec was immediate and decidedly negative. Catholic
officials curtly dismissed Fraser's unflattering interpretation of events, the
Jesuit journal *Relations* being particularly hostile. The vehemence of such
attacks, a strong indication that his conclusions had hit home, must have
comforted Fraser, a man with little respect for institutionalized religion at
the best of times. In contrast to church spokesmen, neither the premier nor
his associates showed the slightest outward concern over the article, but
then the article had been directed more towards the church than the government, anyway.[63] And as Fraser had predicted, certain *nationaliste* quarters would henceforth disparage Fr Lévesque as the darling of Anglo-
Canadians like himself, the sort of French Canadian who told the English
what they wanted to hear.[64] There were Quebeckers, however, who were
pleased with Fraser's revelations about Fr Lévesque's predicament and
the larger divisions within the church itself. Murray Chipman, Maclean-
Hunter's senior management representative in Montreal, informed the
Toronto office that even some senior churchmen agreed that 'it was a good
article which, as one of them said, had the unfortunate virtue – from the
Catholic viewpoint – of being very close to the mark.'[65]

'The distinguishing characteristic of *Maclean's* in its best times,' Peter
Newman has observed, 'has been an uncompromising attempt to record and
authenticate the Canadian experience for Canadian readers.'[66] During the
postwar decade, the magazine enjoyed many such moments. Certainly
Maclean's spoke to Canadians in Canadian terms; it had to, for without that
nationalist identification it would never have survived, as its publishers
knew only too well.[67] Under the guidance of editors Arthur Irwin and Ralph
Allen, and through the writing of Blair Fraser in particular, *Maclean's* made
a real effort to try to dissolve regionalism and the bitter inheritance of paro-
chialism they associated with it. In its place, they sought to create a truly
national feeling and a national consensus. This was assuredly the magazine's most significant contribution. In hindsight, of course, their faith that
the centrifugal forces acting on Canada could be overcome seems naïvely
optimistic, while their belief that regionalism was by definition almost anti-

Canadian possessed more than a tinge of arrogance. Maclean-Hunter and the magazine's staff believed that *Maclean's* was a prime mover and not simply an agent of national change. That the magazine should overrate its own importance was perfectly natural; similar sentiments assumed epidemic proportions in Canada during the postwar decade, and few members of the English-Canadian establishment did not fall victim. That said, the magazine's persistent efforts to confront Canadians with a more challenging view of their country and the need for a distinct identity deserve credit.

The 'golden postwar decade' was an era of pervasive, comfortable middle-class optimism. Canadians elected Liberal governments with their efficient, pragmatic tone to ensure that this happy state of affairs would continue. *Maclean's* recorded and endorsed these postwar developments, and in the process reinforced the consensus for their continuation. Therein lies the basis for the oft-repeated allegation that *Maclean's* was an apologist for the government. But in every sense, *Maclean's* was independently a part of that consensus: an instrument, yes, but an apologist, no. Irwin and Fraser, and Allen to only a slightly lesser degree, were virtually in complete agreement with what Ottawa and especially the mandarins were attempting to carry out. Their views on what sort of Canada there should be and how to bring it about were indistinguishable, as was their elitist, pan-Canadian nationalism. All three persistently tried to enhance the idea content of the magazine along these lines and to lift readers 'above themselves.'[68] More often than not, Fraser was their chosen instrument, as his efforts to interpret Quebec illustrate. The oft-heard quip of mandarins' wives, 'if it weren't for Blair there wouldn't be anything to read in that rag at all,'[69] was far from being a damning criticism of *Maclean's*. Rather, it simply reflected their recognition that no one was a more articulate or credible spokesman for the liberal and progressive elements of the postwar Liberal-bureaucratic vision of Canada than he.

6

'Avoiding wrong impressions'

The Department of External Affairs,
Lester Pearson, and the Press

Among the small band of correspondents and editors who could write intelligently about Canadian foreign policy and international relations during the 1940s and 1950s, Canada's commitment to internationalism was an article of faith. These journalists were convinced they shared a community of interest with the senior officials of the Department of External Affairs and the leading internationalists in the King and St Laurent governments. This conviction, which was much strengthened by the close personal relationship they developed with these men, and above all with Lester Pearson, the personification of Canadian internationalism during this period, ensured that Canadian foreign policy-makers were able to count almost unfailingly on the timely and eloquent support of this influential group of journalists. The Department of External Affairs and the Liberal government were certainly beneficiaries, and arguably, given the basic soundness of Canadian foreign policy during the postwar decade, so was the nation itself. While the discrediting of isolationism and the postwar emergence of communism as *the* threat to Western democracy were undoubtedly the primary factors responsible for forging a domestic consensus on the country's internationalist posture, the role of the press in deepening and sustaining that consensus should not be underestimated.

In retrospect, the wartime transformation of Canadian foreign relations from an uneasy mixture of isolationism and knee-jerk imperialism to a confident internationalism impatient with tired arguments against foreign commitments occurred with breathtaking speed. By the war's end, it was no longer a question of whether Canada would have an autonomous foreign policy but simply what form it would take – and, in practice, even that was not really a point of debate. By 1945 the Department of External Affairs had assembled a cadre of remarkable young men who, in their sheer ability and ultimate influence over government policy, would match 'Clark's boys' at Finance and 'Towers's boys' at the Bank of Canada.[1] While the 'young Turks' of External Affairs were busy pressing these views on their cabinet superiors, they were also forging a new relationship with the press. This represented a significant departure from prewar practice, which had tried to keep formal and informal contacts to a minimum while ensuring those that occurred were carefully controlled.[2] During the period Dr O.D. Skelton was in control, indiscretions such as Pearson's leaks to Grant Dexter during the Munich Crisis were the exception, not the rule.

With Skelton's death in 1941, Norman Robertson, his protégé, became departmental undersecretary. Secretive by nature, Robertson held strong views on how diplomacy should be carried out, and the cultivation of public opinion through the press, which he dismissed collectively as uninformed and unreliable, did not figure prominently in his plan. About all he was prepared to do was brief those he considered the best of the resident Ottawa men: Blair Fraser of *Maclean's*, Ken Wilson of the *Financial Post*, and Grant Dexter of the *Winnipeg Free Press*.[3] Robertson never appreciated that in a capital as intimate as Ottawa, stories were bound to get out, and the real trick was to keep on top of the disclosures and even use them to your department's advantage. Despite his aversion to overfamiliarity with the press (many in the gallery would have questioned the necessity of the modifier 'over'), Robertson did make a point of increasing External's formal contacts with journalists, for instance by substantially increasing the frequency of press conferences and setting up a rudimentary press bureau. But these measures elicited little interest from their intended constituency. With the exception of those few conferences which guaranteed a front-page story, rarely did more than a handful of reporters turn out. Indeed, it became something of a standing joke in the gallery that the only reporters External could absolutely count on to attend these sessions were the two stolid Russians from TASS and the inevitable representative from the government's own Wartime Information Board.[4]

In sharp contrast to Robertson, Lester Pearson understood the importance of good press relations only too clearly, but he spent most of the war in London and Washington where opportunities to cultivate Canadian journalists were limited. When he did pass through Ottawa, however, his more candid and enthusiastic approach impressed younger colleagues and reporters alike.[5] Departmental press relations would change dramatically when Pearson replaced Robertson as undersecretary, but, as the war neared its end, that was still some months away.

In addition to Fraser, Dexter, and Wilson, journalists who would make their mark during the postwar decade covering Canada's entry onto the international stage included Bruce Hutchison[6] and Max Freedman of the *Winnipeg Free Press, Maclean's* editor Arthur Irwin, *Montreal Star* editor George Ferguson, and, itself clear evidence of the fundamentally nonpartisan character of postwar Canadian foreign policy among elite journalists, Norman Smith of the Conservative-leaning *Ottawa Journal*. Significantly, all but Hutchison were active members of the Canadian Institute of International Affairs. Probably the CIIA's signal contributions during this period were its complementary roles as an independent foreign policy 'think tank' and as a training ground for able university graduates bent on careers in diplomacy or other government departments where a firm grasp of international relations was now considered important. The CIIA itself had concluded that the stimulation of public discussion on Canada's postwar international role – in other words, getting Canadians 'thinking internationally' – was its highest priority.[7] Despite the fact that a November 1943 Gallup poll indicated fully three-quarters of Canadians favoured an active Canadian role in maintaining world peace even if it meant using force,[8] the institute's leadership still shuddered at the public's lack of awareness. Casting about for ways to remedy this deficiency, they could not help noticing that at least part of the solution was already at hand – namely, the 'many ... leading editors and writers' who were active CIIA members.[9] For Fraser, Dexter, Ferguson, and their peers, the CIIA was by no means the only influence in shaping their internationalism. Still, their stimulating discussions with the institute's bright young minds and a few wise old heads like Edgar Tarr served an important role in helping to impart ideas, mould attitudes, and build friendships with their country's current and future diplomats and not a few up-and-coming political figures as well. In the process, these journalists were imbued with an almost evangelical sense of mission to spread the internationalist gospel. Dexter's experience was not untypical. In wartime Ottawa, his matchless knowledge of the domestic political scene made him much in demand at the informal gatherings of institute members and their friends, and he absorbed the ideas being bandied about at these free-for-all sessions like a sponge. Not surprisingly, his book, *Canada and the Building of Peace*, published under CIIA auspices in 1944, read like a primer of the bureaucracy's postwar thinking.[10]

Dexter and Ferguson and to a lesser extent Hutchison had the added benefit of having directly absorbed the world view of J.W. Dafoe, by war's end a sort of patron saint of Canadian internationalists – at least those with a collective security bent. For Ferguson and Dexter the war, and especially the manner of its coming, intensified their commitment to an international order based upon such a system, while for Hutchison, by his own admission once a 'complete isolationist,' the same sad train of events had been his conversion.[11] Admittedly, when Ferguson scanned the international political horizon as the end of the war neared, he found it difficult to avoid either 'appearing to dwell in cloud-cuckoo land,' as he put it, or 'falling into [the] pit of destructive criticism.' In the end, he concluded that one could only hope that the internationalists' postwar schemes would prove their worth, or, more to the point, would be given a chance to do so. For Dexter, there were far fewer doubts. The much-hoped-for new age would dawn; as he readily admitted, his superabundance of idealism simply left no place for 'the exigencies of postwar realities.'[12] In Dexter's defence, idealism and optimism were rampant in Canada in 1945, and he was certainly not alone in succumbing. Fraser, too, rejected isolationism and appeasement – Who in English-speaking Canada did not? His hopes for the postwar world were shaped by an idealism rooted in humanitarian instincts and a conviction, shared by Ken Wilson, that rationally the war *must* have unleashed the forces of logic and morality.[13] When one compares these perspectives, it is the similarities among these journalists, not the differences, which are the more striking. Like their friends and mentors in the civil service, theirs was a very confident Canadianism demanding international expression. Canada was primed to embark on a foreign policy revolution in 1945, and no group was more determined to be a part of it.

In April 1945 representatives of the soon-to-be-victorious allies met in San Francisco to draw up the United Nations charter, the basic framework of which had already been agreed to by the great powers. An editorial penned by Ferguson to mark the occasion expressed the sentiments shared by millions of ordinary Canadians. Surely, he offered, 'the nations must have ... learned the lesson of the past.'[14] The high level of public awareness and expectation pleased External officials immensely; determined to see Canada play an active role in the postwar international order, they had recognized that establishing a broad basis of government and hence public support for their plans was essential. By any standard, this story was widely covered by the Canadian media, with no fewer than fifty Canadian newspaper, magazine, and radio correspondents attending the conference's opening sessions. As their diligent efforts to ensure that Fraser would also be heard over the CBC showed, Canada's diplomats were determined that the men they were counting on to get their story across at home were given the chance.[15] The *Winnipeg Free Press,* of course, could be counted upon to do its duty. Sifton's three ablest reporters were California bound, Dexter and Hutchison to cover the vital behind-the-scenes story and Bert Richardson to report on the day-to-day goings-on. Over the next few weeks, an outsider could easily have mistaken Dexter and Hutchison, along with Fraser and the *Ottawa Journal*'s Norman Smith, for a wing of the official Canadian delegation.

King had already concluded that the proposed United Nations was too impractical to work, so his attendance at the early sessions was largely for appearance's sake, to defend Canadian interests, and, one suspects, to keep a watchful eye on his diplomats. Hutchison, Dexter, Fraser, and Smith, however, were not especially interested in what Mr King was thinking; they gravitated towards the men who were doing the real work of the delegation, starting with Robertson, Pearson, Hume Wrong, and Escott Reid, and who, unlike their aging prime minister, were 'believers.' Moreover, they were more than willing to cooperate. After all, they and the press were committed to the same objectives: a viable United Nations and the maximum Canadian involvement in its undertakings.

To meet the Canadian journalists' needs, either Pearson or Reid held formal press briefings daily. These were little more than opportunities for reporters to obtain the basic information for their stories, but with the main conference sessions and numerous subcommittees sitting simultaneously there was a great deal for them to absorb. Unfortunately, as Canadian diplomats were quick to realize, many of the Canadian journalists were in over their depth covering a major foreign policy story, and, of necessity, the civil servants sought out the more able ones privately, usually in some of the more convivial surroundings cosmopolitan San Francisco offered.[16] If during these casual get-togethers the journalists were provided with additional background to explain the Canadian positions at the conference and, in more general terms, the broader implications for Canada of the United Nations as a whole, surely everyone benefited. This, at least, was the rationale for such favoured treatment. In a post-conference note to Fraser, Pearson would allude to 'our work together [there]';[17] it was a candid aside which said a great deal about the nature of their relationship at San Francisco. In return for such consideration, Fraser, Hutchison, and Dexter passed on the appraisals of the domestic political situation and public opinion eagerly sought by External officials. The prevailing mood of press and public alike in English Canada assured favourable coverage of the launching of the UN, but the fact that the reporting and commentary were so enthusiastic and, for the most part, so accurate was a bonus which owed much to External's hard work.

Despite the widening gulf between the Soviet Union and the Western allies, which was already casting a pall over the UN's longterm prospects, Canadian diplomats were united in their determination to try to make the organization work. Political realities, in particular Soviet obduracy, forced them to adopt a pragmatic approach – for instance, accepting the great-power veto. But ordinary Canadians might easily interpret such pragmatism as appeasement, and avoiding such 'misunderstandings' required a certain subtlety in presentation. Even though personally he considered them 'a small step sideways' and not the 'great step forward' Reid and the others were heralding, Richardson sheepishly confessed to his wife that 'after talking to our delegates' he had decided to write an 'impressive' editorial on the veto 'concessions' wrung from the Soviets.[18] Dexter, of course, required no friendly arm-twisting to see the sunny side of practically every development at San Francisco; he had all but declared the conference a success before it started and it was going to take considerably more than Molotov's intransigence and the doubts of the cynics to shake his faith in the new world order. Nor were Hutchison's commentaries or Ferguson's editorials much more questioning. But the crucial concern was to prevent the UN from being stillborn; perfection, after all, could be pursued later.

The summer of 1946 brought Fraser to Paris as one of the handful of Canadian journalists covering the peace conference, External Affairs personnel having made every effort to ensure he would attend.[19] From the outset, the deliberations proved to be a major disappointment, reflecting the grim state of relations between the erstwhile allies little more than twelve months after the end of the European war. For Fraser, the poisonous atmosphere was a revelation, confirming his worst fears about the 'new age.'[20] But if the conference depressed him, there was at least fine summer weather and the delights of Paris to explore with close friends in the Canadian delegation like Arnold Heeney and Charles Ritchie. Despite the diplomatic deadlock, neither Fraser nor Irwin considered his presence in Paris to have been a waste of time. This had been Fraser's first serious exposure to the life of a foreign correspondent and, as such, a valuable experience in itself. It had also given given him ample opportunity to draw even closer to Heeney, Robertson, and the other diplomats, who had put in long hours and performed well, if rather quietly. Their diligence and competence impressed him deeply, and it showed through in his reports.

To many thoughtful Canadians, the onset of the Cold War seemed sure to end their country's role on the international stage almost before it had begun. Some, including the prime minister, were reassured by this thought. In a rambling interview with Dexter shortly after he had returned from Paris, Mackenzie King spelled out his views with rare candour. The United Nations he matter-of-factly dismissed as nothing more than a façade for traditional power politics – in other words, a somewhat tarted-up version of the League.[21] Dexter knew that few of his friends at External were prepared to accept such a gloomy prognosis quite yet and, personally, he remained almost a utopian on the UN's prospects, so such talk made him furious. His first impulse was 'to take after King with an axe,' but, after cooling down, he admitted that ripping the prime minister would not advance the cause of the UN – and that remained the *Free Press*'s foremost objective. Trying to pull his thoughts together, and perhaps also rationalize his subsequent actions, Dexter confided to Hutchison that for readers who had been led to 'believe King is going straight, [a] sudden, and direct attack would not be understood.' Moreover, and perhaps more to the point, 'we would be cut off with no hope whatsoever of influencing [him].' Clearly the best course was 'to nudge him, to discuss the problem, to exploit every incident which helps – but keep our tone low-pitched and steady.' For Dexter, the whole point, after all, was 'not to miss a single opportunity of sowing the seed.'[22] In a year-end editorial recapitulating the accomplishments of the United Nations thus far, he dismissed the 'credulous cynical [observers], expecting either impossible miracles ... or else magnifying every difference of opinion into a barrier against peace.' Canada's own performance, he offered, had been 'sensible and helpful' but at the same time 'not very active' when 'a more outspoken policy ... might have better interpreted the needs of the time and better expressed the needs of the Canadian people.'[23] In comparison with Dexter, Hutchison was gloom personified on virtually every international question, and, while he went along with the official *Free Press* line, he was much more openly pessimistic about the UN's short-term prospects.[24]

Blair Fraser was saying the same things but without Dexter's subtleties. In a 'Backstage' column appearing in the magazine's 15 January 1947 issue, he pointedly noted that while 'officially, Canadian public men are all sup- posed to believe in the United Nations – it's an article of political piety, like belief in motherhood or full employment,' the unvarnished reality was that 'a good many of them are pretty pessimistic about it.'

In September 1947 King appointed Louis St Laurent as his replacement in the External Affairs portfolio. Many civil servants and certainly most journalists with an interest in foreign policy had secretly hoped that Brooke Claxton would get the job. One of the Liberals' rising stars, Claxton was energetic, intelligent, and passionately nationalistic, and had the added plus in many eyes of having been a longtime stalwart of the CIIA with a firm grasp of international relations. In contrast, St Laurent was still relatively unknown in English Canada and, as a French Canadian, automatically sus- pect in the eyes of many government insiders as a probable isolationist. Nevertheless, in the coming months St Laurent's performance as a tireless and effective spokesman inside and outside the cabinet for an active Cana- dian role abroad would silence all doubts. A second change, and arguably the more far-reaching, saw Pearson promoted to undersecretary. At a time when the comings and goings of deputy ministers were not normally fare for the country's editorial pages or news columns, it was revealing that the press would greet this appointment with such enthusiasm.[25]

A month after Pearson and St Laurent assumed their new duties, another welcome development occurred for Canada's foreign policy-makers when George Ferguson was hired as editor of the *Montreal Star,* the most widely read English-language daily in Quebec. Drained by a bitter eighteen-month editorial power struggle with publisher Victor Sifton, Ferguson had resigned from the *Winnipeg Free Press* the previous year. Despite its nominally Liberal leanings on domestic issues, the *Star* had traditionally followed a 'my Empire right or wrong' foreign policy line. However, with communism now the paramount threat to Western civilization, not to mention the capitalist system, J.W. McConnell, the newspaper's tycoon owner, had no difficulty endorsing the Cold War and Canada's wholehearted participation in it. For Ferguson there was a practical result: if it was a foreign policy story, he would be able to operate with considerably more editorial latitude than would otherwise be the case during his early years at the *Star.*[26]

Ferguson had long been fascinated with international relations and considered himself something of a student of the subject, which indeed he was. Through his long involvement in the CIIA, he knew virtually everyone of importance in the country's foreign policy establishment and was especially close to Claxton, Pearson, Wrong, and Robertson. As an intellectual and Oxford man with more extensive contacts in academic circles than any of his peers and, of course, the 'right ideas,' Ferguson fit comfortably into the milieu of the foreign policy mandarins. While C.D. Howe might flippantly dismiss 'External types' for their obvious delight in raising problems simply to discuss their paradoxes,[27] it was precisely this intellectual bent that impressed Ferguson and, one might add, Fraser, Wilson, Hutchison, and Dexter, too. In the Department of External Affairs, there was no question that Ferguson's sharp insights into the domestic side of foreign policy and his well-deserved reputation for bluntly expressing them had earned him wide respect. In the aftermath of his 'resignation' from the *Free Press,* Robertson and Claxton seriously considered him for various UN posts and even the vacant high commissionership in Australia. Robertson, whose praise was always carefully measured, privately thought him 'the ablest newspaperman in Canada,' an assessment with which few of Robertson's colleagues would have quibbled.[28] Ironically, in turning down diplomatic opportunities, Ferguson chose to stay where he could do his friends far more good in the long run. Certainly coverage of international affairs in the *Star* during his tenure as editor enjoyed a high profile (it was the only Canadian daily which kept a full-time UN correspondent in New York) and was considered first rate by the experts in Ottawa.

The same could be said of the *Free Press*. Ferguson's departure and Dexter's elevation to the top job in fact opened the way for Sifton to emerge as the real power. Unfortunately, the best that could be said about Sifton as a journalist was that he made a good businessman. In the coverage of foreign policy, however, the increasingly glaring editorial weaknesses of the Sifton-Dexter team, and the newspaper's overall decline, were barely evident. Both men had an unshakeable belief in free trade, which ensured their support of economic multilateralism, and they had also absorbed Dafoe's unflinching commitment to internationalism and collective security. For Dexter especially, these positions, with their pronounced moral and idealistic overtones, were matters of principle that permitted no deviation whatsoever.[29]

During the crucial months of 1947 and 1948 the St Laurent–Pearson team confronted a world situation that was deteriorating alarmingly. The fact that the prime minister seemed bent on reverting to isolationism at the very time when they were becoming convinced that Canada's security lay in increased, not reduced, international commitments was exasperating.[30] As the government began to consider collective security alternatives to the deadlocked UN, neither Pearson nor St Laurent doubted that the press had the potential to smooth the way or cause considerable grief, depending, of course, on how skilfully it was handled. There was a real danger in appearing to push too forcefully the argument that the United Nations was incapable of performing its collective security role. Clearly, the central figure in any 'educational' campaign would have to be St Laurent, whose avuncular manner and air of authority and stability would give any pronouncements added credibility and, in the process, garner maximum publicity.[31]

As undersecretary, Pearson was now able to apply his talent for press relations on a department-wide scale. The fact that he was a charmer, with a natural talent for influencing people, gave him a huge advantage in the press-relations game. Whether one-on-one or with groups, his refeshingly straightforward approach and self-deprecating wit seldom failed to win over all but the most hardened listeners. Of course, just how straightforward the results actually were for reporters was another matter. Measures were always taken to ensure that Pearson would know which reporters had asked what questions of department staff during the preceding week in order better to shape his press conference agenda and responses, not to mention avoid the embarrassment of being caught unprepared.[32] Often he revealed nothing at all, but somehow even nothing sounded better when Mike Pearson said it.[33]

Pearson transformed the regular weekly press conferences for the Ottawa press corps. Unlike his predecessors, the new undersecretary saw them as an opportunity, not a duty, and, whenever possible, Pearson, assisted by his newly appointed information chief, Saul Rae, and one or two other press-oriented juniors, handled the sessions personally, a practice he continued even after he became minister in 1948. Although several of his colleagues displayed a flare for handling the press conference format – Reid, Dana Wilgress, John Holmes, and Jules Léger particularly – Pearson's skills were unmatched. Attendance increased steadily, a reflection of both the deteriorating international situation and the 'Pearson revolution.'

His briefings were invariably wide-ranging affairs and usually quite candid, though he carefully protected himself by spelling out in advance what could be attributed directly, what was provided for background 'off the record,' and what had to be attributed to the usual euphemisms for authoritative sources: 'informed circles,' 'a Canadian spokesman,' and 'sources close to the Canadian delegation.'[34] One of his favourite tactics was to reveal 'off the record' sensitive information he believed one or more journalists were on the verge of discovering, safe in the knowledge that compromising confidential sources was simply not done by a reputable gallery man. The few who bridled, it was duly noted in the department, represented Conservative papers. Gratton O'Leary, editor of the *Ottawa Journal* and an influential voice in Tory inner circles, was the best-known offender, but despite his periodic indiscretions his friendship with Pearson never suffered and he remained an unabashed admirer of Pearsonian diplomacy.[35] Breaches of confidence were very much the exception, however; the press seldom balked at Pearson's restrictions, with the welcome result (for the East Block) that embarrassing leaks of Canada's diplomatic secrets were a rare occurrence.[36]

External's efforts at information management went far beyond regular press briefings in Ottawa or at international conferences. There was a growing awareness in the department that the press were out there and could be helpful – and likely *would* be helpful if they were encouraged to be so. As one External official put it: 'we might as well try to encourage accurate and well-informed stories and do everything possible to keep the press friendly.' More to the point, as a thoughtful memo on handling press relations at international conferences noted: 'Although the presence of newspapermen may sometimes appear to create problems ... it will often be in the Department's interest to assist the press so as to ensure an appreciation of the Canadian viewpoint ... a knowledge of Canadian initiatives and an intelligent reporting to the Canadian public and to other countries where it may be necessary to explain our position.'[37] External quickly identified those publications they considered especially influential, or at any rate widely read by opinion-makers and important segments of the public, and then diligently monitored their news and editorial content. In English Canada, these included the

Toronto Star and *Globe and Mail*, the *Montreal Star* and *Gazette*, the *Ottawa Citizen* and *Journal*, the *Winnipeg Free Press* and the *Financial Post*, as well as *Maclean's* and *Saturday Night*.[38]

Pearson promptly complied with requests for special briefings by those setting off to cover international conferences or United Nations sessions. In general, he tirelessly encouraged reporters and their editors to cover international events, including first and foremost his own trips abroad, where their accounts could be expected not only to outline the facts but spread a desirable interpretation, too. If his readiness to be nabbed by journalists in the corridors after meetings ensured, as one colleague wryly pointed out, that he would be at or near the centre of the resulting story, well, Pearson's career was hardly being harmed.[39] Self-serving though it might have been, Pearson's tone clearly set the example for the entire department when it came to cultivating solid and mutually profitable relations with Canadian journalists. Grateful newspapermen could hardly be unimpressed. As the *Ottawa Journal*'s Norman Smith once put it, the co-operation forthcoming from External staff 'certainly eases a tough job and rather puts it up to us to deliver the goods.' In a capital city whose bureaucracy was known for its openness to the fourth estate, External Affairs would earn the best reputation of all. 'Press coverage shouldn't be left to chance,' as one External memorandum succinctly put it, and during the Pearson era it most certainly was not.[40]

Within the department's small but increasingly self-important information division there was growing anxiety over the propensity of some journalists to bypass 'official' channels and piece their stories together by 'innocently' seeking out more senior members of the department directly. Not surprisingly, the officials who were actively encouraging the development of such 'special relationships' did nothing to stop the practice. Pearson, who took the brighter journalists seriously and developed genuine friendships with most of them, was particularly 'guilty.' It was a state of affairs which caused some strain within the department but served his (and its) purposes well.[41]

For Pearson, the precedent had been set during his wartime posting in Washington, when he had had ample opportunity to see firsthand just how useful competent, informed, and sympathetic journalists like James Reston and Walter Lippmann could be, whether as conduits of information, political advisers, or educators of public opinion. Indeed, during his sojourn in the U.S. capital, he had established a relationship with Reston very much along these lines, one he and colleagues used shrewdly in succeeding years to the considerable benefit of Canadian foreign policy interests.[42]

As Pearson recognized, there was no reason why, with a little effort, similar relationships with influential journalists could not be duplicated in Canada. Once likely candidates had been indentified, he spared no effort to cultivate them, and his senior officials, especially Wrong, Robertson, and, later, Heeney, fully sympathized with his plans.[43] In one respect, this simply entailed preferred treatment, ranging from last-minute accommodation for Wilson and Fraser at a Washington ministerial conference in 1949 to special confidential background reports for Wilson and Smith in 1951 and 'a word from the right quarter' to guarantee Smith and Fraser the necessary press accreditation at the UN security council session in 1946.[44] In fact, the examples are endless. But, more importantly, it meant that for this select group of journalists the formal process of briefing became the more mutually productive and informal process of consultation. There was never any attempt to hide what was going on, at least within government circles; it never crossed Claxton's mind, for example, that Fraser, after returning to Canada from the Paris Peace Conference, was not being kept informed on all the salient goings-on 'from the people around the East Block.'[45] By the late 1940s, this two-tier structure of press relations comprising a small group of 'authoritative voices' and a larger group of *les autres,* with Pearson at the centre of both, was a *fait accompli*; no one in Ottawa, least of all the journalists who benefited from the arrangement the most, seemed to think it was in the slightest way unusual. Unquestionably, the prevailing journalistic ethics which underlay the responsible, civilized relationship placed Pearson in control. But the arrangement also ensured that reporters were well informed, and the best ones who became part of External Affairs' journalistic 'inner circle' were very well informed indeed.

Despite the considerable effort expended by External personnel to inform and influence the press, they considered the results from the great majority of journalists disappointing. Foreign policy, except during crises, remained a hard sell in Canada during the immediate postwar years. Exhausted by the war, the public were not interested in reading about problems in distant places, or so most editors and publishers seemed to believe. Pearson and his colleagues despaired that such attitudes would ever change, particularly in the press gallery, where most of the reporters seemed obsessed with domestic politics virtually to the exclusion of anything else. Contemporary memoranda are laced with endless grumbling about the press gallery's need to be 'spoon fed to get the story right ... [or even] to see there's one at all'; catching the Canadian angle, if their bureaucratic critics are to be believed, was as far beyond their grasp as atomic physics.[46] The Canadian Press was held in the lowest regard of all because of its excessive reliance on American wire-service reports which invariably downplayed Canada's significance in any international story. Understandably, gaffs like the assignment of a sports reporter to cover the Paris Peace Conference did not enhance the news agency's reputation in the East Block.[47]

Surveying the supposed dearth of talent in the Ottawa press corps in 1950, Arnold Heeney, one of the ablest mandarins and then the department's undersecretary, confided to Bruce Hutchison that only two gallery regulars – Blair Fraser and Ken Wilson – could get a foreign policy story straight and comment intelligently on it. Unfortunately, he lamented, neither of them wrote for a daily.[48] Even allowing for the ingrained External arrogance, Heeney's frank assessment was not all that far off the mark; certainly, it would not have been disputed at the senior levels of External, where Fraser and Wilson were highly regarded. Max Freedman, Dexter's gallery replacement and later the *Free Press*'s Washington correspondent, Michael Barkway, who would assume the Ottawa editorship of the *Financial Post* after Wilson's death in 1952, and the *Journal*'s Norman Smith were considered a notch below. Hutchison, Dexter, and Ferguson were all editors and thus not included in Heeney's informal survey.

Beginning in 1947 and through the next two years, the Pearson–External Affairs publicity apparatus was fully engaged in marshalling public support behind Canada's and the West's vital Cold War interests – namely, the Marshall Plan and the North Atlantic treaty.[49] St Laurent made a clear statement of Canadian interest in a defensive alliance to contain communism and link the United States and Canada to Western Europe at the United Nations, but, as Reid later noted with barely concealed disbelief, 'the significance of this statement was not appreciated at the time by newspapermen who were covering the Assembly.'[50] However, the message was not lost on Grant Dexter. While he was lauding the UN and Canada's 'unshakeable' support for it as a 'resolute answer to anyone who may have lost heart in the power of the Charter to keep the world at peace,' most of his friends at External, with Pearson in the forefront, had already done just that.[51] The *Free Press*, in contrast, had always regarded a workable system of collective security, with or without the Soviets, as *the* objective, and Dexter had found merit in an earlier observation by St Laurent that peace should depend on suiting the pace of international cooperation to 'democratic unity' and 'not to Russian obstinacy.'[52] As for the *Montreal Star* and *Maclean's*, for some time they had been adamant that collective security, and not the United Nations per se, must have the highest priority.

By the end of 1947, attitudes were clearly changing. Hutchison merely stated the obvious in his year-end review of the international situation when he observed that recent events had shown that the underlying premise of UN optimists was faulty – clearly Moscow had no intention of cooperating with the West.[53] In a watershed editorial following on the heels of the communist *coup d'état* in Czechoslovakia, Dexter himself acknowledged that Moscow had frustrated the UN's purpose and that a functioning collective security pact, spanning the Atlantic, was needed to make the Russians more reasonable. For readers who might have found this apparent abandonment of the United Nations by such a leading supporter difficult to accept, he offered the reassurance that an 'Atlantic pact' would actually 'be strengthening the United Nations by giving collective security its real chance to operate.' For Ferguson the sad events in Prague aroused the strongest emotions. 'Are we still appeasers?' he questioned angrily, invoking the bitter memories of 1938.[54] Thereafter, the *Star* editorial page argued loudly for the speedy conclusion of some form of North Atlantic defensive alliance. The rhetoric employed by Dexter and Ferguson closely matched that which St Laurent, Pearson, and others were using to build support for just such a pact. It was no accident that Dexter and a few trusted journalists were aware that the government remained sharply divided over the St Laurent–Pearson initiatives; the pact's supporters had kept them informed in the obvious hope they would alert an already sympathetic public opinion and thus bring pressure to bear on the doubting politicians.[55]

On 19 April 1947, speaking in the House of Commons, St Laurent made his most impassioned plea yet for a North Atlantic collective security arrangement; this time, his comments received wide coverage in the press. The *Free Press* printed his statement verbatim and welcomed his assurances that Ottawa was determined not to abandon the UN. Ferguson saluted his statement as 'historic' and 'remarkable.' Communist aggression was a reality and, pending the strengthening of the United Nations, Canadians must act with the rest of the free world to defend themselves. 'Canada,' he concluded approvingly, 'has declared a foreign policy which sweeps aside the isolationism, the half measures, the weasel words [of appeasement].'[56] Evoking the sad train of events of the late 1930s was more than just an effective editorial tactic. For utopian internationalists the preceding three years had brought a succession of bitter disappointments and equally bitter disillusion, and now the inevitable reaction had come in full force. The Reids and Pearsons either had already become hardened cold warriors or were well on their way,[57] and Dexter and Ferguson were going through a similar metamorphosis. Fraser's postwar expectations had been less sanguine and certainly less moralistic, but he, too, was deeply disturbed by developments in Europe and their implications.

Through the summer and autumn of 1948, editorial commentary favouring the Atlantic security pact proposals in the *Star, Free Press, Financial Post,* and *Maclean's* became, if anything, more pressing. Ferguson's defence was typical. Such an arrangement, he admonished his readers, would not be 'charity' but 'common sense,' 'an effective form of fire insurance, and the only one available.' While 'this revolutionary concept' had clearly already won 'majority acceptance in this country,' he also warned darkly of the existence of an 'obstinate hard core of people [a clear reference to contrary voices in the cabinet] who delight to live exclusively in the past.'[58] With the crude Soviet effort to blockade West Berlin spurring everyone on, 'defence multilateralism' was now being promoted with the same conviction that its economic brother had been since the end of the war. Indeed, 'the very highest sources' had assured Wilson that the Canadian government was determined the security pact would 'contain definite obligations for ... economic cooperation.'[59] During succeeding months, this linkage between economic and military security – the European Recovery Program and the Atlantic pact – would become a major theme both at External and in the editorials and news columns of the *Financial Post*.

With Mackenzie King's retirement on 15 November 1948, St Laurent became prime minister. Two months earlier, to almost no one's surprise – the move had been mooted off and on for almost two years – Pearson had entered the cabinet as secretary of state for external affairs. This appointment presented his many admirers in the press with an opportunity to express their support publicly for both the man and his collective security agreement; in private exhanges, their encouragement and offers of assistance were even more unrestrained. Ferguson hoped 'that now and again in the next few years I'd be able to help,' while Gillis Purcell, the Canadian Press chief, only half-jokingly warned Pearson that 'now you'll be able to prove you're as good as all your newspaper friends have claimed for so long.'[60]

By February 1949 the North Atlantic treaty negotiations had reached their most delicate stage. In this instance, the favoured Canadian strategy of quiet diplomacy was not paying off. Still, there was anger over the flood of State Department leaks to James Reston which were appearing almost daily in the *New York Times*, leaks that implied a watering down of the military terms of the pact and the outright elimination of the economic provisions so dear to East Block hearts. 'Our boys are thinking it may be time for a calculated indiscretion by our government,' Hutchison confided to Dexter from Washington. 'This is pretty important stuff it seems to me and I am given the green light to write it as I please.' Just in case Hutchison needed extra encouragement, Pearson arranged a combination pep talk and briefing, and, judging by the reporter's reaction, it must have been a vintage Pearsonian performance. 'Whatever happens the hockey player [Pearson's nickname in *Free Press* memoranda] ... would prefer defeat to any compromise ... [and] this sounds good to me,' Hutchison reassured Winnipeg.[61] Needless to say, he and Dexter agreed to do what they could to help in the common cause.

Within a month, the negotiations had been completed. The drafting and ratification of this agreement marked the coming of age of Canadian foreign policy and were unquestionably a personal triumph for St Laurent, Pearson, and the senior officials at External Affairs. George Ferguson extolled the pact's merits and confidently predicted that Canadians would need 'no long course of public indoctrination to persuade us to make the military and other commitments now called for.'[62] Dexter could not quite bring himself to admit that NATO had supplanted the United Nations as the ultimate guarantor of the free world's security, but he acknowledged it was the best solution at hand and for that reason deserved the country's full support. When parliament approved the NATO treaty with only two dissenting votes, it was a clear indication of the degree to which fear of communist aggression had forged a foreign policy consensus in Canada. Nonetheless, the efforts of External Affairs and the media during the preceding two years to build public support for this particular initiative had certainly played their role.[63]

In the afterglow of NATO's establishment, many Canadians seemed seduced by the comfortable illusion that the Cold War was manageable and perhaps even won. Once again, the public's supposed unwillingness to 'think internationally' was furrowing brows at External Affairs, and publications like *Maclean's*, which were trying to play up Canadian foreign policy developments, were encountering the same disconcerting complacency.[64] The outbreak of the Korean war in late June 1950 rudely shattered such illusions. By a singular bit of diplomatic good fortune – a Soviet boycott of the Security Council – the Americans were able to get North Korea branded an 'aggressor' and the UN to authorize its first 'police action.' Obtaining UN sanction may have largely been a public relations stratagem to cloak Washington's plans in international legitimacy. In Canada, however, UN legitimacy mattered a great deal to both the St Laurent government and public opinion.[65]

In the minds of true believers, here was the all-but-moribund UN's chance to fulfil its promise, and an aroused public opinion clamouring for tangible Canadian support of the American-UN position was soon pressuring Ottawa to act. While the decision to commit Canadian forces was made quickly enough, Pearson's department still faced two serious problems. The first had been candidly outlined to Ken Wilson by Arnold Heeney only a few weeks after the outbreak of the conflict. Ottawa saw Korea as a Cold War sideshow, Heeney stressed, but was desperately concerned that the Americans would lose their sense of perspective and get 'carried away.' At the same time, he revealed, some members of the Canadian government did not recognize the danger the war posed to Western (and Canadian) security, and their failure to appreciate the gravity of the situation was complicating Ottawa's task.[66] The second problem was to keep an increasingly heated domestic public opinion under control, an absolute necessity if the government's efforts to influence American policy along a more moderate course were to have any chance of success. As it wrestled with these problems during the coming months, the Department of External Affairs found to its chagrin that some of its closest friends in the press, men whom it naturally hoped – and more to the point, expected – would play a supportive role, turned out to have their own agenda.

Both the *Montreal Star* and the *Winnipeg Free Press* immediately joined in the general chorus clamouring for unconditional Canadian support of the military effort Washington was hastily mounting under the UN flag.[67] As absolutely committed proponents of collective security, Ferguson and Dexter subscribed to the view that the whole postwar system would collapse if even one aggressor was not stopped. Hand-wringing and moral support were not good enough, and any evasion of the country's responsibilities was intolerable. What better means of forcing the issue than an aroused public opinion?[68] Throughout July, Dexter pounded home the collective security argument in a succession of emotional editorials. Ferguson, meanwhile, adamantly proclaimed that Canadian participation in the ground fighting 'should be taken for granted.' After all, 'there is more than a moral obligation involved ... the fact [is] that effective collective security remains the only safe way of protecting ourselves.'[69] Public opinion, at least in English-speaking Canada, seemed to agree and was growing increasingly restive over the appearances of foot-dragging in Ottawa.[70] A formal commitment for ground forces came in early August, though, with the military cupboard empty, it would be 1951 before any number of Canadian soldiers would be ready for combat. Neither Dexter nor Ferguson was prepared to take the Liberals to task for this woeful state of unpreparedness, rightly feeling that all Canadians bore a share of the responsibility for the drastic postwar rundown of the country's armed forces. But even government insiders admitted they had badly bungled the public relations side of the whole contribution-of-forces episode.[71]

At least the Korean crisis had solved one of the Department of External Affairs' long-standing complaints: public indifference towards and the resulting media undercoverage of Canadian foreign policy. After several years of cutbacks in *Maclean's* coverage of international affairs, for instance, newly appointed editor Ralph Allen was pressing for extra resources to satisfy readers' demand for world news while Fraser, the magazine's recognized foreign affairs expert, was being inundated with requests for speaking engagements from across the country.[72] In such speeches he could provide a reasonably indepth explanation that had immediate impact, but he could reach only a limited audience; in contrast, his CBC radio commentaries, while overcoming the latter problem, were inevitably too brief to do justice to complex problems. As for *Maclean's,* Fraser found it difficult at the best of times to keep his 'Backstage' columns timely, and a fast-breaking story like Korea only magnified his problems. Nevertheless, by drawing on his extensive network of civil service contacts and his astute political instincts, Fraser was able to report on the Canadian diplomatic effort during the early stages of the crisis with remarkable accuracy and surprising currency. His strength, of course, was that he *did* know what was going on in Ottawa, virtually as it was happening and not infrequently even before. Such was the confidence External Affairs officers vested in his judgment, skill, and, one might add, sympathy. Fraser's approach to journalism emphasized the explanation of the roots of policy and the basis of the government's decisions. Since both looked much clearer from close up than from afar, his columns could not help but place the government's Korean policy in a more favourable light.

In contrast to *Maclean's,* and alone among the country's major English-language dailies, the *Winnipeg Free Press* had been consistently providing extensive coverage of Canadian foreign policy since the end of the war. Its reliably pro-internationalist slant and, although these were somewhat less reliable, its Liberal sympathies, made it a favourite in civil service and intellectual circles.[73] Thanks to both Hutchison and Freedman, the *Free Press* had led its competitors in providing original, up-to-date coverage of the diplomatic side of the Korean conflict. Freedman, whom the long-suffering Dexter once compared to 'a great artist [who] on his rare appearances ... steals the show and no doubt is worth all the trouble,'[74] had cultivated an extensive network of sources in the American capital, thanks in no small part to the helpfulness of Canadian ambassador Hume Wrong, whose own relations with the State Department were excellent. By allowing American officials to vet his copy, Freedman regularly gained access to sensitive background information, an arrangement he, Dexter, and Hutchison naturally found extremely helpful. Of course this tie-in was also useful to Wrong and his staff. Freedman was accommodating, knowledgeable, and serious enough to get most stories right, and, moreover, his paper was perceived to be so influential in Liberal party circles by the State Department as to be accepted by them as an 'authoritative voice.'[75] The arrangement could prove especially helpful when the Department of External Affairs wanted a particular story aired, clarified, discredited, or suppressed. One incident, which occurred in the spring of 1948, illuminates the nature of the relationship. Freedman, relying heavily on information supplied by Wrong, had written a series of articles on some crucial discussions then under way between the Truman administration and Congress over precisely how Canada would be allowed to benefit from the Marshall Plan. When Wrong noticed that one of these articles misrepresented American policy in a way that might embarrass Canada's friends in Washington, he promptly telephoned Ottawa and got an official there to explain their problem to Freedman. 'These are little things,' the latter cabled Dexter apologetically, 'but I am so friendly with External that I would very much appreciate having them cleared up [and] will send on a little sub-edit when I receive the text of Hume's suggested amendation tomorrow.'[76] Freedman's usefulness extended further. Wrong made little effort to conceal his dismissive view of Ottawa 'as an asylum of subnormal and rather mischievous children' and was not above using the *Free Press* and its local man to assist in some foreign policy-making of his own when his frustration with Ottawa's line became too much to bear.[77]

Hutchison's presence was even more useful to Ottawa's diplomats and her friends in the American capital. His reputation as one of Canada's foremost political analysts and an influential adviser to Liberal party heavyweights gave him real status in the United States, while most of the Americans he encountered found his unaffected, outgoing manner and unabashed admiration for all things American downright irresistible. By 1950 he had already accumulated a great deal of experience covering the American scene and fancied himself a first-rate analyst of foreign policy. Certainly no Canadian journalist could match his string of official and unofficial contacts in the United States. Hutchison's forays to Washington and New York provided him with the background he later used to pry explanations out of Ottawa officialdom or to flesh out his own columns and Dexter's editorials.[78] Like Dexter, his principal interest was the domestic political implications of Canadian foreign policy, and that emphasis suited his country's diplomats at the United Nations and Washington perfectly. Both saw him as a useful ally and, via the *Free Press,* as a pipeline to a significant chunk of Liberal party and public opinion; consequently, they went out of their way to try to help him. Hutchison, naturally enough, basked in the attention.[79]

Among Hutchison's American journalist friends were Lippmann and Reston, the two leading foreign policy commentators of the day. Both men were kept exceptionally well informed by the Truman administration and the Congress, and they were frequently used as authoritative voices, kite flyers, confidential intermediaries and even in a quasi-advisory role by their bureaucratic and political patrons. In a Canadian context, it was the role Hutchison, and to varying degrees Dexter, Ferguson, Fraser, and Wilson, had begun to see themselves performing, and indeed had already begun to perform with every encouragement from Pearson and other senior men at External, the Department of Finance, and the Bank of Canada. The pressures of the Korean crisis merely served to cement the relationship more firmly than ever.[80]

The Korean War entered a new period of crisis in November 1950 when Chinese communist 'volunteers' routed the overconfident and overextended United Nations forces as they rashly pressed towards the Manchurian frontier. Pearson's worst nightmare – the prospect of the Americans embarking on some crusade to punish the iniquitous Chinese Reds – now threatened to become reality. For the next few months, limiting the damage to the larger Western cause which the Chinese intervention threatened to inflict and containing the American response within reasonable bounds were the pressing concerns.[81] Dealing with Washington was problem enough, but Pearson had to contend simultaneously with a large segment of Canadian public opinion angered over the East Block's failure to support the hard-line American position.

Pearson's plan for negotiations between the UN and China, announced on a national radio broadcast on 5 December left George Ferguson unimpressed. 'I understand the line is that the Red Chinese are not as other Reds – a theory I gravely suspect, and that if we do this or that, we can come to an understanding with them,' he confided sceptically to a friend, 'but I fancy it is to be our side that will do the thises and thats, leaving the Peking boys ... to break any agreement ... which they'll do as and when it suits them.'[82] Ferguson was now a thoroughgoing cold warrior, and his convictions showed. Still, like Wilson and McEachern, he was prepared not to question openly the wisdom of Pearson's approach for the time being. Dexter, however, had a much harder time restraining himself. Pearson's statement had left him disappointed, perplexed, even angry. China was clearly an aggressor, and this was hardly the time to be tentative.

When ceasefire negotiations broke down early in the new year, the rationale for Pearson's go-slow approach evaporated. Ominously, the Americans stepped up the pressure for their 'aggressor' motion more vigorously than ever. To deflect what the East Block considered Washington's misplaced zeal, Canadian diplomats responded with a bevy of stratagems designed to delay any vote on their ally's proposal. Their hope, growing steadily dimmer, was a compromise resolution capable of extricating the West from the Korean morass and less likely to alienate opinion in the non-aligned camp.[83]

Dexter waited a week, then took a swipe at the Liberal government the likes of which it rarely had to absorb from the *Free Press.* 'What is needed now,' he stated bluntly, 'is a declaration, in unmistakable terms, that this country, like the United States, is determined to stand up to aggression.'[84] During the next three weeks, Dexter restated this point with rising indignation, on 25 January, for example, bluntly querying whether 'Red China ... [should] be formally condemned for aggression or should the crime be whitewashed in deference to counsels of expediency.' By this point, even Ferguson had begun to wonder whether Canada was drifting away from its firm commitment to collective security. Finally, on 26 January, Pearson, after an exhausting diplomatic effort which had produced minimal results, announced that Canada was prepared to support the U.S. motion condemning China, albeit with certain 'reservations.' Various explanations of this change of heart were put forward, but the simple truth was that the course he had been diligently pursuing had reached a dead end and was now becoming more divisive, at home and abroad, than opting to support the Americans.[85]

Dexter greeted Pearson's statement with a conspicuous lack of enthusiasm. After dismissing the minister's recent diplomatic exertions as mere 'appeasement,' he noted sarcastically that 'it is good to have Mr. Pearson on the record and it would be still better if he and his colleagues would cease and desist forthwith from further efforts to delay.'[86] The next few days saw no move to soften the criticism. Dexter was making his point – with silence – and for those cold warriors who felt the government was not showing sufficient resolve, the *Free Press*'s indictment was refreshing indeed.

Ferguson, in contrast, was obviously much relieved that Canada had finally fallen into line, and now went out of his way to explain the reasoning behind what he called the 'stalling tactics' of recent weeks. His basic point, and it had the advantage of being true, was that Ottawa had been trying to keep Korea from fatally distracting American attention at the expense of Europe, the decisive Cold War front. According to the *Star,* 'only undue simplification of the basic principles of Canadian foreign policy can make Mr. Pearson out to be wrong,' and criticisms of his recent actions consequently were 'wholly unmerited.' Writing in *Maclean's,* Fraser offered a defence of the government's performance which was rather less emotional than Ferguson's but stressed the same points.

Dexter's sharp attacks on Pearson and his Korean policy during December and January, and particularly the implication that Ottawa had been dabbling in appeasement, had left Pearson and his colleagues more than a bit miffed.[88] English-language editorial comment had been almost universal in condemning the Chinese as aggressors, but none had pursued the government's 'refusal' to go along as relentlessly as Dexter. Even Ferguson, with his intimate knowledge of the internal workings of the '*Free Press* mind,' was hardpressed to fathom the paper's motives. It was possible that Dexter was simply determined Canada not be left off the hook on the condemnation of China. Still, it was clear to Ferguson that this had never been Canada's intention, and with Freedman at the UN throughout, he found it hard to believe that Dexter was unaware of this point.[89]

The truth is that during January Dexter had become alarmed that Pearson and the government were backing away from their commitment to achieving collective security through the United Nations.[90] It was a view which seemed to be corroborated by a few others, including John Deutsch, a senior bureaucrat with considerable international expertise in the economic sphere and strong opinions on just about every subject. Deutsch exerted a tremendous intellectual influence over the *Free Press* editor's thinking. Pearson himself had inadvertently added credence to Dexter's suspicions when he showed Freedman a confidential discussion paper prepared at Heeney's request by John Holmes, a junior member of Canada's permanent UN delegation. Holmes's memorandum dealt with the implications the Korean War held for collective security, and concluded pessimistically (if realistically) that the UN had little practical future as anything more than a talking shop. Pearson had merely wanted Dexter's confidential opinion, presumably on the domestic political implications of any abandonment of the UN ideal for out-and-out reliance on regional security pacts like NATO. It was assumed Freedman and Dexter would not confuse the memo's contents with any finished ideas, and certainly not settled policy. Discussion paper or not, Dexter was appalled that such heresy had crept into the department's thinking, and Freedman's unfortunate comments that the ideas, which he dismissed derisively as 'selective collective security – with Canada deciding where and when and if we will do anything under the [UN] Charter' – seemed to be swaying Pearson, deepened the misunderstanding.[91] Only in March, when Dexter met with Pearson and some of the others in Ottawa, was he finally reassured. Reid 'was ... absolutely solid on the main point of resisting aggression and standing up to Russia,' Dexter recorded with obvious relief, and, as for Pearson, 'he did not complain about our editorials and so far as I could discover he is not in favour of appeasement.'[92] Moreover, Dexter now had a clearer appreciation of how hard St Laurent, Pearson, and Claxton had had to fight to achieve as much as they had and it sobered him considerably. Interestingly, Hutchison seems to have shared none of his friend's anxieties about the leadership of Pearson or the government, and apparently had no doubts about their motives and objectives.[93] Swaying Dexter, if in fact he tried, had obviously not been easy.

During the postwar decade, hard-edged criticisms of Pearson and Canadian foreign policy were the exception, not the rule. This support reflected more than anything else the absence of fundamental, longterm differences of opinion between the top echelon of journalists and the bureaucratic and ministerial architects of Canadian foreign policy. Throughout this period the professional relationship between these two groups was mutually beneficial, and such friction as periodically occurred should not obscure this basic reality, for it certainly did not at the time.

The partnership rested on two pillars, with the first being a shared perspective on the fundamentals of Canada's postwar international role. When asked what was wrong with Canadian foreign policy during these years, Fraser's stock response was simply that 'there was not enough of it'[94]; Dexter and the others would have readily agreed. In this regard, one cannot underestimate the pervasive support for the 'new internationalism' which, certainly in English-speaking Canada, characterized the postwar decade.[95] As Holmes later recalled, 'a new body of Canadian professionals – foreign service officers *and students of foreign policy* [author's emphasis] – were feeling their oats, aspiring to a place nearer the seats of power.' Surely Fraser, Hutchison, Dexter, Wilson, Irwin, Freedman, Smith, and Ferguson could have been mentioned in this context as well; Pearson and his colleagues in the Department of External Affairs certainly thought of them in this way.[96] For these men, as for a majority of English Canadians, Pearson articulated and symbolized the hopes of a nation and, through his diplomatic achievements, made Canada mean something in the world, in the process earning the respect of his countrymen. At least until the Suez Crisis of 1956, even the Conservative opposition had difficulty disputing anything more substantial than the details of Pearson's and the government's handling of Canadian foreign policy. Indeed, some, like Donald Fleming and James Macdonnell, felt that in the tense international climate of the late 1940s and early 1950s the national interest dictated they support the government when at all possible. A few of the party's leading lights were actually enthusiastic admirers of Pearson's diplomatic abilities, although such sentiments were obviously not widely advertised. Both views, moreover, were shared by some Conservative-leaning journalists.[97]

The second factor at work was the journalists' perception of their responsibilities. Certainly nowhere was the responsible, civilized relationship more in evidence than in the elite press's dealings with the Department of External Affairs. The principal concern of the journalists was to educate Canadians internationally; getting the story straight necessitated the closest of contacts with the establishment that formulated and implemented foreign policy. In the environment of postwar Ottawa and even more so abroad, this led to a blurring of the social and professional relationship between the two groups until, in the minds of the journalists and undoubtedly many of the diplomatic professionals as well, the distinction all but disappeared.[98] Admiration for the brainpower and dedication External possessed in officials such as Wrong, Robertson, and Heeney was eclipsed only by the degree of respect and affection the press, and especially the top-ranked men, had for Pearson. Indeed, this esteem had no equal anywhere else in the government and, not infrequently, bordered on hero worship. George Ferguson's assessment that, as minister, Pearson was the best and the brightest of the 'politician-experts,' a man who in effect stood above politics, was clearly shared by Ferguson's peers.

Diplomats and journalists had a common vision of Canada's role in the postwar world, and both accepted that the press had a role to play in translating that vision into reality; the actual arrangements that followed were very much a function of the journalists' own attitude. For Canadian diplomats, the objective was clear: they wanted to build a consensus in English-speaking Canada for an assertive internationalism. As for the French-speaking quarter of the country, it was simply expected – or at any rate hoped – that St Laurent would somehow manage to keep Quebeckers on side in any crunch.[99] In carrying out the former task, however, the necessary consensus was largely forged by developments abroad and the absence of credible alternatives, with the press playing a distinctly secondary role. Nevertheless, at the time this was not so clear, and the supporting role of the press was deemed sufficiently important to merit a considerable effort by Canada's diplomatic professionals. In return for encouraging and assisting the press, and particularly the press elite, Pearson and his associates received useful publicity and other often valuable forms of behind-the-scenes cooperation, not to mention helpful political counsel. Both sides considered it a fair bargain.[100]

In January 1953 Bruce Hutchison had written to Pearson requesting an interview 'to our mutual advantage.' Hutchison had a contract to put together a series of articles for *Maclean's* and expected to be writing extensively for several newspapers as well, including the *Financial Post*. 'It is probably desirable that I should write with reasonable accuracy and with proper guidance,' he pointed out to his longtime friend, and 'if you can spare time to give me off the record some of your views of events I think it will prevent me from going off the rails and creating wrong impressions.'[101] Even allowing for the obvious attempt at flattery, the phrasing of Hutchison's proposal neatly encapsulates the assumptions which underlay the intimate relationship that developed between the country's leading public affairs journalists and its diplomats during the postwar decade – a relationship that went a long way towards ensuring that the coverage of Canadian foreign policy seldom went 'off the rails' or created any 'wrong impressions.'

7

'We comment with some degree of impartiality'

The Emergence of a Liberal Press Establishment

The *Maclean's* 1957 post-election issue reached subscribers just days after the 10 June polling date. Publication deadlines meant editor Ralph Allen had had to write his editorial almost two weeks earlier. By that point in the campaign, Blair Fraser had sensed that the incumbents, tired and arrogant after twenty-two unbroken years in power, would lose many seats and perhaps win only bare re-election. It seemed unthinkable they would actually lose. So it was that Allen penned his editorial, admonishing his readers: 'For better or for worse, we Canadians have once more elected one of the most powerful governments ever created by the free will of the electorate.'[1] No great admirer of the Grits, Allen's intention had been to rap Canadians' collective knuckles, but few readers grasped that. Instead, *Maclean's,* Allen, and especially Fraser, whose assessment, most assumed, had been Allen's inspiration, were red-faced. The unthinkable had happened. Never had the content of an editorial (or its writer's intent) been more misunderstood. For many in the country, Allen's words merely seemed to confirm that the 'Liberal press establishment,' in which *Maclean's* and Fraser had occupied leading positions for years, had been as arrogant and out of touch with Canadian opinion as the haughty Liberals themselves. For Conservatives, CCFers, and independents, not to mention many Liberals, the existence of a journalistic establishment favouring the Liberal party was an article of faith, as much as that other political 'fact' of the postwar decade – the existence of a Liberal-leaning bureaucratic establishment.

At least until the last term of the St Laurent government, many members of the English-language press, and certainly all but a handful of the ablest, had clearly admired the Liberals' competent administration and had broadly agreed with the direction in which Louis St Laurent, C.D. Howe, and Mike Pearson were leading the country.[2] Traditional political partisanship was an important factor in the attitude displayed by some – Grant Dexter and Bruce Hutchison, for instance – and a factor for all. But beyond this connection lay the increasingly intimate interaction between a highly competent bureaucracy and a party which nurtured it on the one hand and an evolving journalistic philosophy or style on the other. The product of this interaction between press and government, the responsible, civilized relationship, was an authoritative and certainly sympathetic press, but not one that was politically subservient.

The close relations between the abler reporters and editors and their mandarin sources in the 1945–57 period had their roots in the journalists' perception of how they should report the complexities of government administration in wartime. Out of both personal conviction and a sense of professional responsibility, these journalist insiders were predisposed to cover their subject favourably. In the event, it would prove difficult to comment favourably on the government policies shaped in and administered by the senior civil service without appearing to comment just as favourably on their political masters – a fact that greatly benefited the Liberal party.

By the late autumn of 1943, however, publicizing their obvious wartime successes was less of a priority for the Liberals than ensuring that the Canadian public had a favourable opinion of their capacity for postwar administration, and in particular for managing the transition from a wartime to a peacetime economy.[3] Led by Brooke Claxton, one of the party's most politically astute minds and the leader of the progressive faction in caucus, the Liberals began to fashion an appealing reconstruction plan based on activist economic and social measures crafted to pre-empt the growing political threat from the left as well as to satisfy Clifford Clark, Graham Towers, and other senior economic mandarins.[4] In generating a groundswell of support among the voters, the endorsement of influential segments of the press would be clearly invaluable.

During the three years following its narrow re-election in 1945, the Liberal government faced formidable challenges in both domestic and foreign policy, and mastered the majority with conspicuous success. Their record of achievement left even cabinet ministers breathless and certainly convinced a large section of the population that the Liberals, backed by the expertise of the senior civil service, were a very able administrative team.[5] As one awed young Liberal later wrote, 'what one had come to marvel at most in Canadian Liberalism was its efficiency, its splendid imperturbability, the infallibility of both its fortune and its genius ... It was a new politics of pragmatism made more compelling for its graceful power.'[6] It was hardly surprising that many of the abler journalists would be similarly swayed. After all, not only were they in close contact with the very politicians and civil servants who had masterminded all this success, but ideologically speaking most were part of the broad political centre the Liberals all but monopolized during the postwar decade. In the face of an accepting public and a press that almost daily, with a few exeptions, seemed to become more outwardly sympathetic to the government, selling an alternative explanation of events to Canadians was going to be, as one Conservative glumly put it, 'a man-sized job.'[7]

Obviously, the task was not going to be made easier by the emergence of a Liberal press establishment, a process many observers considered well under way during the early postwar years. Nevertheless, several developments during 1948 added substantially to the Tories' woes and certainly shifted the sympathies of several members of the country's journalistic elite even farther towards the government camp.

The first was made possible by the long-awaited retirement of Mackenzie King as Liberal party leader. The septuagenarian King's decision to step aside was met with open relief by most Liberals, but none felt it more keenly than the 'young Turks' of the party led by Brooke Claxton and Douglas Abbott. Increasingly, they had chafed under the restraining hand of King and the group of basically conservatively minded ministers he had assembled around himself during the 1930s. Having decisively beaten back the CCF (at least for the time being) and weathered the worst of the postwar transition, in both instances largely thanks to policies they had pressed on their older colleagues, Claxton and the others felt the Liberals had every right to be satisfied with their performance and much reason for optimism. More to the point, they were eager to put their own stamp on the 'Government party.'

Dexter had been growing increasingly worried about one aspect of the 'Liberal revolution' – the growing power of the state over Canadians' lives – and, urged on by Crerar, Macdonald, Power, Lambert, and others who had his ear, he saw the leadership transition as more than simply an exercise in political theatre. It was also an opportunity, and perhaps the last, to push the party back onto the rails of 'true liberalism.'[8] In fairness to Power and Lambert, their concern was not the welfare state heresy; both men strongly supported the Liberals' measures. Rather, they feared, as did Victor Sifton, Dexter, Hutchison, and for that matter even Mackenzie King, that the government's growing reliance on faceless, unaccountable advisers was a dangerous departure from democratic liberal principles.[9]

Tom Crerar, Angus Macdonald, the deep thinkers of the *Free Press,* and the other remnants of 'encrusted Whiggism,' as Chubby Power aptly characterized them,[10] might rue the Liberal party's postwar leftward slide, but, fortunately for the party's electoral fortunes, theirs was not a mainstream view. A quarter of the population were under thirty years of age and most Liberals rightly saw the CCF, despite its recent setbacks, as the chief threat to their political hegemony. As Norman Lambert shrewdly put it: 'First, there must be definiteness about leadership and secondly, the position of the party in this postwar world must be restated in terms of a sound forward-looking policy.' This sort of talk was pretty hard for someone weaned on 'bow-and-arrow' liberalism like Hutchison to take. 'I was amazed to find this conservative guy come out for what he called Social Democracy – a leftward movement of the Liberal Party which he believes is demanded by history,' he confided to Dexter. 'To have N.L. in the general camp of the brain trust and Pickersgill is at least a novelty and may be a straw in the wind.'[11]   And indeed it was. However, despite doubts about the party's direction, which he so freely aired in private, Dexter's editorial pronouncements positively bubbled over with optimism about a Liberal rebirth under their splendid new leader and, even though they amounted to the progressive platform virtually *in toto*, about the new policies, too.[12]

When the Liberals assembled in Ottawa for their convention, *Maclean's* greeted the delegates with a pointed editorial provocatively entitled 'Is the CCF Winning by Default?' in which Irwin took the government to task for dragging its feet on social programs, particularly health insurance. The progressive wing of Liberaldom must have beamed at such criticism. As soon as the Liberals had made their choice, Blair Fraser, who had never made a secret of his personal admiration for St Laurent, hailed his election as proof that 'courage, ability and integrity can bring a man success in politics.'[13] Although the *Financial Post* confined its comment to a single editorial, McEachern filled it to the brim with superlatives, describing St Laurent variously as 'a Canadian with outstanding qualities of head and heart,' 'one of the towering characters of the generation,' and a 'man who will stand tall and important in any gathering of world political leaders.'[14] George Ferguson, who like Irwin, Wilson, McEachern, and Fraser had covered the convention in person, privately doubted whether St Laurent had either the flexibility or the progressive instincts needed to best the CCF. Nevertheless, he wholeheartedly endorsed his candidacy and welcomed the selection of Quebec's native son for reasons that 'transcend[ed] politics.'[15] In the face of such press acclaim, Conservative predictions that King's retirement would create a crack in the Liberal monolith 'that will soon be open for vital attack' seemed premature.[16]

The Liberal leadership convention had hardly dispersed when the party scored another publicity coup: Lester Pearson's appointment as secretary of state for external affairs. With Cold War tensions mounting dramatically, it was a move that further enhanced the government's already strong reputation for foreign policy competence. Pearson was 'probably the most popular man in Canada, among those who know him at all,' to quote Fraser's appraisal, and Liberal insiders had long believed that arranging his entry into the cabinet would provide their party with a political asset of the first order.[17] Privately, Pearson's army of journalistic admirers could hardly contain their pleasure at the news. But when this spilled over into print, frustrated Conservatives saw their suspicions of Liberal bias confirmed yet again.[18]

Sandwiched between St Laurent's selection as Liberal leader in August and his assumption of the prime ministership in November, Conservatives had gathered for their own leadership convention. John Bracken, in whom so many party moderates had invested their hopes six years earlier, had proved an uninspiring and ineffective leader, and, increasingly, the performance of the caucus in the House of Commons had been an embarrassment. As one party insider bluntly put it: 'The "new look" worn by the Progressive Conservative Party is somewhat similar to the "new look" portrayed by today's dress style. Too much is hidden – the body appears all out of shape – an atmosphere of uncertainty and disillusion is reflected – the background is vague – a target for sympathetic gibes and condolences.'[19] Clearly Bracken had to go, but, unfortunately for the party's wider prospects, far too many Canadians viewed the leader of the anti-Bracken forces and the man who was emerging as his most likely successor, Ontario premier George Drew, as nothing more than the front man for Tory Toronto. Drew had few admirers in the national press and, in fact, a great many journalists, Fraser included, despised him. Professionalism dictated that Fraser try to be objective in print, but privately he could hardly conceal his delight when a CCF temperance candidate defeated Drew in the 1948 Ontario election.[20]

Maclean's, the *Financial Post,* the *Montreal Star,* and the *Winnipeg Free Press* all spent the weeks preceding the Progressive Conservative convention lamenting the party's sad state and the pressing need, to use Irwin's words, for a strong 'progressively minded free enterprise' alternative to the governing Liberals as 'the best insurance against socialism.'[21] When, as expected, Drew swept to the leadership on the first ballot, the initial reaction of the independent and the independent Liberal press was predictably congratulatory, although the tone of the commentary was far more restrained than that St Laurent had enjoyed. Dexter echoed the private feelings of Liberal sympathizers (and Drew-haters – Dexter fell into both camps) when he noted, tongue firmly in cheek, that 'the emergence of a clear dividing line between the two great parties ... will be welcomed everywhere and by none more warmly than by Liberals.'[22] Clearly, any revival of the Conservatives' electoral prospects hinged on Drew's ability to rehabilitate the party's image in the press, and this obviously had to start with his own tarnished image. Favourable post-convention comments meant little; the real tests of his and his party's relations with the fourth estate lay ahead.

St Laurent wasted little time in seeking his own electoral mandate and the Conservatives, with their own new leader at the helm, entered the 1949 campaign buoyed by their usual misplaced optimism. Drew's strident criticisms of the Liberals' extravagance and autocratic tendencies rallied only the converted. To the majority of Canadian voters, most of whom, after all, had never had it so good, gloom-and-ruin speeches bore no resemblance to reality. Moreover, Drew's well-publicized efforts to forge an electoral alliance with the Union nationale – coined the Drew-Duplessis axis by the ever-vigilant Dexter – caused an inevitable backlash in English Canada. At the same time, a generally prosperous economy and fear of a Tory resurgence gravely undermined the CCF's appeal. In contrast, the Liberal organization lacked no resources and needed no issues, save the promise of more of the same success at home and abroad. It was enough to bathe in the reflected glow of adulation for Prime Minister St Laurent, the quiet, competent statesman who was 'above politics,' or so it was alleged. The campaign was an exercise in image-making: 'Uncle Louis' versus 'Tory George.' Under the circumstances, the results of the 27 June poll were thoroughly predictable – a landslide victory for the Liberals.[23]

The *Free Press* had conducted an unabashedly anti-Drew campaign, one made all the more bitter as a result of the personal and political enmity between the Sifton brothers and the new Conservative leader. Both Dexter and Hutchison considered Drew a positive danger to the country and worked hand in glove with the Liberal backroom to defeat him.[24] In editorial after editorial, they hammered away at Drew's supposedly isolationist, protectionist, and reactionary policies and the need for majority government, the latter being a none too subtle reminder to wavering free enterprisers that they did not have the luxury of voting against the Liberals if they wanted to ensure that the CCF were defeated. In the end, the newspaper's advice to the voters was presented as simple common sense: 'trust the management of [your] affairs to the party which has shown by its performance that it knows how to look after Canada's interests.'[25] In deference to the priorities of its owner, the editor of the *Montreal Star* devoted most of his editorial energies to denunciations of the CCF, and nothing was said of the Drew-Duplessis axis. But as the polling date neared, Ferguson threw the paper's full weight behind St Laurent, the 'son of Quebec,' and, like the *Free Press,* emphasized the government's 'efficient and sensible record of administration.'[26] Meanwhile, in his 'Backstage' columns, Fraser strove to put the Conservative campaign in its most favourable light. 'Up to now,' he wrote midway through the contest, for example, the feeling that the Liberals had been in long enough had 'been frustrated by a lack of real alternatives [but] this year the alternative is there.'[27] Still, the result seemed to indicate most Canadians had trouble seeing it.

Surveying the magnitude of the Liberals' victory – 192 seats in a 265-seat House – and with an eye on the deteriorating international situation, Ferguson welcomed the election of a government which could command support nationwide (that is, had substantial support in Quebec), though he questioned whether the mandate might have been too sweeping. As for Dexter, he gloated quietly. With the Liberals assured of another four years in the government benches, he could safely speculate on the unfortunate implications for Canadian democracy of the Tories' seemingly permanent weakness.[28] In its election post mortem, the *Financial Post* also stressed the Conservative party's irrelevancy. More than anything, McEachern and his employers had wanted to see the CCF crushed, and, realistically, the Tories' short-term role in such a strategy was to ensure an ample Liberal majority by winning as few seats as possible themselves. In that light, the election verdict can hardly have been disappointing. It certainly did not help that McEachern thoroughly disliked Drew and openly confided to friends that too often the Conservative leader had a limited acquaintance with the truth.[29]

Sifting through the electoral wreckage, J.M. Macdonnell attributed his party's disastrous showing to four basic factors: prosperity and the fear 'manipulated by the Liberals' that the Conservatives would bring a depression; the success of the Liberal 'hate campaign' against Drew; the decline of the CCF's appeal; and the inadequacy of their own publicity efforts in the face of the Liberal party's 'originality ... attractiveness ... and unscrupulousness.'[30] As bitterly disappointed party members scanned about for scapegoats, it was easy to lash out at those publications which had favoured the incumbents. Recounting a heated exchange he had had some months before the election with George McCullagh, an ardent Tory and publisher of the *Globe and Mail,* Clifford Sifton confided to his brother that 'I got the feeling ... [it] ... reflected ... an inability to accept the fact that we could honestly prefer [the government] to the Conservative opposition.'[31]

There is no question that during most of the postwar decade a virtual state of cold war prevailed between the Progressive Conservative party and the great majority of journalists covering national affairs. Most Conservatives pointed accusingly at the blatant partisanship of the journalists themselves, with the Liberal press establishment, naturally enough, ranking as the most blatant and certainly the most damaging offenders. But to a large degree it was a self-serving explanation; apart from any merits the Liberals possessed, much of the Conservatives' poor image with and in the press was their own fault. Macdonnell, one of the most intelligent and moderate men in the party's inner circle, ruefully estimated that 90 per cent of the press gallery was already against Drew when he became leader, and Macdonnell was probably an optimist. Still, he thought the situation could be reversed. First, Drew had to make more of an effort to cultivate the publishers and editors of the large circulation dailies already sympathetic to the party – the *Toronto Telegram* and *Globe and Mail*, the *Ottawa Journal*, and the *Montreal Gazette*. Second, Drew and other MPs had to become more accessible to individual reporters and editors. 'They love attention,' he reminded his colleagues, 'and within six months a majority of the Gallery might be won over.'[32]

Macdonnell's estimate of six months was about five-and-a-half years off the mark, but his emphasis on adopting a less adversarial approach at least pointed the party in the right direction. Initially, Drew did make attempts to improve his relations with reporters. Any favourable impact this might have had was quickly undone by an extremely partisan, combative political style which inevitably came off second best in confrontations with the civilized, patrician St Laurent. Almost as ill-advised were his repeated attempts to bait the senior members of the civil service. Five months after becoming leader, he had warned a McGill University audience that 'we are fighting for personal and economic freedom here in Canada today [and] are in a very real danger of losing that fight to the bureaucrats who accept the basic philosophy of Karl Marx no matter what political name they may adopt.'[33] Although unwilling to name names, he foolishly persisted in hurling the accusations. For the Ottawa press corps in general, and particularly for the so-called 'elite' journalists, Drew's baseless attacks on men they often knew as friends, certainly men they respected as public servants in the finest sense of the term, and men who were in no position to defend themselves were deemed completely unjustified. It is little wonder that, suspicious of Drew and his party to begin with, Fraser, Wilson, and Ferguson, for instance, increasingly dismissed the Drew-led Tories as an uncivilized rabble whose elevation to government was an appalling prospect.[34]

In practice, few Conservative MPs reached out beyond gallery loyalists, and during the late 1940s and early 1950s there were few enough of these. A notable exception was newcomer George Nowlan, one of the small group of reform-minded Conservatives in the caucus. For Nowlan, the obvious impact on public opinion when stories favourable to his party appeared in independent publications 'simply show[ed] how absolutely essential friends in the Press Gallery are, and how dependent all parties must be upon having the best possible publicity placed upon all of their actions.'[35] The contacts he forged with Blair Fraser, a fellow Nova Scotian and Acadia University alumnus, showed relations could be put on an amicable basis even with someone whom most Tories considered to be at the very centre of the Liberal press establishment. But most of Nowlan's colleagues were content to nurse their grievances, one of which was that a great press army of Liberal flacks was permanently arrayed against them.[36] During St. Laurent's first term, it was difficult for a columnist like Fraser to avoid dwelling on the glaring weaknesses of the official opposition; no matter how balanced the approach, besieged Conservatives were bound to feel resentful.[37] At the same time, most of the leading journalists, Fraser included, never tried very hard to establish contacts within the Conservative caucus, a step that might have broken down at least some of the ill-feeling. Partly this was because the caucus members were not newsmakers of any significance, but obviously a dislike of certain Conservative personalities and the unconstructive 'opposition' mentality they displayed did not help.[38]

Even if the Tories' worst fears of a Liberal press were exaggerated, the Liberals had every reason to be pleased with their relations with the fourth estate. Of course, they started with several distinct advantages. First, they were the government, which meant that reporters, in the normal course of their work, had to cover what the Liberals were doing. It only remained for the government to administer the country's affairs with a reasonable degree of competence and some flair, and the bulk of the news converage and commentary was bound to be favourable. But the Liberals were not content to leave matters there. Unlike their Conservative opponents, they went out of their way to ingratiate themselves with journalists across the country – especially those who, as H.E. Kidd of Cockfield and Brown, the Montreal public relations firm which masterminded Liberal party publicity, concisely phrased it, 'are prepared to help us.'[39] Among those, according to a contemporary Liberal source, were George Ferguson, Grant Dexter, and Bruce Hutchison. Convinced that the government could carry public opinion if it could only get the story of its impressive day-to-day achievements told, the wiser heads in the party organization emphasized the need for favourable or fair news coverage – the Liberals tended to view the terms as synonymous. Not coincidentally, this was precisely the approach Hutchison and Dexter had urged them to adopt.[40]

A key element in the Liberals' success in the press relations game was the contribution the prime minister and most of his cabinet ministers were able to make. To reporters weary of dealing with his temperamental, suspicious predecessor, St Laurent was a breath of fresh air. But behind the 'Uncle Louis' façade, itself a press creation, lay the real St Laurent: reserved, proper, intensely private, certainly more the *seigneur* than corporate lawyer in his dealings with journalists.[41] The new prime minister approached the press with supreme self-confidence, and with the considerable talents of the ubiquitous Pickersgill never far from his side. Press conferences were formal, carefully controlled affairs which resembled audiences more than anything else, and private interviews were little different. As long as the questions (and questioners) were serious and conformed to his notoriously narrow views of what was proper subject matter for a prime minister's attention, St Laurent exuded charm and affability. But for the unfortunates who broke his rules, the Gallic charm quickly evaporated. One of the forbidden topics was family vacations at St Patrice in the Gaspé, and when an American reporter ventured to write a straightforward account of one such visit, St Laurent was furious. Back in Ottawa, he interrupted his first press conference to dress down the offender with a curt reminder that 'people here know what to publish and what not to publish.'[42] Neither the *Chicago Tribune* nor its man in the gallery was popular in Ottawa – both were widely dismissed as reactionary red-baiters – but the fact no one rose to his defence is revealing nonetheless. Such rebukes were the exception, however; the behaviour of the Ottawa press corps rarely departed from the norms St Laurent expected. The Ottawa press corps, like much of the country, was simply overawed by the man. After all, these were the Liberal 'happy times,' years when, as an admiring Hutchison astutely observed, St Laurent stood astride Ottawa like 'God Almighty and the whole Trinity combined.'[43]

But St Laurent was not the only Liberal politician to enjoy success influencing the press. For Pearson, press relations were just another form of the diplomatic arts which were his strong suite. Finance Minister Douglas Abbott, who endeared himself to journalists of all stripes by introducing the 'budget lock up,' was not far behind Pearson in cultivating a favourable image for himself and his department. Minister of National Defence Brooke Claxton was well liked in the gallery and favoured key reporters with invitations to informal Sunday afternoon briefings at his Ottawa home. As for the indefatigable Jack Pickersgill, once he had made the jump into the cabinet in 1952 he had more good ideas than he knew what to do with in this area as in most others. Even the imperious C.D. Howe got on relatively well with the press corps during the Liberals' ascendant years, and his association with a few, especially Ken Wilson, was very close indeed.[44]

Press access to deputy and assistant deputy ministers and other senior civil servants was also considerable during the late 1940s and early 1950s.

Departmental public relations arrangements were rudimentary at best and pride of authorship and administrative pragmatism ensured that the bureaucrats, generally with their ministers' approval, were only too willing to explain the ramifications of government policy to inquiring reporters. These contacts were most formally developed, socially and professionally, by the men who were acknowledged to be at the top of the gallery heap by the late 1940s, Ken Wilson and Blair Fraser, and did much to deepen the common outlook which already existed between the two groups.[45] Given the paternity of much of the government's policy, the implications in terms of favourable press coverage for the Liberals were obvious.

During the early St Laurent years, the press gallery was a cozy club with about seventy accredited members. Full membership was restricted to those representing dailies, leaving the likes of Fraser and Wilson to be content with a vague associate status. Determined to protect their earnings as part-time commentators for radio (and later television) and to preserve their competitive news advantage, a majority favoured barring representatives of the electronic media outright from membership until 1958. During the early 1950s, a quarter of the gallery worked for the three wire services. Except for the Ottawa dailies, only five Canadian newspapers (including the *Montreal Star* and *Winnipeg Free Press*) kept more than one of their own reporters in Ottawa full time, and in the face of the phenomenal increase in the complexity of government administration, single-person bureaus severely restricted what even the hardest-working reporter could adequately cover.[46] While the quality of the reporters assigned to the gallery was generally well above average, there was a disproportionate number of older men in the gallery, many of whom were traditional in their approach. This served to reinforce the perception that a parliamentary reporter was in Ottawa to cover only politics. Regardless, a significant number lacked the training to keep up with the increasingly important non-political stories Ottawa-based journalists had to tackle. This, of course, was a constant lament of the new-style journalists like Fraser and Wilson, not to mention of the senior civil servants and cabinet ministers.[47] The end result was that much of the gallery reporting was mediocre, with little effort expended on analysis or interpretation. Abler press observers certainly recognized that the institution had deficiencies.[48] To a large degree, the top journalists in Ottawa operated at arm's length from the gallery, while the country's leading editors continued to carry on their own dialogue with the government.

From the Liberals' perspective, however, news 'poisoned at the source' by partisan reporting was a much more serious problem than real or imagined deficiencies in gallery members' competence or work habits. National Liberal Federation officials kept an up-to-date list of Ottawa newspapermen they considered either were outright Tory sympathizers or regularly slanted their copy to the government's detriment.[49] Liberal insiders all seemed to agree that the Canadian Press, the most important conduit of news to the daily press and, through a subsidiary, to radio as well, was a nest of Tories. Another frequent target was the *Financial Post*, compromised supposedly by the existence of a malign Maclean-Hunter-Drew axis which, of course, was almost exactly 180 degrees from the truth.[50] These Liberal stalwarts were just as suspicious of the CBC, although in this case over its preoccupation with fairness, having convinced themselves that the corporation's policy was 'to be so honest that it leans over backwards against the government.'[51]

Yet fret as some of the government's supporters might over its press image, any objective observer could see little danger of the Liberal juggernaut being derailed as the 1953 election neared. Although the St Laurent administration was showing obvious signs of becoming intoxicated with its own success, its aura, comprising equal parts managerial competence and sheer arrogance, continued to mask any governmental failings. Still, more prescient Liberals and Liberal sympathizers found these trends disturbing.[52] Even Jack Pickersgill, a partisan Liberal's Liberal, confided to his close friend Bruce Hutchison that the Conservatives' weakness and the negative effect it was having on the government made him very sad; 'how sad, you can imagine,' his listener added wryly. However, Hutchison was honestly concerned, partly because he recognized that a strong opposition would be good for the Liberals and Canada, too, and partly because the government's drift away from liberal doctrines and its growing preoccupation with spending and administration worried him. 'Do not tell me [the government] has no principles,' he sarcastically pointed out to Dexter after one long diatribe against the ills of big government. 'It has and will defend to the death the principle of staying in office.'[53] But Hutchison was not the only 'Liberal' journalist to show signs of disenchantment. 'The Grits grow very complacent and arrogant,' Ferguson grumbled to a confidant, 'and this may just prove their undoing.' Everyone looked to St Laurent and Howe, but, with few exceptions, Pearson being the most obvious, the younger men were an ordinary lot. As for 'radical or liberal thought,' as far as he could see it had utterly disappeared from the government's priorities.[54] Blair Fraser had been alluding for some time in his 'Backstage' column to the frustrations of Liberal backbenchers with their own government, but he was an exception. None of the others had aired their concerns in public.[55]

All that was realistically at stake in the election called for 10 August 1953 was the dimensions of the Liberal majority. Indeed, so confident was the party that it budgeted only half as much for advertising as it had in 1949.

'They will have to meet the usual spate of charges of extravagance and waste, over-taxation, complacency and what not, but that's about all, [and] will win again, [though] I hope with a smaller majority,' Ferguson groused privately.[56] Michael Barkway, Wilson's replacement at the *Financial Post* and another journalist who was already on the edge of the Liberal press establishment, confided to a senior diplomat that he, too, had 'a sad jumble of feelings about how he would like the election to turn out.'[57] Hutchison and Dexter, despite their reservations about the direction the government was heading, quickly rallied to the cause. Hutchison, who had formally tendered his services to the party in December 1952, was candid about his reasons for supporting the incumbents.[58] Like Victor Sifton and Grant Dexter, he was convinced that a Tory victory would simply push the Liberals further left. And then, as always, there was the problem of Drew. Hutchison could not stomach the thought of his becoming prime minister; 'My sense of humor,' as he put it, 'doesn't go that far.'[59] Fortunately for Hutchison's peace of mind, he was certain that Drew's presence at the Tory helm made the Grits invulnerable.[60]

Despite its pious mid-term exhortations on the pressing need for a stronger Conservative party, the closest the *Financial Post* came to offering direction during the campaign was an editorial highlighting business confidence entitled 'Honest Gloom Is Hard to Find,' hardly the sort of endorsement Drew and his party were hoping to receive from Bay Street.

Meanwhile, the *Montreal Star* played its 'usual game,' as Ferguson coyly put it, meaning 'we comment ... with some degree of impartiality [and] I fancy ... will come down for St. L[aurent] ab[ou]t the beginning of Aug[ust] ... As J[ack] Pickersgill remarked to me early this year, "we appreciate y[our] 70 p[er] c[ent] support."'[61] Sure enough, on 1 August the Liberals received their endorsement from the *Star*. Thereafter, Ferguson's editorials stressed the incumbents' achievements in foreign and economic policy and their fine administrative record. While the *Star* would have supported the Liberals regardless of his preferences, Ferguson's endorsement was sincere. If his enthusiasm for some of the government's social policy initiatives was waning, on vital foreign policy questions he felt the Liberals under St Laurent and Pearson were performing brilliantly. In the final analysis, neither of the opposition parties measured up.[62]

For his part, Fraser was convinced that Canadians recognized the growing irascibility of the Liberals for what it was: a clear sign of just how tired they had become, and he felt that this, combined with the obvious need for a stronger opposition, would cut their majority. More than ever, his political attachments were to personalities, not party, although it must be said that most of the political personalities he respected, starting with Pearson, happened to be Liberals. Fraser's own philosophy, which he often confided to friends, was to vote for the gang who could do the least damage, and obviously for him the Liberals still fit that description best. In his final 'Backstage' column, he frankly outlined the dilemma voters faced: 'Nobody knows better than the Liberals that the Liberals have been in office too long. Their cabinet ministers are aging and tiring and they've had enough of power to dull the keen edge of appetite for the top job when Prime Minister St. Laurent retires. Their backbenchers are bored, frustrated and devoid of hope. The queues are too long at every conceivable opening for advancement.' As for the Conservative party: '[It] no longer knows how to oppose. Too long away from the routines of administration, deprived of the formal "intelligence service" which opposition parties get from the civil servants they appointed, the Conservatives allow the Liberals to get away with murder and even the Liberals know it's a bad thing for the country.'[63] Editor Ralph Allen agreed that a Liberal defeat was remote and could only cast about for ways of strengthening the Conservatives in their seemingly permanent opposition role.[64]

Election day saw the Liberals returned with a substantial, though reduced, majority. Once again the combination of 'Uncle Louis' and the government's generally sound record – even many Conservatives acknowledged the latter point – had prevailed over the 'unrelenting belligerence' and 'apocalyptic views' of Drew and his party.[65] Of the many views offered to explain the Conservatives' defeat, Fraser was probably closest to the mark when he noted simply that no one could beat St Laurent. Hutchison predictably lamented the demise of the two-party system, while Ferguson joined the *Financial Post* in warning the victors against the dangers of overconfidence.[66] It was a faint hope. As a 'knowledgeable correspondent,' probably Ferguson, had told Claxton just weeks before the election, if the voters believed that their affairs were being well administered, they also believed the government '[was] out of touch with them without much regard for their feelings.'[67] Another landslide was hardly likely to humble the 'Government party.'

Nevertheless, on the surface, the next two years passed uneventfully enough for the government. A February 1955 Gallup poll showed that midterm Liberal support, at 51 per cent, was marginally ahead of their 1953 vote.[68] Yet the St Laurent government, grown increasingly cautious and disinclined to re-examine its old policies or adopt new ones, was dying from self-satisfaction. The first outward sign of trouble came in June 1955, when the government stumbled badly in a hamhanded effort to force through amendments to extend indefinitely the emergency powers of C.D. Howe's Defence Production Act. Before saner heads in the cabinet prevailed and worked out a compromise, the opposition had had a field day railing against the Liberals' 'arrogance of power' and 'contempt for Parliament.' That the episode had occurred at all 'startled many thoughtful people,' one veteran Liberal grumbled.[69] Yet the Liberal inner circle, with whom Hutchison remained in close touch, seemed to learn nothing at all from the incident.

The press, however, were considerably more astute. During the previous few months, Hutchison had seen and heard enough in Ottawa to realize that 'the Old Man [St Laurent] is really through and the sooner a new one is found ... the better.' Now, with the Defence Production brouhaha, the government had '[made] an egregious ass of itself.'[70] Hutchison was writing a regular national affairs column for the *Financial Post* and he pulled no punches in dismissing the legislation as 'quite indefensible' and in congratulating the Conservatives for forcing a 'humiliating, salutary and inevitable' retreat on the government front benches.[71] A Liberal partisan to be sure, he rightly felt that the government's friends were doing it no good in attacking honest critics like himself. Happily back in Ottawa after six frustrating, disappointing, and not very successful years as *Free Press* editor, Dexter's solution was to dump the entire responsibility for the débâcle at the feet of a 'stubborn and irrational' C.D. Howe, who, as Dexter knew from his still impeccable cabinet sources, fully deserved the blame.[72]

The new editor of the *Free Press* was Tom Kent, a brilliant young English newspaperman Sifton had recruited to rehabilitate his paper's sliding reputation. After having all but smothered Dexter, Sifton had given in to Kent's demand for what amounted to complete editorial independence. It would be, to say the least, a turbulent relationship. On this issue of Liberal 'bad manners,' Kent tried to play down the whole affair, mildly chiding the government and offering only the slimmest credit to the Tories. Yet despite the brave front, Kent was far too intelligent an observer not to be shocked and disappointed by the government's obvious loss of political touch. Ferguson's editorial path was even more tortuous. At first, he, too, had been mildly critical of the Liberals. But as the Conservatives' attacks mounted, the *Star* abruptly changed its tune. After a month of so-called Conservative obstruction, Ferguson openly urged the government to invoke closure.[73] Privately, however, he admitted they had 'made a fine botch' of the whole business and was especially alarmed at the cabinet's obvious disunity.[74] As for *Maclean's*, Fraser's personal feelings were made very public. C.D. Howe, he wrote pointedly, had finally learned the answer to his oft-quoted jibe: 'Who will stop us?' It was a stupid humiliation that could and should have been avoided. Fraser's patience with certain members of the Liberal establishment had been wearing thin, much to the irritation of the latter. Now he reported that a small minority of Liberals were pondering the previously unthinkable: that the septuagenarians St Laurent and Howe were liabilities and that it would be better for the party to lose the next election fighting on a platform of the future, not the past.[75]

For once, the support they had received from the press actually satisfied the Conservatives, for it had made all the difference in enabling them to present themselves as the champions of parliament and the people against the dictatorial, power-hungry Grits. Some of the faithful even saw a light, albeit still only a glimmer, at the end of the political tunnel.[76] Many journalists still had little confidence in the Tories' capacity to govern, but there had been a growing realization in the minds of gallery members in particular that the opposition needed help in cutting the government down to size, help which they, and perhaps they alone, were in a position to give. The fact that too many Liberals had grown contemptuous of the gallery was also beginning to have its effect.[77]

During the winter of 1955–6 Hutchison tried to put a favourable gloss on Liberal prospects, although like Fraser he seemed to be looking for reasons to say something vaguely complimentary about the new George Drew and the Conservative party's apparent revival. But a private assessment of the Liberals he shared with Grant Dexter told a quite different story: 'I form an increasing impression that the Great and Good Government is slipping badly ... I don't see many positive mistakes but I see a growing inability to decide anything. This may be quite unfair and untrue but it is certainly the impression that most people form ... In short, it seems to me that the country ... is just bored to death with the old faces.'[78] Blair Fraser's confidants heard a similar story. At a private dinner in Bonn he frankly suggested to a rather surprised Charles Ritchie that the Liberals would lose the next election. Not the least of the signs they were in serious trouble, he stressed, was the support they were losing among 'the small group of publicists, professors, civil servants, and men of influence [that they] have depended [upon] for much of their influence.'[79] It was a revealing comment, and quite probably an autobiographical one, too.

Events – in the seemingly innocuous form of a pipeline project – would soon confirm the premonitions of Liberal disaster which Fraser, Hutchison, and other newspapermen had been unable to shake. The trans-Canada pipeline was to be Howe's last great initiative at economic nation-building. Smarting from the previous year's Defence Production Act humiliation, Howe made the passage of an $80 million government loan to finance the construction of a portion of the pipeline by an American-dominated consortium a matter of personal credibility and a test of party loyalty. At least 'if the Liberal Party goes down,' he confided to Tom Crerar in March, shortly after the announcement of the government's plans, 'it will go down in a good cause.'[80] One suspects most Liberals preferred not to go down at all, but the idea of compromise simply did not enter Howe's thinking. In a triumph of administrative over political priorities (and with some simple bad luck thrown in), Howe had convinced the rest of the cabinet that they had to push the measure through parliament within three weeks. Faced with Conservative and CCF filibuster pledges, Liberal parliamentary strategists Walter Harris and Jack Pickersgill decided on a solution that was long on ingenuity but short on common sense: the government would impose closure at every stage of the bill's passage, if need be clause by clause. To clear-headed observers, it was as good an indication as any yet of just how completely the Liberals' once infallible political touch had deserted them.[81]

Howe introduced his bill on 14 May and promptly invoked closure, before there had been any debate at all. Initially, the press in general and certainly most members of the gallery supported the St Laurent government's pipeline plans. The *Financial Post,* long an admiring supporter of Howe's schemes and of the pipeline in particular, acidly dismissed the opposition efforts 'to mislead and befuddle the Canadian public in the hope of making political profit for the next election.'[82] Writing in the same issue, however, Hutchison was quick to point out that the Liberals, unused to real opposition inside or outside parliament, had 'totally and comically mismanaged everything' and, perhaps more ominously, had underestimated the gravity of what was happening to them. Ferguson reacted negatively to the government's use of closure, but on the grounds that it would only give credibility to Drew's 'baseless' charges of 'dictatorship.' For Dexter, the latest turn of events was 'an amazing departure for a Liberal government,' though he was quick to stress that the opposition's tactics were equally dubious. During the preceding weeks, *Free Press* editor Tom Kent had offered only lukewarm endorsement of the loan scheme and criticized the overzealous application of closure – 'foreclosure' he called it derisively – as a certain way to guarantee that the bill's merits would receive little public attention.[83]

At Ottawa, the debate rapidly degenerated into a rancorous exchange where, as Kent had predicted, the merits of the Liberals' natural gas policy were lost amid the opposition din on the rights of parliament. Never an outstanding parliamentarian, the seventy-four-year-old St Laurent was plagued by bouts of severe depression which left him apathetic for weeks on end and could provide no direction during the debate. Howe had never tried to mask his contempt for House scrums or the honourable members across the floor and was an outright liability, while the younger men like Pearson, Martin, and Harris were either too inexperienced and intimidated by Howe or, as in Pickersgill's case, too ingenious and partisan. Everyone seemed to agree that the government backbenches contained no useful debating material at all. The retirement of abler debaters (and wiser heads) like Abbott and Claxton was now being deeply felt.[84]

Simply watching the daily battles between the Tory and CCF Davids and the Grit Goliath was bound to have an effect on the gallery. As closure motion inexorably followed closure motion, the opposition's emotional condemnations of Liberal arrogance and dictatorship were gaining credibility. Such was the disarray in Liberal ranks that no one in the caucus even tried to explain the government's position to ordinary gallery members, whereas the two leading opposition strategists, Stanley Knowles of the CCF and Davie Fulton of the Conservatives, kept in constant touch with the press. Since gallery members supplied the bulk of the political commentary on CBC radio and television and on private radio as well, their growing disgust with Pickersgill's intrigues and Liberal steamroller tactics in general was extremely damaging to the government's cause.[85]

The unfolding disaster posed a delicate problem for the government's more prominent friends in the fourth estate. To Fraser and Dexter, the Liberals' uncivilized behaviour, not to mention stupidity, came as a rude shock.[86] One could obviously stand by loyally, though at a heavy price in reader credibility, or one could criticize the government 'firmly' but 'constructively' in the hope of saving it from itself. The choice for the *Free Press*, as Victor Sifton noted with some understatement, 'was difficult for us.'[87] As late as 22 May, eight days after the bill's introduction, Kent had been bravely pledging support 'for an imperfect Liberal Government over a Conservative party that gets almost every national issue as wrong as Mr. Drew has got the pipeline.' Two days later the *Free Press* had had enough. If and when the bill passed, the Liberals still 'will have suffered a moral defeat of major significance,' Kent indignantly told his readers. 'One can only hope that the lesson restores, to a Government suffering from the slackness and intolerance of long success, a closer adherence to the principles that its supporters stand for.'[88] The wrench had come for Dexter, too. Four days later, in an unsigned editorial, he spelled out 'why [the government's] friends across the country are so disturbed': its repeated use of closure had prevented a fair debate of the pipeline's merits. It was typical that Dexter, whose liberalism and Liberalism had always been hopelessly intertwined, was still unable to decide whether the government's intentions or the style of their execution was more disturbing.

While admitting that its repeated application 'can be questioned,' Ferguson defended closure in principle and took pains to remind *Star* readers that 'filibuster and blockage' were just as damaging to parliamentary democracy as anything the Liberals had done.[89] By the mid 1950s Ferguson enjoyed considerable editorial freedom to comment on national politics and he was not being held back by his publisher on this issue. It was certainly not out of partisan allegiance to the Grits, either; that had long since worn thin. Rather, Ferguson deeply respected Howe and was convinced that the pipeline plans were fundamentally sound. This, combined with an absolute loathing of the Conservative party, was probably enough to keep him on side.

Throughout the debate, the *Financial Post* never deviated from its position that the pipeline bill deserved speedy passage. Announcing closure before the debate opened might have been an ill-advised manoeuvre, McEachern agreed, but 'the trouble with the Opposition is not that it has been gagged but that it has been unconvincing and unconstructive.'[90] Meanwhile, Hutchison's columns in the *Post* remained noticeably silent.

One 1 June, the pipeline tragicomedy reached its nadir. This was the infamous Black Friday, when Speaker René Beaudoin, under what seemed suspicious circumstances suggesting government interference, reversed a procedural decision of the previous day and literally attempted to turn back the parliamentary clock. Faced with this unbelievable performance, House decorum utterly broke down. The humiliation of the government was now complete and nowhere was this more clear than in the gallery, where only one English-speaking member, Alex Hume of the *Ottawa Journal,* a particularly sycophantic Grit, could be found who still defended closure. Everyone else joined in the chorus of denunciations, albeit some more enthusiastically than others.[91] Kent forthrightly blamed the government and its bulldozer tactics for this latest débâcle, while Dexter admitted the sincerity of the opposition members' sense of outrage.[92] Ferguson reacted by lamely calling for 'orderly debate' and blaming both sides for the breakdown – valid enough in theory, but under the circumstances missing the point.

By the early hours of 6 June, the government had its pipeline, but it was a Pyrrhic victory. Publicly, Ferguson was unrepentant, and in one of the braver and certainly least accurate editorial predictions of his distinguished newspaper career he insisted that 'when its contribution to the Canadian economy is fully realized, a good many people will be wondering in amazement what all the shouting was about in May–June 1956.' Privately, however, he felt disillusioned and, one suspects, even betrayed by the whole performance. It was all the proof one could ask for, he fumed, surveying the previous month's disaster, that 'the government had gone nuts.'[93]

Having chastened the Grits, Sifton, Kent, and Dexter now appeared to panic that they had gone too far. If the government could only get a breathing space, many Liberals (and quite a few others) confidently expected the crisis would blow over.[94] From wishful thinking, if not firm conviction, Kent tried to downplay the longterm damage that the government had suffered, offering the opinion that while 'there are some points of justice in part of [the Liberal arrogance] argument ... it is difficult to see Mr. Drew making an effective election issue out of that alone [and] he has nothing else.'[95]

Because of its lengthy lead times, Maclean's had to comment after the fact, but this merely affected the timing, and not the tone, of its coverage. Allen, who was not over-fond of the Liberals, categorized their closure strategy as 'a piece of bad judgement so gross as to be immoral' and condemned 'the blind unawareness that there was any impropriety in thus getting [their] own way.'[96] Fraser's friends sensed that he felt personally betrayed by the government's crude use of power. Indeed, after one particularly depressing session of the debate, he had taken aside Southam bureau chief John Bird, a close friend but a man whose private sympathies for the Conservative party were certainly well known, and angrily informed him that it was now the duty of every Canadian to turf out the Liberals in the next election.[97] In 'Backstage,' he had calmed down only slightly, concluding that a Liberal defeat at the polls in 1957 'would not be due to their pipeline policy ... but because they failed to observe the proper limits of power.' From valid premises – an invincible majority – the Liberals had drawn a 'wrong' and 'dangerous' conclusion: that they could do as they wished with parliament. And how far did one have to look for proof? In what amounted to a personal confession, Fraser supplied his own answer: 'Normally, in this civilized town, the government tends to have more friends than enemies – most people, probably far more than in other parts of Canada, agree with its policies most of the time. But if the Liberals have a single defender on this issue, I haven't happened to meet him.'[98]

During the previous month, as one of the Conservatives' abler strategists would later observe, the government's 'image of competence and wise benevolence had evaporated.'[99] Certainly the impact of the pipeline debate on the press was enormous. Overnight, the Liberals squandered the ample reserve of respect and goodwill they had built up over a decade or more. By the end of the debate, most reporters considered it self-evident that the opposition's course had been right. Moreover, the government's heavy-handed response confirmed suspicions a number had already held that the St Laurent regime needed knocking down a peg or two. That the Liberals let it be known they felt unfairly treated by the press added to the strain by reinforcing the view of a lot of reporters that far too many members of the government felt the press had been 'under control.'[100] Unquestionably the crisis had been a watershed in the breakdown of the responsible, civilized relationship between press and government; things were never the same again.

During the twelve months between the pipeline debate and the general election, however, Liberal fortunes gave the appearance of reviving, thanks in large part to favourable reviews by national opinion-makers, including those in the press.[101] As late as April 1957 the party's popularity still topped 47 per cent, and three-quarters of the respondents polled claimed to be satisfied with the government's performance. Yet appearances were deceiving. Much of the support was soft, given more out of habit than conviction. The 'Uncle Louis' of 1949 and 1953 had become a distinct liability. John Diefenbaker's selection in December 1956 as the ailing George Drew's successor highlighted this change. Although sixty-two himself, Diefenbaker was the picture of vigour while St Laurent appeared even older, some would have said considerably older, than his seventy-five years. While most Liberals smugly dismissed Diefenbaker as a second-rater, Hutchison wondered aloud whether 'the Government has underestimated both him and its own troubles.'[102]

Such telltale signs of looming political trouble were a cause of real concern to Mike Pearson's legion of admirers in the press and elsewhere who recognized that St Laurent had to go – and the sooner the better for their man's chances. Fraser quite openly advanced this view in his 'Backstage' columns.[103] For such men, Pearson's accession to the leadership was the obvious means to ensure a speedy return to a happy state of Liberal competence and virtue. It was a conviction Pearson's recent diplomatic *tour de force* mediating the Suez crisis had considerably strengthened. But by the spring of 1957 the old Liberal confidence – or was it overconfidence – had returned, blinding all but a handful of party faithful to the political dangers that loomed ever closer.[104] The party braintrust was determined to fight one more election under the St Laurent–Howe banner, and Pearson's day would have to wait. There would be no promises and no new programs; just the Liberal record. Or as Brooke Claxton sarcastically put it, it was going to be 'you ain't ever had it so good – and we're the boys you have to thank for it.'[105]

At the outset of the 1957 campaign the accepted wisdom gave the Conservatives substantial gains, but no one considered an outright victory possible.[106] The previous autumn the *Financial Post* had begun debunking the 'time for a change' argument and during the early stages of the contest had confined its editorial comment to the predictable calls for a strengthened two-party system. But that meant the defeat of the CCF, not the humbling of the Grits. Hutchison, meanwhile, had been using his weekly *Post* column to praise the government's overdue rediscovery of fiscal responsibility and to attack Diefenbaker's wild-eyed economic populism.[107] To those who were not prepared to re-elect the Liberals, Hutchison's advice was simple: vote Conservative and eliminate the political curse of splinter parties.[108] One suspects, however, that he didn't intend for many of his readers to heed his call. George Ferguson greeted the election with a half-hearted dismissal of the Tory's principal campaign issue – Liberal arrogance and disrespect for parliament – and lapsed into silence until the last days of the campaign. In contrast, the *Free Press,* with Dexter in the forefront, was pro-government and, perhaps more to the point, ardently anti-Conservative right from the start.

After only a couple of weeks of campaigning, it was becoming clear that the public mood was more volatile than anyone had ever expected. Chagrined Liberals had to concede that the Diefenbaker-led Conservatives were showing dismaying signs of life. Memories of the pipeline had not faded, nor had the pension parsimony of 'six-buck Harris's' 1956 budget. Moreover, the Suez crisis, while it certainly embellished Pearson's reputation, had tarnished the government's image in parts of English Canada. To make matters worse, the Liberal party, from St Laurent and Howe down, seemed completely at a loss over what to do to reverse the slide. In fact, there was hardly any facet of the Liberal campaign, including their handling of the crucial new medium of television, which was not hopelessly inept.[109] A worried Hutchison could not fathom the 'posture of confidence, almost of indifference' which passed for Liberal strategy.[110] As he dutifully recorded Tory successes and Liberal failures, only the performance of his hero, Pearson, plus the hope that 'the poll will come soon enough to rescue us,' provided any cheerful news.[111]

As Dexter surveyed the floundering Liberal campaign with half a month to go, he was no longer willing to dismiss the increasingly confident assessments of Conservative friends as the usual unfounded Tory optimism. 'We may be going over the dam,' he admitted to his old confidant, Tom Crerar, and in his columns practically began to plead with 'Liberals with a bad conscience about the pipeline affair' not to desert the party.[112]

As the last days of the contest wound down, the *Montreal Star,* as Ferguson carefully explained it to a friend, 'weaved a careful course suggesting that people might vote the man and not the party' and 'that the world would not come to an end if the Grits were licked or weakened.'[113] However, one suspects that weakening was clearly the preferred alternative. Meanwhile, in its final pre-election editorial, the *Financial Post* all but endorsed the Liberals, noting sarcastically that 'the fact that an election is being held disposed of the argument that dictatorship has been established in Canada and that Parliament has become a cipher.'[114] To no one's surprise, the *Free Press* endorsed the incumbents as far and away the superior alternative.

Despite the fact 'that some Ministers have been there too long,' Kent's thinly disguised jibe at Howe and St Laurent, 'a Liberal vote is a vote ... for a Government that includes ... [one] young man [who in proven] ability far outshines anyone else in any party – Mr. Pearson.'[115] Only among the Liberals' tired ranks would the sixty-year-old Pearson have been considered a 'young man.'

Constrained as usual by its publishing schedule, *Maclean's* covered the campaign only in its final pre-election issue. Like Hutchison, Fraser had quickly grasped how the momentum was shifting to the Conservatives. He had no use for Tories in the collective and very serious reservations about Diefenbaker, yet the thought of another overwhelming Liberal mandate was pretty discouraging, too. Moreover, he really did believe the Liberals deserved to lose. Much of Fraser's credibility lay in his knack of sensing and then expressing the unarticulated views of his readers. In this case, they were likely his own views as well. Many Canadians, he argued, did not want the Liberals out so much as humbled, and 'the more the Liberals talk about the inevitability of a Liberal government, the more they reassure these fifty-one-percent Liberal voters ... [that] it's quite safe to vote Tory and take the self-satisfied smirk off [the Liberals'] faces.'[116] During the final days of the campaign Fraser had become convinced that the Tories might actually squeak in, although virtually nobody else, the pollsters included, considered it possible.[117] Pressed by Ralph Allen to predict the outcome ten days before the vote, Fraser guessed another Liberal victory, though probably a very narrow one. The resultant 'post-election' editorial was intended to be a swipe at the Liberals and the voters alike.

By the early hours of 11 June, it was clear that Diefenbaker had engineered a stunning political upset. Analysing the election coverage on CBC television, Fraser, like virtually everyone else in Canada, had been unable to disguise his astonishment. Canadians who had wanted a stronger opposition, he later quipped sardonically in *Maclean's,* had gotten their wish, though not precisely in the way they had anticipated.[118] Although anti-Liberal feelings had obviously run strong in the electorate, the Conservatives had also run a masterful campaign. By focusing on Diefenbaker's leadership and 'vision' and downplaying the unpopular anti-state postures which had sunk earlier Tory efforts, party strategists had made it easy for disenchanted voters to buy the argument that it really was 'Time for a Diefenbaker Government' and that, in effect, they could have Liberal-style government without the irritation of Liberals running it. Favourable press coverage, long the ally of the Liberals, had certainly helped, as the party's media friends were quick to point out.[119]

Although both the *Free Press* and the *Financial Post* could not resist tak-

ing a swipe at the winners, the post mortems of the Liberal press establishment were surprisingly unemotional. Ferguson paid his respects to the
outgoing administration and lamented the loss of Pearson in particular, but
privately he admitted he 'had had enough of the old gang.'[120] Talk that the
government had been defeated accidentally, so comforting to disbelieving
Liberal loyalists, struck him as absurd, a dangerous remnant of their power
complex.[121]

Hutchison sensed the same delusion among many of his Liberal friends,
but being more of a partisan he was much more concerned about its long-
term implications for the party. His preoccupation now was Liberal regen-
eration and what route it would take. Despite having spilled a sea of ink
over the last ten years criticizing Liberals' (and now Conservatives') slide
into fiscal immorality, he accepted politically that the Liberals would now
have to shift even further to the left. To believe anything else, he sighed,
was 'mere nostalgia.'[122] Still, if Hutchison was powerless to steer the Liberal party away from further economic apostasies, he could at least use his
influence to ensure Mike Pearson's selection as party leader.

Indeed, apart from whether the new government would fall on its face,
something Dexter, for one, believed likely after consulting with a few mandarin friends, the Liberal leadership succession was now *the* political question.[123] For the likes of Fraser, Ferguson, Dexter, and Hutchison, whose
perennial boosting of Pearson had become almost a full-time sideline to
their regular work, seeing he got the top job became an obsession. As
Hutchison had enthused in the aftermath of Suez, 'the tide in the affairs of
men seems to be sweeping him inevitably into the Prime Minister's office.'
Tide or not, 'without Pearson,' as Fraser bluntly put it, 'the Liberals would
be in sad shape indeed for a 1958 election.' Ferguson, who was presumably
attempting to be a little more subtle, pointed out rather transparently that
the new Liberal leader '[would] have to be a man of great character and pervasive charm.'[124] As for the *Free Press* braintrust, Kent, Victor Sifton, and
his similarly conservative chief lieutenant, Dick Malone, were bound
together by little more than a desire to see Pearson become prime minister.[125]
While Dexter had been eased out of the inner circle, he still retained access
to the editorial page and he intended to do everything he could 'to help
Mike shine.'[126] At the same time, Dexter felt it was imperative that he and
other 'true liberals' like former mandarin John Deutsch convince their man
to reject the dangerous leftish nonsense of the Walter Gordon crowd that
increasingly seemed to have his ear. Dexter's concerns certainly were not
shared by Kent; after all, he would soon be spouting 'leftish nonsense' to
Pearson himself. Undoubtedly he *was* feeling guilty over his part in the
'critical job that had to be done on the late government.' Now was the time

to aid the party regardless of its faults, and most obviously by securing the leadership for Pearson.

It was not enough merely to promote Pearson, however. The candidacy of Paul Martin, Pearson's only serious rival, had to be derailed, and anti-Martin sentiments certainly formed a strong undercurrent in their individual coverage of the leadership campaign. While all of them considered Martin an egoist and a self-promoter – in other words, too 'uncivilized' – the overriding reason for opposing him was that he dared to challenge their favourite's steady advance to the top.[127]

The Liberals gathered in January 1958 and duly embraced Pearson as their new leader. Having turned down the chance to deliver the convention's keynote address on, among other grounds, his pious conviction 'that we newspapermen should not thus publicly engage in partisan politics and thereby lose whatever reputations we may have for impartiality and hence any influence,' Hutchison nonetheless had openly canvassed delegates on Pearson's behalf, as had Dexter.[128] In the warm afterglow of Pearson's victory, any doubts about the party's policy direction or contrition for past sins were promptly set aside by the *Free Press*. The important thing, as Dexter said, waxing optimistic, was that the Liberal party 'once more is on the march.'[129] Privately, Ferguson was extremely pleased at getting 'our man in,' but in print he took pains to warn party faithful they had to offer the electorate more than just a new list of names. Judging by the general tone of convention rhetoric, he noted pointedly, the 'Government party,' like the Bourbons, seemed to have learned nothing from their recent reverses. For Hutchison, the new direction spelled out in the Liberal platform was a major disappointment; while he drew solace from Pearson's election, there was little else to cheer about.[130]

Once again, political events would move too rapidly for Fraser to comment in *Maclean's*. On 20 January, fresh from his convention victory, Pearson had introduced a sort of want-of-confidence motion contrived by Pickersgill which basically called for the Conservatives to hand power back to the Liberals without the bother of an election. Observing this latest manifestation of Liberal arrogance from his seat in the gallery, Dexter must have recalled a prediction he had made five years earlier that Pickersgill's love of political intrigue would eventually 'land [him] on his face in the street.'[131] Politically, it was an absolutely monumental blunder. The Conservatives had prayed for such an opening and were quick to capitalize on it. Dexter and Kent strove mightily to put Pearson's *faux pas* in a favourable light, while McEachern, who had been ventilating his dissatisfaction with the new government's spendthrift ways and calling for an early election, dryly observed that 'the prudence of [Pearson's] first move … [was] debatable.'

On this occasion, Ferguson preferred editorial bluntness over subtlety. 'Like all slick tricks,' the *Star* reflected cooly, 'this one backfired.'[132]

Within a matter of days, Diefenbaker had called an election and launched his assault. There was little to speculate about other than how far down Diefenbaker would bury the Liberals and their new leader, so predicting the final standings became popular sport for journalists. Fraser guessed 170 seats publicly, and privately a sweep. Hutchison felt that 'a substantial Tory majority' was likely, and not such a bad thing, he concluded, since 'we want Dief in with no alibis to stew in his own promises and ruin himself.'[133] Dexter must have felt there was already enough to be pessimistic about, and as the débâcle neared he cheered himself with an estimate that the Tories would only garner a 'modest majority' of 140 seats.[134]

If anything, the Liberal effort on the hustings this time was even more muddled than in 1957 – no mean achievement. The press, now broadly sympathetic to Diefenbaker and the Tories, hardly needed to embellish what was actually happening, while the Liberals, convinced that the fourth estate had been persecuting them since 1955, behaved as if their erstwhile friends were temporarily deranged.[135] At first the *Free Press* appeared oblivious to what was happening, but when reality finally dawned the paper soldiered on loyally. The *Financial Post* offered little comment save the usual enjoiners about the need for a majority government. On this occasion, however, McEachern pointed out that a majority government could be achieved 'if there is a marked swing one way or the other.' Since a swing of any kind to the Liberals, marked or otherwise, did not seem likely, this might be construed as a cautious endorsement of the Diefenbaker team. The closest Fraser came to an overt display of partisanship in any of his columns during the campaign was a backhanded slap at the new prime minister's decision to make public, for partisan ends, a confidential report on the country's economic prospects prepared for the late St Laurent government by senior civil servants. Diefenbaker employed the document with devastating effect, accusing the Liberals of having suppressed the study because it had predicted an economic slowdown and higher unemployment by the end of the decade and had thus contradicted rosy Liberal campaign claims of an endless Grit-engineered prosperity. Revealingly, however, Fraser focused his criticism on the harm being done to both the public's perception of civil service impartiality and the tradition of confidentiality in civil service–cabinet dealings, and not on the sullying of the political image of the Liberal party.[136] Early on, the *Montreal Star* called for a 'strong government' and a 'decisive mandate'; then, ten days before the poll, Ferguson announced without mustering any great enthusiasm that 'the circumstances of today dictate the over-riding need to give the Conservatives a real chance.'[137]

The 1957 and 1958 elections, fought within 294 days of each other, were really two parts of the same contest, with the latter simply completing the destruction of the King–St Laurent dynasty the former had begun. As returns rolled in, it was clear that Canadian voters had engineered a rout of unprecedented proportions. Seeking suitable punishment for the Liberals' arrogance of power, Canadians seemed to have relegated the party to a generation in the political wilderness. Conservatives were everywhere triumphant, or so it seemed. Unquestionably a new era in Canadian political life had dawned.

In the autumn of 1957, only a few months after the defeat of the St Laurent government, Escott Reid stopped to have a drink with Blair Fraser, whom he had bumped into at the United Nations headquarters in New York. A veteran External hand, Reid was one of the diplomats attached to the Canadian delegation while Fraser was there to report for *Maclean's* and CBC radio. They were friends of long standing and their meeting was completely innocent. But Conservatives MPs in the Canadian delegation caught wind of their get-together and were not amused. The rules of behaviour, as they informed the nonplussed Reid, had changed: Fraser was a Grit journalist and it was no longer acceptable for Canadian civil servants to be seen socializing with him.[138] It was a petty over-reaction, but it also revealed how deeply the conviction ran among Conservatives that a Liberal press establishment had shamelessly conspired with senior civil servants and Liberal ministers to further the interests of the Liberal party during the past twenty-two years. Now things would change. Such incidents, however, were an ominous beginning to the new government's relations with the press.

During the postwar decade, the perception that there was a group of journalists, encompassing some of the ablest editors and correspondents, who were openly sympathetic to the Liberal government and in turn openly favoured by them was widely accepted. In a very real sense, the perception itself made the existence of a Liberal press establishment a fact. But it was more than just a perception: such a group did exist and they did enjoy a special relationship with government insiders. In some instances, out-and-out partisanship was hard to deny; but in other cases, where very different factors were at work, such an explanation is simplistic.

During and after the war, the English-speaking press elite adopted a style of journalism which stressed information and informed analysis over opinion. A professional got his facts correct, and that meant winning the confidence of those with access to such information. During the 1940s and 1950s this access increasingly meant the senior levels of the civil service rather than the government or opposition benches. Furthermore, the resultant evolution of close relations among the press, bureaucracy, and more 'modern' Liberal ministers reinforced at the personal level ties of sympathy which already existed at the policy level. By and large, among the so-called establishment journalists, there was enormous respect for the mandarins and their work, and for the Liberals for being intelligent enough to let them do it. In these circumstances, it would have been hard to cover the government without also becoming too close to it, or at least appearing to be so, and without seeming to be an outright supporter.[139] By the early 1950s the Liberals had been in power and the Conservatives out for almost two decades, and that fact alone made it difficult for journalists, no matter how independently minded, not to come to think of the incumbents as the 'Government party.' Moreover, just as the press were able to assist in the creation of the public consensus nurtured and tapped by the Liberals, they were not immune from becoming swept up in it themselves.

Partisanship certainly played its role in the Liberal press establishment's perception of public affairs. Frequently, however, this stand took the form of a negative response to Toryism and CCF-style socialism as much as any favourable disposition towards the Liberal party, with its inevitable elements of partisanship and coarseness, at least as distinguished from the Liberal government, with its aura of competence, nonpartisanship, and public service. This distinction, when defined in these terms, *was* important to these journalists; most of the time they tried to make it in their public writings, although with varying degrees of success. Of course, the nature of the responsible, civilized relationship itself placed great pressure on the insider journalists; even those like Fraser, Ferguson, and Wilson who attempted very hard to walk the slippery path between being a responsible, informed, independent commentator and simply an informed spokesman were bound to find it difficult. By the 1950s, none of them, least of all Dexter and Hutchison, were succeeding consistently. That said, however, the fact remains that policy supported in conscience does not make one a partisan. In this regard, columnist Douglas Fisher's apt description of Fraser – that he 'had an open mind that went with his establishment frame of reference' – has more general application.[140]

As for the influence exercised by the Liberal press establishment over the political attitudes of English-speaking Canadians, this remains very difficult to assess. Their true impact, whether as partisans or as independents sympathetic to the Liberal agenda, undoubtedly lay considerably below the estimates of Conservative party stalwarts. Thanks to the inroads being made by radio and television, newspapers and magazines were no longer pre-eminent in informing Canadians or in shaping their opinions. As the pipeline debate and the federal elections of 1957 and 1958 would show dramatically, television in particular would soon emerge as the dominant medium for political news. The Liberals recognized that the influence of the print media was in decline, yet they continued to cultivate editors and reporters and were most concerned that they not be left without strong, credible support there.[141] While the Conservatives persistently exaggerated the importance of these journalists, clearly the latter did influence the public's perception of the government. That perception was rarely unfavourable, but it was also not decisive in determining the political winners and losers of the postwar decade.

In the cases of Ferguson, Wilson, and Fraser as well as Kent, Irwin, McEachern, and to some extent Allen, one sees 'Liberal' journalists who favoured the government chiefly because they favoured its policies and personalities and because the available alternatives were far less desirable for the country and certainly less congenial personally. Political partisanship in the traditional sense was definitely a secondary motive. For Hutchison and Dexter, however, policy, especially on the domestic front, was secondary, whereas personalities and traditional partisan loyalties linked to a profound distrust of Canadian Conservatism and a fear of socialism played a more central role in sustaining their support of the Liberal government and its program. In the end, however, the results were hardly distinguishable.

Conclusion

A Responsible, Civilized Relationship

Throughout the postwar decade, the perception that the press was pro-government or pro-Liberal was widespread. Indeed, the two were normally seen as synonymous even though one could obviously favour specific government policies without believing Canada's Liberals had a monopoly on leadership or ideas. There was even wider agreement on the existence of an establishment press composed of most of the leading journalists, men who unquestionably favoured and were favourites of the Liberal government. Given that the Liberals, in their guise as 'Government party,' were alleged to have successfully co-opted the senior civil service and seduced the leading figures of business and finance as well, it would hardly have been surprising if another elite group had also succumbed. However, the reality of the situation in all cases was more complex.

For the most part, the press was incapable of covering thoroughly the increasing complexities of wartime and postwar government. Bruce Hutchison's lament to Grant Dexter that 'a lousy press is this nation's worst weakness'[1] was unfair, but by mid century the calibre, expectations, and especially the resources of the average journalist covering national affairs increasingly fell short of what was required and achieved in the government itself. Like any government, the Liberals were concerned about their image and sensitive to criticism. And there was no question that, regardless of the collective level of competence displayed in their day-to-day reporting and analysis, the Ottawa press corps could still inflict serious damage on the government's image. Coverage of the 1956 pipeline fiasco had clearly shown that. One must also remember that daily newspapers boasted a combined circulation outnumbering households during these years[2] and in matters of public affairs were a leading source of news commentary and analysis. True, by the end of the Liberal era, television had made enormous inroads as a news source, with obvious political implications, but it had not yet supplanted the printed word. Even earlier, radio had cut into the print media's dominance, but again not decisively.[3] Under the circumstances, then, the Liberals clearly had to be aware of the press. In practice, that meant accepting it for what it was, and making the best of the situation. When it appeared for a time in 1955 that the *Toronto Star,* reliably Liberal and with the country's largest circulation and an immensely popular weekend edition, might fall into 'the wrong hands,' party insiders were terrified and understandably so. After all, some publications, basically those with the largest or most influential audiences, were 'more efficient [for image-making] than others ... and from experience,' as one Liberal organizer matter-of-factly boasted, 'we have a pretty good idea of who they are.'[4]

Until the last two years of the St Laurent administration, the simple truth is that the Liberals rarely had anything to worry about in their relations with the fourth estate. First, the wartime and postwar Liberal administrations, with the assistance of a very competent group of senior civil servants, governed well. In the circumstances, bad news was infrequent and even major challenges, such as the war effort itself and postwar reconstruction, served to strengthen the Liberal government's reputation for competence, integrity, and firm leadership. While diehard Conservatives might see a conspiracy, particularly in the press's consistent support of foreign policy,[5] the broad policies followed by the Liberals here, as in other areas, were for the most part either logical or inevitable or both and were seen as such by a great majority of the press and public alike.

Second, even if ordinary press representatives covering national politics did not face the dilemma of a Bruce Hutchison, who, after one of his whirlwind visits to Ottawa, boasted to his editor that 'the only trick here is to escape the people who want to see and entertain you,'[6] the Ottawa environment was not conducive for lone journalists bent on maintaining an absolute independence of observation and action. The relative openness and accessibility of ministers and senior bureaucrats, the mingling of social and professional contacts, and the reporters' growing dependence on government sources who seemed permanently entrenched in power worked subtly to undermine the independence of all of them, from the able to the mediocre.[7] Indeed, the primary purpose of parliamentary reporters – to report on what the government was up to – at a time when the government was competent and self-confident inevitably drew the press into the government orbit, even if not firmly into the government camp. This tendency was reinforced by the preferred approach to public affairs journalism, at least among those of the mandarins' generation, which emphasized informed explanation rather than uninformed opinion, respected authority, and dismissed the traditional adversarialism (or 'opposition playing') that characterized so much of American political journalism as un-Canadian and unprofessional.[8] Explaining what the Liberals were doing usually made them look good while at the same time further entrenched the image of the Conservatives as perpetually weak, disorganized, and out of touch with the Canadian mainstream. If the Conservatives and their sympathizers should complain that darker forces were at work,[9] the fact remained that favourable reporting generally reflected the recognition of competence far more than partisanship. Realistically, after all, in the broad areas of economic, social, and foreign policy, the Conservatives offered either variations on Liberal policies or less appealing (and less credible) alternatives. In this regard, it is worth noting that when the Liberals began their rapid descent into the political abyss in 1956, the members of the press gallery, supposedly domesticated on a steady diet of government 'pap,' proved remarkably spirited in their criticism. While hardly categorical evidence, it seems to support the conclusion that although most political journalists may have harboured Liberal sympathies, far fewer held Liberal loyalties.

But what of the leading journalists, the so-called Liberal press establishment? Cabinet ministers, especially those most in tune with the ideas of the senior bureaucrats, had every reason to cultivate these men or, more accurately, to allow themselves to be cultivated by them. To implement policy successfully and earn the kudos for it required that the public be made aware of what they were trying to accomplish. This, in turn, necessitated winning the support of those articulate, influential elements in the media with access to the audiences the policy-makers wished to reach.[10] Similarly, the senior bureaucrats had a direct interest in responding to journalists who could competently explain the intricacies of the new style of government they were keen to implement.[11] Both politician and bureaucrat gave these select reporters and editors preferential treatment, with the understanding that in return they would receive fair, complete, and timely coverage. This relationship unquestionably gave journalists like Wilson, Dexter, Hutchison, Ferguson, and Fraser, and through them others like Allen, Irwin, and McEachern, access to the most privileged and useful background information; in the process, the journalists gained prestige as 'authoritative voices.'[12] As Hutchison liked to remind colleagues, the first duty of a reporter of public affairs was to be read, and clearly being close to the government made that much more likely.[13] Of course, some powerful Liberals had trouble seeing where the line should be drawn, and so did some prominent journalists.

Ultimately, however, the close relationship with political powerbrokers

mattered less to these journalists than the professional and personal closeness they maintained with senior officials in the civil service. This was a situation which obviously had the blessing of most senior Liberals and merely
served to confirm the existence of a 'Liberal Trinity' in Conservative
minds.[14] Certainly the mandarin–press tie had a far-reaching impact on how
these journalists, and consequently Canadians as a whole, saw their country and its national government. One does not have to subscribe to the view
that the wartime and postwar Liberal administrations were thinly disguised
government-by-bureaucrats to recognize that the able civil service was just
as much an asset in building the image of Liberal competence in the minds
of the press insiders as among other groups.[15] The deep respect of these
journalists for the civil service and its influence, particularly on foreign and
economic policy, was apparent in their reporting and commentary. Without
question, they fell into the category of those Canadians who, as historian
J.L. Granatstein has observed, 'saw [the mandarins] as public servants in
the best sense of that term, men who changed the way government operated
and whose overall influence and impact were positive in the extreme.'[16]
They were proud to call the mandarins friends, and it was hard not to think
of them almost as colleagues.

For Blair Fraser, George Ferguson, and Ken Wilson, in particular, all
three of whom (Wilson the most, Ferguson the least) were enamoured of the
growing expertise and scope of government, the Liberals' chief redeeming
virtue was their common-sense respect for the mandarinate's talent and
sophistication. Not surprisingly, the Liberals they most admired were Pearson, Abbott, Claxton, St Laurent, and, before his political collapse, Howe
– the ones best equipped to master this dynamic new political environment
with its growing emphasis on policy-making and administration. Corres-
ponding to the admiration was an ingrained fear that the Conservatives were
uninterested in mastering the complexities of government and, more dis-
turbingly, perhaps not even capable of doing so. Drew's frequent attacks on
the civil service and the generally reactionary tone of his and his party's
pronouncements confirmed the visceral sense Ferguson, Wilson, and Fraser
had that Goethe could just as easily have been thinking of the Tories when
he wrote 'there was nothing more frightening than ignorance in action.'[17]
Until the Liberals discredited themselves and the Conservatives became
more 'responsible' and 'civilized,' such men were not going to shift far
from their broad endorsement of the 'Government party.'

Both Grant Dexter, whom John Diefenbaker once curtly dismissed as
'one of the icons of Canada's Liberal press establishment,' and Bruce
Hutchison were unquestionably partisan Liberals.[18] Both immersed themselves in the Liberal cause with an enthusiasm that should have satisfied

even a Pickersgill.[19] As George Ferguson observed with only modest exaggeration, it was an astonishing quality of Dexter's objectivity that in the end it 'always [seemed] to show that the Liberals were right.'[20] Certainly Dexter acknowledged his party sympathies; indeed, he was frequently recruited as the 'Liberal-leaning' analyst for public affairs panels on CBC radio and television programs. Hutchison tried harder to appear nonpartisan, and with some success: he was considered sufficiently independent to be offered the editorship of the once hard-Tory *Toronto Telegram* when new owner John Bassett, Jr, was attempting to recast the paper's image in the early 1950s. He was also approached about becoming a Liberal candidate in the 1953 federal election, an offer he declined only after having considered it for some time.[21] Both men preferred to consider themselves 'independents,' albeit with strong and admitted Liberal sympathies. Under these circumstances, the journalist's problem, as Hutchison clearly recognized, was how to avoid becoming publicly identified as a 'public stooge and minstrel endman for the Liberal Party.'[22] Dexter, and Hutchison even more so, subscribed to a small-L liberal philosophy that was increasingly anachronistic in the postwar Liberal party, and they knew it.[23] Thus, while both men admired the intellect and integrity of the mandarins and their kindred spirits in the cabinet, especially Pearson, the Liberals' (and the mandarinate's) steady march towards 'more welfare, more Danegeld, more Keynes and more of everything I don't like,' as Hutchison put it despairingly, deeply troubled them.[24] Hutchison professed respect for some individual Conservatives – Jim Macdonnell, for example – but he had none for Tories in the collective, and he certainly saw no political alternative to the Liberals. As a consequence, his growing dissatisfaction received a considerably more spirited airing in private than in public, though there were enough oblique references to Liberal arrogance to earn him a measure of respect from moderate Conservatives, something that eluded Dexter. On occasion, Dexter could be a thunderous critic of the Liberals, but his normal editorial behaviour made it difficult for acquaintances, not to mention *Free Press* readers, to discern whether 'we' meant 'the government, the government and Dexter, or just Dexter,' as Ferguson rather cuttingly put it.[25] In the end, the fact that they were so attached to the Liberal party, and not just the government, compromised both Dexter and Hutchison.

George Ferguson's journalistic views underwent a considerable evolution after he left the *Winnipeg Free Press* in 1946, not in the least his opinion on the proper role of the press *vis-à-vis* the government. With a few exceptions, Pearson being the most notable, he would approvingly reaffirm the cynical maxim that the only way a journalist should look at a politician was down. Among his peers, he came closest to recognizing the natural tension that should exist between press and government, yet he rejected the idea that the press should consistently be some sort of opposition. What he really aspired to was independence. Certainly as editor of the *Montreal Star* during the 1950s the sort of party messenger work, Liberal name-dropping, and active pleading for the 'Government party' that Dexter and Hutchison, his one-time colleagues at the *Free Press,* frequently indulged in and that he, too, had once practised, left him cold.[26] Nevertheless, as Ferguson scanned the political horizon for alternatives to the increasingly tired and arrogant Grits, he found it empty. So while he could and did withhold the sort of automatic support the government had come to expect from its journalist friends, on most issues he still seemed to endorse the Liberals in the end as the country's best hope and his most ideologically compatible home.[27]

Unlike Ferguson, who had the advantage of being able to avoid Ottawa and hence at least some of the guilt of direct association with the Liberals,[28] Blair Fraser and Ken Wilson, being based in the capital, enjoyed no such luxury. Wilson pioneered economic reporting in Canada and, in essence, the coverage of modern government itself. Despite his intimate ties with the mandarinate as well as Howe, Abbott, and Pearson, he escaped most of the accusations of partisanship so frequently levelled at his Maclean-Hunter colleague. In part, this had to do with the focus of his coverage, for the usual contemporary perception was still that economics was distinct from politics. Furthermore, since he did not need them to the same degree, Wilson maintained relatively few close contacts on the political side. Indeed, if anything, he was perceived as being too much under the influence of the bureaucrats.[29] Of course, had Wilson not died prematurely in January 1952, before the perception of a Liberal press elite became so firmly entrenched, he, too, would have come in for much more criticism on those grounds.

Because of his public profile with both *Maclean's* and the CBC, Fraser was the most attractive target of all for critics of Liberal establishment journalism. Covering politics meant he had to cover politicians. But he never tried to get as close to them as Hutchison or Dexter did, nor nearly as close as he was prepared to get to civil servants. Like the other leading members of the Liberal press establishment, he practised a style of journalism that emphasized solid interpretation and analysis and left him open (and sensitive) to the accusation of Liberal partisanship or at least a Liberal bias.[30] And, like them, he developed personal sympathies that made it more likely he would criticize only obliquely or in private those he admired and often considered his friends. Even then, as he readily acknowledged, such chiding was done more in sorrow than anger. Yet Fraser's so-called loyalty to the Liberals was ultimately based on policy considerations, a shared nationalism and internationalism, and his belief that they were civilized and competent and that the Tories were not.[31] Fraser's coverage of national affairs highlighted this broad agreement, and certainly the Liberals and the senior civil servants were confident that he identified with their goals. Among those more critical of the government, however, the perception of Fraser's motives was predictably different.[32]

By the time of the 1955–7 'Gritterdammerung,' Fraser, Hutchison, Ferguson, and Dexter, along with several associate members, were firmly identified as members of a Liberal press establishment. All believed in the Liberal government and, to varying degrees, in the Liberal party. By reason of long service, competence, and sympathy, all enjoyed the social and professional perks of their special position. Finally, all were comfortable in the Ottawa milieu – that is, among the mandarins and the 'better class of Liberal' – and, after all, as some political outsiders queried, was not Ottawa a place where only Liberals could feel at home?[33] The longer the Liberals remained in power and governed well, the more firmly the relationship had been cemented and the more deeply these men had become coloured with the perspectives of the Liberal-bureaucratic establishment. This was the sort of 'Rockcliffe mentality' which dominated the St Laurent era in particular and which all of them, but Fraser especially, came to epitomize. For Fraser, Ferguson, and Wilson, political partisanship had ultimately counted for very little in their coverage of national affairs, in keeping, appropriately enough, with the 'Government party's' own 'renunciation' of politics.[34] To Hutchison, despite mountainous rationalizations, it counted for a great deal more, and so, too, for Dexter.

The so-called responsible, civilized relationship increasingly characterized press-government relations during the Liberal years. The style of the elite journalists manifested it most clearly, and ultimately it became all but synonymous with the existence of a Liberal press, even though the most respected Conservative journalists, including Grattan O'Leary, John Bird, and Norman Smith, were also adherents to all but the relationship's overtly Liberal aspects. Civilized, responsible men dealt with one another in a civilized, responsible fashion. In the hands of able, conscientious journalists, and as long as the government was also able and conscientious, the public was kept remarkably well informed on matters of public policy. Adversarialism was irresponsble and unprofessional, and seemed increasingly irrelevant in an age of consensus and competence. Nonetheless, such a style of journalism was vulnerable to manipulation, not so much by conscious or even unconscious design as by its sheer comfortable familiarity.[35] It could, and by the early 1950s undoubtedly did, become too civilized and no longer responsible enough, and in succeeding years it became discredited in the eyes of the public and a new generation of journalists alike.[36]

Writing to Fraser a year after the 1958 Diefenbaker sweep, H.E. Kidd, a prominent Liberal insider, reminded him that 'Canada needs the direction of men of character, competence and intellectual integrity. Perhaps that is a lot to ask for in a democracy such as ours,' Kidd demurred, 'but that is what the people have had during the Mackenzie King and St. Laurent regimes.'[37] Kidd was hardly an unbiased observer, but there was much truth to his statement. A brilliant senior civil service, a discredited and disorganized opposition, a pervasive national consensus at least within the dominant English-speaking elite, and a particular collection of personalities gave rise to the responsible, civilized relationship. And therein lay the foundations of the Liberal press establishment of the war years and the postwar decade.

Notes

ABBREVIATIONS USED IN THE NOTES

AO	Archives of Ontario
BUA	Bishop's University Archives
CHAR	*Canadian Historical Association Report*
CHR	*Canadian Historical Review*
CJEPS	*Canadian Journal of Economics and Political Science*
CS	Correspondence Series
DEA	Department of External Affairs Records
DF	Department of Finance Records
HHC	Horace Hunter Correspondence
IJ	*International Journal*
JCS	*Journal of Canadian Studies*
JICH	*Journal of Imperial and Commonwealth History*
MHP	Maclean-Hunter Papers
NAC	National Archives of Canada
NLFP	National Liberal Federation Papers
PCPP	Progressive Conservative Party Papers
QQ	*Queen's Quarterly*
QUA	Queen's University Archives
UBCA	University of British Columbia Archives
UCA	University of Calgary Archives
UTA	University of Toronto Archives

Note on the style of the notes. Opening entries followed by a period indicate the citation of a quotation in the text or refer to the last passage preceding the note. In compound entries, interviews are listed first, followed by the remaining citations in alphabetical order.

INTRODUCTION: The Changing Landscape

1 J.L. Granatstein and Paul Stevens, eds., *A Reader's Guide to Canadian History*, vol. 2: *Confederation to the Present* (Toronto 1982), 41
2 Interview with Charles Peters (publisher of the *Montreal Gazette* during the 1940s). Paul Rutherford, *The Making of the Canadian Media* (Toronto 1978), 124–5
3 Paul Rutherford, *A Victorian Authority: The Daily Press in Nineteenth-Century Canada* (Toronto 1982), 212 and 220–1
4 A.H.U. Colquhoun, *Press, Politics and People: The Life and Letters of Sir John Willison* (Toronto 1925), 20
5 Rutherford, *Victorian Authority*, 42 and 190. Ramsay Cook, *The Politics of John W. Dafoe and the Free Press* (Toronto 1963), 15–16
6 Colquhoun, *Press, Politics and People*, 54
7 Quoted in Richard Clippingdale, 'J.S. Willison, Political Journalist: From Liberalism to Independence, 1881–1905,' (PhD dissertation, University of Toronto 1970), 422. Ibid., 390–2
8 Hector Charlesworth, *More Candid Chronicles: Further Leaves from the Notebook of a Canadian Journalist* (Toronto 1928), 163. Clippingdale, 'J.S. Willison,' 451
9 John S. Willison, 'An Address Delivered before the Political Science Club of Toronto University,' 23 Nov. 1899. Wilfrid Kesterton, *A History of Journalism in Canada* (Toronto 1979), 83, and Rutherford, *A Victorian Authority*, 225–6
10 Ross Harkness, *J.E. Atkinson of the Star* (Toronto 1963), 23
11 Willison, 'An Address Delivered,' 8. Clippingdale, 'J.S. Willison,' 405–6
12 Charles A. Bowman, *Ottawa Editor: The Memoirs of Charles A. Bowman* (Sidney, BC 1966), 9; Wilfrid Eggleston, 'Leaves from a Pressman's Log,' QQ 63, no. 4 (winter 1957), 562; Kesterton, *History of Journalism*, 162–3; and John S. Willison, *Reminiscences: Political and Personal* (Toronto: McClelland and Stewart 1919), 121–2
13 Paul Bilkey, *Persons, Papers and Things* (Toronto 1940), 49. Sandra Gwyn, *The Private Capital* (Toronto 1984), 397–402, and Willison, Reminiscences, 124–8
14 Clippingdale, 'J.S. Willison,' 401–5; Rutherford, *A Victorian Authority*, 79–82; and NA, Sir Clifford Sifton Papers, v. 55, J.S. Willison file, Willison to Sifton, 4 July 1898, and v. 74, 1 Oct. 1899, and v. 115, Sifton to Willison, 7 Feb. 1901
15 Rutherford, *A Victorian Authority*, 223–4

16 Rutherford, *The Making of the Canadian Media*, 69. Interview with Wilfrid
Eggleston; Kesterton, *History of Journalism*, 69–83
17 Wilfrid Eggleston, *While I Still Remember: A Personal Memoir* (Toronto
1968), 154
18 Cook, *Politics of John W. Dafoe*, 55. Ibid., 17 and 189
19 NA, Brooke Claxton Papers, v. 67, Tarr file, Claxton to Dexter, 2 Dec. 1950;
Cook, *Politics of John W. Dafoe*, 189
20 Interviews with Arthur Irwin and Peters
21 Interviews with Fraser MacDougall, Victor Mackie, and Peters; Eggleston,
While I Still Remember, 155–64
22 Interviews with Eggleston and Irwin; Rutherford, *The Making of the Canadian
Media*, 95–6
23 Frank Underhill, 'Canadian Liberal Democracy in 1955,' in *Press and Party
in Canada: Issues of Freedom* (Toronto 1955), 33. Interviews with James
Coyne and Hugh Keenleyside

CHAPTER 1: The *Winnipeg Free Press* and the Road to War

1 The *Manitoba Free Press* had changed its name to *Winnipeg Free Press* in
December 1931.
2 On Dafoe's early career, the best source is Ramsay Cook, *The Politics of
John W. Dafoe and the Free Press* (Toronto 1963). Also useful are Murray
Donnelly, *Dafoe of the Free Press* (Toronto 1968), and George Ferguson,
John W. Dafoe (Toronto 1948).
3 George Ferguson Papers (Toronto), unpublished memoir draft. Interview with
David Ferguson and Thelma LeCocq, 'Editor Ferguson,' *Maclean's*, 1 April
1947, 41
4 Interview with Ferguson; Ferguson Papers, unpublished memoir draft;
Arnold Heeney, *The Things That Are Caesar's* (Toronto 1972), 15
5 Christina McCall-Newman, *Grits: An Intimate Portrait of the Liberal Party*
(Toronto 1982), 197–8
6 NA, Frank Underhill Papers, v. 34, file 174a, transcript of a speech by Dafoe,
16 Oct. 1943. Ferguson interview; Ferguson Papers, unpublished memoir
draft; Ferguson, *Dafoe*, 4–5; Le Cocq, 'Editor Ferguson,' 38
7 Interviews with Ferguson, James Gray, and William Metcalfe; Ferguson
Papers, unpublished memoir draft
8 Interviews with Alice Dexter, Gray, Bruce Hutchison, and Metcalfe; NA,
Brooke Claxton Papers, v. 18, F correspondence 1921, 1923–37 file, Ferguson
to Claxton, 10 May 1937
9 Interview with Metcalfe. Interviews with Samuel Freedman, Gray, and Burton Richardson; James Gray, *Troublemaker! A Personal History* (Toronto
1978), 65 and 141–2
10 Interviews with Victor Mackie, Metcalfe, and Richardson; Ferguson, *Dafoe*,

122–6; NA, Burton Richardson Papers, v. 4, file 43, Richardson to Donnelly,
15 Dec. 1959; QUA, Norman Rogers Papers, CS, v. 1, 1937 file, David to Norman Rogers, 10 January 1937
11 Interviews with Alice Dexter and Wilfrid Eggleston; QUA, Grant Dexter
Papers, v. 1, file 7, autobiographical memorandum, undated; Wilfrid Eggleston Papers (Ottawa), memo on Dexter, 24 Nov. 1949
12 Interview with Eggleston; Dexter Papers, v. 3, file 21, Dexter to Ferguson,
20 Jan. 1942; Ferguson Papers, unpublished memoir draft
13 Interviews with Alice Dexter, Susan Dexter, Eggleston, and Wilfred Kesterton
14 Interview with Freedman; Cook, Politics of *John W. Dafoe*, 183–4, 235–6,
and 238–40; NA, J.W. Dafoe Papers, CS, 1935–7, Dafoe to Stewart, 17 Jan.
1936
15 For Dafoe, internationalism and active support for collective security as a
practical (or realistic) means of preserving world order were synonymous.
Many Canadians who believed their country must be involved in world
affairs – for example, pacifists and others in the peace movement – did not
accept the validity of such a linkage. Dafoe and his sympathizers considered
such people naïve, merely 'internationalists on the sidelines.'
16 NA, Clifford Sifton, Jr Papers, v. 2, Ferguson 1936 file, Ferguson to Sifton,
4 and 14 Aug. 1936 and Sifton to Ferguson, 22 Aug. 1936 and 5 Aug. 1937;
Victor Sifton 1936 file, Victor to Clifford Sifton, undated [Sept. 1936]
17 Claxton Papers, v. 18, Correspondence F 1921, 1923–37 file, Ferguson to
Helen Claxton, 28 Nov. 1939. Freedman and Escott Reid interviews; Dafoe
Papers, CS, 1935–7, Dafoe to Stevenson, 17 April 1936
18 Cook, *Politics of John W. Dafoe*, 244–5; James Eayrs, *In Defence of Canada*,
vol. 2: *Appeasement and Rearmament* (Toronto 1965), 27–8 and 37–9; and
C.P. Stacey, *Canada and the Age of Conflict*, vol. 1: *1921–1948, The Mackenzie
King Era* (Toronto 1981), 180–6 and 188
19 Donald Page, 'The Institute's "Popular Arm": The League of Nation's Society
in Canada,' *IJ*, 33, 1 (winter 1977–8), 58–61. Isolationism, like internationalism, was a complex concept with many nuances. Some isolationists in Canada,
particularly in French Canada, took the term quite literally. For many others,
however, it simply meant an unwillingness to become actively involved in
resolving international disputes, as distinct from not being concerned about
them at all. For the *Free Press*, 'isolationism' became a broadly applied term
of contempt which could be used as a label for virtually everyone who did
not subscribe to the orthodox collective security views of the paper's principals. In other words, many 'internationalists' were, from Dafoe's perspective,
indistinguishable in practice from 'isolationists' in the sense he used the term.
20 Dafoe Papers, CS, 1935–7, Dafoe to Stewart, 28 July 1936. Dafoe quoted in
Robert Bothwell and Norman Hillmer, eds., *The In–Between Time: Canadian*

External Policy in the 1930s (Toronto 1975), 25-7; Dafoe Papers, CS, 1935-7, Dafoe to Dawson, 4 Dec. 1936, Dafoe to Harris, 12 June 1936, and Dafoe to Toynbee, 10 Jan. 1936; R.A. Mackay and E.B. Rogers, *Canada Looks Abroad* (Toronto 1938), 269-70; and F.H. Soward, *Canada in World Affairs: The Pre-War Years* (Toronto 1941), 29-32

21 Stacey, *Canada and the Age of Conflict*, 186. Cook, *Politics of John W. Dafoe*, 246-7; Dafoe Papers, CS, 1935-7, Dafoe to Dexter, 30 Oct. 1936, and Dafoe to Glen, 22 Oct. 1936; *Winnipeg Free Press*, 1 Oct. 1936. Privately, Dafoe disparaged King as the 'appeaser from appeaserville.' Bruce Hutchison, 'The Greatest Man in Canada,' *Fortune*, 25, June 1942, 107

22 Dafoe Papers, CS, 1935-7, Martin to Dafoe, 8 Oct. 1936; Dexter Papers, v. 1, file 13, Dexter to Ferguson, 12 Nov. 1937; Clifford Sifton, Jr Papers, Victor Sifton 1936 file, Victor to Clifford Sifton, undated [Sept. 1936], and Ferguson file, Ferguson to Sifton, 7 Oct. 1937

23 Interview with Alice Dexter; Dexter Papers, v. 1, file 2, Dafoe to Dexter, 30 Oct. 1936; Ferguson Papers, unpublished memoir draft. Even two years later during the height of the Munich Crisis there were only five Canadian correspondents based in London. They represented the *Montreal Star*, the *Toronto Telegram* and *Star*, the Southam chain, and the Canadian Press and British United Press news services. Carlton McNaught, *Canada Gets the News* (Toronto 1940), 128-31

24 Dexter Papers, v. 1, file 13, Dexter to Ferguson, 12 Nov. 1937

25 On Voigt, see Phillip Knightly, *The First Casualty* (New York 1975), 198.

26 Dexter Papers, v. 1, file 13, Dexter to Ferguson, 10 April 1937

27 Dafoe Papers, CS, 1937-9, Dexter to Dafoe, 15 May 1937; Dexter Papers, v. 1, file 2, Dafoe to Dexter, 23 Jan. 1937

28 Dexter Papers, v. 1, file 2, Dafoe to Dexter, 5 June 1937

29 Clifford Sifton, Jr Papers, Ferguson 1937 file, Ferguson to Sifton, 28 Dec. 1937. Foreword by Dafoe in Mackay and Rogers, *Canada Looks Abroad*, vii

30 Claxton Papers, v. 18, F correspondence 1921, 1923-37 file, Ferguson to Claxton, 20 Dec. 1937

31 Dexter Papers, v. 8, Diaries, 23 Feb. and 1 and 17 March 1938; John English, *Shadow of Heaven: The Life of Lester Pearson*, vol. 1: 1897-1948 (Toronto 1989); Lester B. Pearson, *Mike: The Memoirs of the Rt Hon. Lester B. Pearson*, vol. 1: 1897-1948 (Toronto 1972), 108

32 Hume Wrong as quoted in McCall-Newman, *Grits*, 197. Claude Bissell, *The Imperial Canadian: Vincent Massey in Office* (Toronto 1986), 55-7; Dexter Papers, v. 1, file 13, Dexter to Ferguson, 12 Nov. 1937; and UBCA, Alan Plaunt Papers, v. 4, file 8, Pearson to Plaunt, 19 Jan. 1937

33 Pearson, *Mike*, 109. Interview with Hugh Keenleyside

34 English, *Shadow of Heaven*, 198-9

35 NA, Lester Pearson Papers, N1 Series, v. 4, Ferguson file, Pearson to Ferguson, 5 Nov. 1937. Dexter Papers, v. 1, file 13, Dexter to Ferguson, 12 Nov. 1937

36 Dexter Papers v. 1, file 13, Dexter to Ferguson, 19 Oct. 1937

37 Ibid., 12 Nov. 1937

38 Ibid.

39 Ibid., v. 8, Diaries, 18 March 1938

40 NA, Mackenzie King Papers, Diaries, 14 March 1938. *Winnipeg Free Press*, 12 and 14 March 1938

41 Interview with Freedman; Dafoe Papers, CS, 1937–9, Dafoe to Shotwell, 13 April 1938; Thomas Slobodin, 'A Tangled Web: The Relationship between Mackenzie King's Foreign Policy and National Unity' (PhD dissertation, Queen's University 1986), 303

42 See, for instance, a particularly hard–hitting editorial in the *Winnipeg Free Press*, 1 Aug. 1938. Cook, *Politics of John W. Dafoe*, 242–3 and 246

43 Massey to Barrington–Ward, 13 Sept. 1938, quoted in Robin Betts, 'George V. Ferguson, Canada and Appeasement,' *The Historian* 7 (summer 1985), 12. Ferguson interview; Dexter Papers, v. 8, Diaries, 11 and 24 April and 2 May 1938

44 NA, Arthur Meighen Papers, Meighen to Knowles, 28 Nov. 1939, 152945–6. Frank W. Peers, *The Politics of Canadian Broadcasting, 1920–1951* (Toronto 1969), 219 and 266–7. *Winnipeg Free Press*, 27 July and 19, 27, and 31 Aug. 1938

45 Pearson to Skelton, 4 Nov. 1938, as quoted in Bothwell and Hillmer, eds., *The In-Between Time*, 165; English, *Shadow of Heaven*, 199–200. Dexter Papers, v. 8, Diaries, 30 Aug. and 2 and 15 Sept. 1938, and v. 1, file 14, Dexter to Ferguson, 24 July and 6 Sept. 1938

46 At least according to Dexter, Pearson had little time for the other Canadian correspondents in London chiefly because he considered them (or their papers) too tainted with imperialist sympathies to be relied upon. Except for some briefings given the visiting editor of the *Financial Post*, which had been arranged by the *Post*'s London 'stringer,' Dexter himself, the *Free Press* was the exclusive beneficiary of this windfall. Floyd Chalmers Papers (Toronto), U.K.–Germany trip file, memo on a conversation with Pearson, 29 Sept. 1938; Dexter Papers, v. 1, file 14, Dexter to Ferguson, 20 Sept. 1938

47 Dexter Papers, v. 1, file 14, Dexter to Ferguson, 20 Sept. 1938

48 Ibid., Ferguson to Dexter, 14 Sept. 1938

49 Ferguson Papers, unpublished memoir draft; Norman Smith, 'Pearson, People and Press,' IJ 29, no. 1 (winter 1973–4), 15

50 Dexter Papers, v. 1, file 14, Ferguson to Dexter, 1 Sept. 1938, and Dexter to Ferguson, 20 Sept. 1938; Ferguson Papers, unpublished memoir draft

51 Dafoe Papers, CS, 1937–9, Dafoe to Ferguson, 1 Sept. 1938. Dexter Papers,

v. I, file 14, Dexter to Ferguson, 14 Sept. 1938. Street sales, usually a good barometer of public interest, did not reflect this conviction.

52 *Winnipeg Free Press,* 9 Sept. 1938. Dexter Papers, v. I, file 14, Ferguson to Dexter, I and 8 Sept. 1938

53 *Winnipeg Free Press,* 10, 13, and 14 Sept. 1938; Dexter Papers, v. I, file 14, Ferguson to Dexter, 14 Sept. 1938

54 QUA, Charles Dunning Papers, v. II, file 94, King to Dunning, 19 Sept. 1938; Eayrs, *In Defence of Canada,* 66–8. *Winnipeg Free Press,* 15, 19, and 20 Sept. 1938

55 Dexter Papers, v. 8, Diaries, 29 Sept. 1938

56 Ibid., v. I, file 14, Dexter cable, 28 Sept. 1938; Ferguson to Chalmers, 7 Nov. 1938; Ferguson to Dexter, 28 Sept. 1938

57 Eayrs, *In Defence of Canada,* 66–8; 'Overseas Reactions to the Crisis – Canada,' *Round Table* 113 (Dec. 1938), 39; and Stacey, *Canada in the Age of Conflict,* 215–18

58 Chalmers Papers, U.K.–Germany trip file, memo of a conversation with Pearson and Dexter, 10 Oct. 1938; Dafoe Papers, CS, 1937–9, Dafoe to Ferguson, 19 Nov. 1938; Dexter Papers, v. I, file 14, Ferguson to Dexter, 29 Oct. 1938; Clifford Sifton, Jr, Papers, v. 2, Ferguson 1938 file, Ferguson to Sifton, 12 Oct. 1938

59 *Winnipeg Free Press,* 30 Sept. 1938

60 Interviews with Ferguson, Freedman, and Metcalfe; Dafoe Papers, CS, 1942–4, Ferguson memo, undated (1943); Ferguson, *Dafoe,* 104; Bruce Hutchison, 'Canada's Gadfly: The *Winnipeg Free Press,*' *Harper's,* April 1963, 86; Richardson Papers, v. I, file 9, Richardson to Mrs Wanda Richardson, 4 Oct. 1938

61 Dafoe Papers, CS, 1937–9, Ferguson to Dafoe, 20 Oct. 1938; UCA, Bruce Hutchison Papers, I.2.I, Hutchison to Malone, 10 Sept. 1961; Hutchison, 'Canada's Gadfly,' 82

62 Plaunt Papers, v. 9, file 1, 'Comment of Principal Canadian Newspapers on the September Crisis,' undated memorandum [Oct. 1938]. Interview with Richard Malone; Frank Scott, *Canada Today* (Toronto 1939), 114–16

63 Claxton Papers, v. 27, Dafoe (I) file, Dafoe to Ferguson, undated [Oct. 1938], quoted in a memo by Ferguson, undated [1944]; Dafoe Papers, CS, 1937–9, Dafoe to Ferguson, 30 Sept., 18 Oct., and 5, 8, and 19 Nov. 1938, and Ferguson to Dafoe, 20 Oct. 1938; Dexter Papers, v. I, file 14, Ferguson to Dexter, 3 Oct. 1938

64 Dafoe Papers, CS, 1937–9, Dafoe to Ferguson, 19 Nov. 1938. Dexter Papers, v. I, file 14, Dexter to Ferguson, 20 Sept. 1938, and Ferguson to Dexter, 3 Oct. 1938

65 Dexter Papers, v. I, file 14, memo, undated [Feb. 1939], and v. 30, text of a

speech delivered to the Winnipeg Bankers' Club, 30 Jan. 1939; Pearson Papers, NI Series, Congratulations 1939–42 file, Smith to Pearson, 10 Jan. 1939; and Richardson Papers, Richardson to Mrs Wanda Richardson, 19 Jan. 1939

66 Dexter Papers, v. 5, file 36, memo on an interview with King, 1 July 1947. Dafoe Papers, CS, 1937–9, Dafoe to Ferguson, 11 Oct. 1938; J.L. Granatstein and Robert Bothwell, '"A Self–Evident National Duty": Canadian Foreign Policy, 1935–1939,' JICH 3, no. 2 (Jan. 1976), 227–30; and Blair Neatby, *William Lyon Mackenzie King,* vol. 3: 1932–39, *The Prism of Unity* (Toronto 1976), 296–300

67 Rogers Papers, I, v. 2, General correspondence M–W file, David to Norman Rogers, 16 April 1939

68 *Winnipeg Free Press,* 15 March 1939

69 Ibid., 24 March 1939

70 Dafoe Papers, CS, 1937–9, Ferguson to Dafoe, 21 March 1939

71 Ibid., 1935–7, Dafoe to Davies, 7 Jan. 1937; 1937–9, Dexter to Dafoe, 23 April1937, Dafoe to Noel–Baker, 29 May 1937

72 Quoted in Eayrs, *In Defence of Canada,* 74

73 Dexter Papers, v. 5, file 36, memo on an interview with King, 1 July 1947. On Skelton's view, ibid., file 32, memo on an interview with Alexander Skelton (Skelton's son), 16 Jan. 1948. Underhill Papers, v. 34, Cook file 169b, memorandum on Cook's dissertation, 18 Dec. 1961, and Dafoe file 174a, comments by Ferguson on Cook's dissertation, undated (August 1961)

74 Clifford Sifton, Jr Papers, v. 2, Ferguson 1939 file, Ferguson to Sifton, 27 Nov. 1939

CHAPTER 2: The *Financial Post* and Rearmament

1 Interview with Arthur Irwin; AO, MHP, HHC, v. 64, *Half a Century of Service* (1953); '75th Anniversary Supplement' to *Newsweekly,* 26 Sept. 1962

2 Floyd Chalmers, *Both Sides of the Street: One Man's Life in Business and the Arts in Canada* (Toronto 1983), 4–5, 23, 35–8, and 49. For another view of the *Post*'s editorial performance during the 1920s, see Paul Rutherford, *The Making of the Canadian Media* (Toronto 1978), 43

3 NA, J.W. Dafoe Papers, CS, 1935–7, Dafoe to Clifford Sifton, Jr, 8 Aug. 1935. Interview with Robert Fulford; MHP, Board of Directors Correspondence, v. 3, minute books, 3 June 1938

4 Dafoe Papers, CS, 1937–9, Dafoe to Ferguson, 18 Oct. 1938. James Eayrs, *In Defence of Canada,* vol. 2: *Appeasement and Rearmament* (Toronto 1965), 119–21 and chap. 5

5 Dafoe Papers, CS, 1935–7, Chalmers to Dafoe, 31 Dec. 1935; MHP, Board of Directors Correspondence, v. 3, minutes, 27 May 1940. For a thorough

analysis of the role of Maclean Publishing in the Bren gun affair, see David
Mackenzie, 'The Bren Gun Scandal and the Maclean Publishing Company's
Investigation of Canadian Defence Contracts, 1938–1940,' JCS 26, 3
(automne/fall 1991)

6 *Financial Post*, 27 Aug. and 3 and 10 Sept. 1938. H. Blair Neatby, *William
Lyon Mackenzie King*, vol. 3: *1932–1939, The Prism of Unity* (Toronto 1976),
300–1

7 Interview with Irwin; Floyd Chalmers, *A Gentleman of the Press*, (Toronto
1969), 300–1; and MHP, HHC, v. 63, Bren Gun Inquiry file, Hunter to Maclean,
17 Sept. 1938, and v. 73, Bren gun file, draft of Hunter's statement before the
public accounts committee, undated [1939].

8 Floyd Chalmers Papers (Toronto), Memoranda, 1939 file, interview with
Lambert, 27 July 1939; MHP, HHC, v. 63, Bren Gun Inquiry file, Moore to
Maclean, 27 Jan. 1939

9 MHP, HHC, v. 73, Bren gun file, editorial conference minutes, 12 Feb. 1939.
Interview with Irwin; MHP, HHC, v. 63, Bren Gun Inquiry file, Moore to
Maclean, 16 and 27 Jan. 1939, and v. 73, Bren gun file, editorial conference
minutes, 22 Sept. 1939

10 MHP, HHC, v. 63, Bren Gun Inquiry file, editorial conference minutes,
25 March 1939. Interview with Irwin

11 Arthur Irwin Papers (Victoria), Hunter memorandum, 9 June 1939, and
Hunter to Irwin, 12 July 1939

12 *Financial Post*, 22 July, 26 Aug., and 2, 9, 23, and 30 Sept. 1939

13 Chalmers Papers, memo of a conversation with Norman Robertson, 2 Sept. 1939

14 Toronto *Globe and Mail*, 24 Nov. 1939. MHP, HHC, v. 73, Bren gun file,
memo, 15 Sept. 1939; draft of letter to King, 16 Sept. 1939; Chalmers to Hunter,
18 Sept. 1939; and editorial conference minutes, 22 Sept. 1939

15 Irwin Papers, Defence interviews file, Winnipeg, 16 Aug. 1939, and Defence
Investigation memoranda, Dexter interviews, 27 and 28 Dec. 1939

16 Chalmers Papers, memo on an interview with Norman Rogers, 3 Nov. 1939;
MHP, HHC, v. 63, Bren Gun Inquiry file, Hunter to Maclean, undated [autumn
1939]. *Financial Post*, 23 Sept. 1939. On Mackenzie, see J.L. Granatstein,
'King and His Cabinet: The War Years,' in John English and J.O. Stubbs,
eds., *Mackenzie King: Widening the Debate* (Toronto 1977), 178–80

17 Dafoe Papers, CS, 1937–9, Dafoe to Clifford Sifton, 12 Nov. 1939

18 *Financial Post*, 7, 21, and 28 Oct. and 11 and 18 Nov. 1939. Irwin interview; Irwin Papers, Tyrrell to Irwin, 26 July 1939, McNaughton interviews,
19 June, 7 Sept., 5 Oct., and 1 Nov. 1939, and Vaughan interviews, 2 and
24 Aug., 6 Oct. and 28 Dec. 1939; Mackenzie, 'Bren Gun Scandal,' 151;
and MHP, HHC, v. 63, Bren Gun Inquiry file, Hunter to Maclean, 16 Sept. 1939,
and v. 73, Bren gun file, memo, 15 Sept. 1939

19 Mackenzie, 'Bren Gun Scandal,' 153
20 Irwin Papers, Campbell file, interview 26 Oct. 1939, Vaughan file, interview
    2 Aug. 1939, and Defence Investigation file, Irwin memos, interview with
    Dexter, 27 and 28 Dec. 1939; NA, Ian Mackenzie Papers, v. 20, file 41–2,
    MacLachlan to Senior, 28 Oct. 1939. Irwin Papers, Defence – Comment on
    Series file, Wilson to Chalmers, 20 Jan. 1940
21 Irwin Papers, Defence – Chalmers interviews file, memo of conversation
    with Thompson, 30 Oct. 1939; Mackenzie, 'Bren Gun Scandal,' 155
22 *Financial Post,* 25 Nov. and 2 Dec. 1939 and 6 and 13 Jan. 1940. Chalmers
    Papers, memo of an interview with Rogers, 3 Nov. 1939; Irwin Papers,
    Roberts file, memo of interview with Roberts, 27 Dec. 1939; Rogers file,
    memo of Wilson interview with Rogers, 8 Nov. 1939
23 MHP, HHC, v. 63, Bren Gun Inquiry file, editorial conference minutes, 29 Jan.
    1940
24 Ibid., v. 81, Maclean file, Maclean to Hunter, 23 March 1940. Irwin Papers,
    O'Leary file, interview with O'Leary, 9 Nov. and 27 Dec. 1939; MHP, Maclean
    Correspondence, v. 52, editorial conference minutes, 1 March 1940
25 *Financial Post,* 2 and 9 March 1940. Confidential interview
26 *Financial Post,* 20 April 1940. Ibid., 30 March 1940
27 Ibid., 2 Nov. 1940. Ibid., 6 July 1940. Michael Bliss, *Northern Enterprise:
    Five Centuries of Canadian Business* (Toronto 1987), 446 and; MHP, HHC,
    v. 87, W file, Hunter to Webber, 20 Sept. 1940
28 Irwin Papers, Campbell file, memo of interview with Campbell, 26 Oct.
    1939, and Vaughan file, memo of interview with Vaughan, 6 Oct. 1939. NA,
    Lester Pearson Papers, NI Series, v. 4, Dexter file, Dexter to Pearson, 27 Jan.
    1940; Reginald Whitaker, *The Government Party: Organizing and Financing
    the Liberal Party of Canada, 1930–58* (Toronto 1977), 128
29 MHP, HHC, v. 87, Wilson file, Wilson to Chalmers, 7 June and 19 and 26 July
    1940; v. 75, Chipman file, Chipman to Chalmers, 10 July 1940. On the adver-
    tiser backlash, see ibid., 20 April and 11 Oct. 1940, and v. 78, Gowdy file,
    Wilson to Hunter, 8 Jan. 1940.
30 Chalmers Papers, memo, 2 June 1940; Irwin Papers, Vaughan file, memo on
    interview by Wilson, 24 June 1940; MHP, HHC, v. 87, Wilson file, Wilson to
    Chalmers, 24 June 1940
31 MHP, HHC, v. 87, Wilson file, Wilson to Hunter, 31 July 1940
32 Robert Bothwell and William Kilbourn, *C.D. Howe: A Biography* (Toronto
    1979), 133
33 Quoted in the QUA, Norman Lambert Papers, Diaries, 23 May 1940. Bothwell
    and Kilbourn, *Howe,* 138 and 144; Dafoe Papers, CS, 1940–2, Dexter to Dafoe,
    26 Jan. 1941
34 Chalmers Papers, memo of interview with Scully (the steel controller) and

MacMillan, 27 Oct. 1940; memos of interviews with MacMillan, 15 Oct.,
18 Nov., and 16 Dec. 1940; Irwin Papers, Defence – Interviews-Ottawa file,
memo on interviews with Bell, 29 and 30 Oct. 1939, and Wilson to Chalmers,
3 Dec. 1940
35 *Financial Post,* 16 and 23 Nov. 1940
36 Bothwell and Kilbourn, *Howe,* 141–2; Dafoe Papers, CS, 1940–2,
Dexter to Dafoe, 5 Feb. 1941
37 *Financial Post,* 14 and 28 Dec. 1940 and 25 Jan. and 18 Feb. 1941. Dafoe
Papers, CS, 1940–2, Richardson to Dafoe, 20 Jan. 1941, and Clifford Sifton
to Ferguson, 22 Jan. 1941
38 Dexter Papers, v. 2, file 19, memo, undated [1940]; Irwin Papers, Defence –
Financial Post Notes – 1940–1, Chalmers memo, 27 Feb. 1941; MHP, HHC,
v. 87, Wilson file, Wilson to Chalmers, 3 Dec. 1940
39 MHP, HHC, v. 74, C miscellaneous file, Hunter to Carmichael, 25 Jan. 1941.
Dexter Papers, v. 2, file 20, memo, 10 Nov. 1941
40 *Financial Post,* 8 and 15 Feb.1941
41 Interviews with Irwin and Wilfrid Eggleston (the chief press censor)
42 Dafoe Papers, CS, 1940–2, Dexter to Dafoe, 4 Feb. 1941
43 Ibid., 5 Feb. 1941; Richardson to Dafoe, 4 Feb. 1941
44 *Financial Post,* 15 and 22 Feb. and 1 March 1942
45 House of Commons, *Debates,* I, 26 Feb. 1941, 1057. Interview with Irwin
46 *Financial Post,* 8 March 1941. Dafoe Papers, CS, 1940–2, Dafoe to Victor
Sifton, 13 Feb. 1941; MHP, HHC, v. 75, Chipman file, Hunter to Chipman,
28 Feb. 1941
47 Dafoe Papers, CS, 1940–2, Dexter to Dafoe, 29 Jan. 1941. *Financial Post,*
10 May 1941
48 MHP, HHC, v. 81, Maclean file, Hunter to Maclean, 1 March 1941. Dafoe
Papers, CS, 1940–2, Dafoe to Dexter, 7 March 1941
49 MHP, HHC, v. 63, Bren Gun Inquiry file, Gordon to Hunter, 6 March 1941,
and Cushing to Chipman, 11 March 1941
50 Chalmers Papers, War Finance 1939–45 file, interview with Dunning and
Chipman memo, 6 Jan. 1941; Irwin Papers, Defence – *Financial Post* Notes –
1940–1 file, Kennedy to Chalmers, 10 March 1941, and Gowdy to Chalmers,
5 March 1941; and MHP, HHC, v. 63, Bren Gun Inquiry file, Cushing to Chipman, 11 March 1941
51 Bothwell and Kilbourn, *Howe,* 75
52 Chalmers Papers, memo of interview with Towers, 12 March 1940
53 NA, Mackenzie King Papers, Diaries, 9 Oct. 1941, 13 Sept. 1940. NA, H.E.
Kidd Papers, v. 14, file 19, Claxton to Wright, 3 March 1941
54 *Financial Post,* 18 Jan. 1941
55 MHP, HHC, v. 79, Donald Hunter file, Horace to Donald Hunter, 11 Jan. 1941

56 Ibid., v. 75, Chipman file, Hunter to Chipman, 19 Feb. 1942
57 *Financial Post*, 5 Jan. 1946. Bliss, *Northern Enterprise*, 447
58 Dafoe Papers, CS, 1942–4, Dexter to Dafoe, 4 March 1942
59 Bothwell and Kilbourn, *Howe*, 149
60 MHP, HHC, v. 73, Bren gun file, memo, 15 Sept. 1939
61 Chalmers, *Both Sides of the Street*, 131. *Financial Post*, 5 Jan. 1946

CHAPTER 3: The *Winnipeg Free Press* and Conscription

1 NA, J.W. Dafoe Papers, CS, 1937–9, Dafoe to Ferguson, 3 Sept. 1939
2 Interviews with James Gray and Paul Martin; Ramsay Cook, *The Politics of John W. Dafoe and the Free Press* (Toronto 1963), 261, 265, and 292–4; George Ferguson, *John W. Dafoe* (Toronto 1948), 17–18 and 109
3 UCA, Bruce Hutchison Papers, 1.2.7, Dexter to Malone, 10 Sept. 1961. Ferguson, *Dafoe*, 5–6 and 57
4 *Winnipeg Free Press*, 1 April 1939. House of Commons, *Debates*, 3, 30 March 1939, 2426 and 2440–1; Toronto *Telegram*, 28 March 1939
5 J.L. Granatstein, *The Politics of Survival: The Conservative Party of Canada, 1939–1945* (Toronto 1967), 24; C.P. Stacey, *Six Years of War: The Army in Canada, Britain and the Pacific* (Ottawa 1966), 111
6 *Winnipeg Free Press*, 9 Sept. 1939. Dafoe Papers, CS, 1937–9, Dafoe to Ferguson, 14 Sept. 1939; *Winnipeg Free Press*, 12 Sept. 1939
7 NA, Brooke Claxton Papers, v. 137, Conscription (B) file, Claxton to Macdonnell, 16 Sept. 1939; QUA, Dexter Papers, v. 2, file 15, memo of Pelletier interview, 5 July 1939, and file 16, memo, undated [Sept. 1939]; George Ferguson Papers (Toronto), unpublished memoir draft; and NA, Clifford Sifton, Jr Papers, v. 3, Victor Sifton Sept.–Dec. 1939 file, Soucisse to MacDermot, 10 Nov. 1939
8 Dafoe Papers, CS, 1937–9, Dafoe to Ferguson, undated [Aug. 1939]; NA, Lester Pearson Papers, N1 Series, v. 4, Dexter file, Dexter to Pearson, 14 May 1939
9 Ferguson, *Dafoe*, 108. Arthur Irwin Papers (Victoria), Maclean's – letters – Hutchison file, Hutchison to Irwin, undated [1940]
10 Grattan O'Leary, *Recollections of People, Press and Politics* (Toronto 1977), 48
11 Dexter Papers, v. 2, file 18, Ferguson to Corbett, 8 Aug. 1940; James Gray, *Troublemaker! A Personal History* (Toronto, 1978), 134–42; NA, Burton Richardson Papers, v. 3, file 26, Gray to Richardson, undated [April 1942]
12 Interviews with Gray, Victor Mackie, and Burton Richardson
13 Interviews with Stephanie Deutsch, Alice Dexter, Wilfrid Eggleston, Wilfred Kesterton, and Martin

14 Dexter Papers, v. 3, file 21, Dexter to Ferguson, 20 Jan. 1942; Gray, *Trouble-maker!* 191

15 Interviews with Gray, Kesterton, and Mitchell Sharp

16 Interviews with Edouard Handy, Hutchison, J.W. Pickersgill, Richardson, and Walter Turnbull

17 Prior to taking up his appointment as American minister, Pierrepont Moffat had asked visiting *Vancouver Sun* editor Bruce Hutchison who was the best-informed newspaperman in Ottawa. Hutchison's immediate response was Dexter and Grattan O'Leary, editor of the Conservative-leaning *Ottawa Journal.* Hutchison Papers, 1.2.1, Hutchison to Dexter, undated [summer 1940]

18 Dexter Papers, v. 3, file 5, Ferguson to Dexter, 4 Sept. 1943. Dafoe Papers, CS, 1942-4, Dafoe to Shih, 24 Feb. 1942

19 Dexter Papers, v. 3, file 21, Dexter to Ferguson, 20 Jan. 1942. Ibid., 17 Jan. 1942 and memo, 27 Jan. 1942; Richardson Papers, v. 3, file 26, Ferguson to Dexter, 19 Jan. 1942

20 QUA, T.A. Crerar Papers, III, v. 104, Dafoe 1936-43 file, Dafoe to Crerar, 13 June 1940; Dexter Papers, v. 1, file 3, Dafoe to Dexter, 16 Oct. 1940; Clifford Sifton, Jr Papers, v. 3, Ferguson 1940 file, Ferguson to Sifton, 26 Jan. 1940, and Sifton to Ferguson, 31 Jan. 1940

21 *Winnipeg Free Press,* 27 March 1940. This was a view shared by other keen observers. Pearson Papers, NI Series, v. 2, Claxton file, Claxton to Pearson, 27 April 1940

22 NA, J.L. Ralston Papers, v. 57, Victor Sifton file, Sifton to Ralston, 7 Nov. 1940; Clifford Sifton, Jr Papers, v. 3, Victor Sifton 1940 file, Victor to Clifford Sifton, 8 Nov. 1940. Richardson Papers, v. 2, file 21, Ferguson to Richardson, 3 Sept. 1940

23 Interview with Charles Peters; Dafoe Papers, CS, 1940-2, Dexter to Dafoe, undated [April 1941]; Granatstein, *The Politics of Survival,* 83-7

24 Dexter Papers, v. 2, file 20, memo, 10 April 1941. Crerar Papers, III, v. 104, Dafoe 1936-43 file, Crerar to Dafoe, 25 April 1941 and Dafoe Papers, CS, 1940-2, Dexter to Ferguson, 11 Nov. 1941

25 Dafoe Papers, CS, 1940-2, Dafoe to Ferguson, undated [April 1941]

26 Dexter Papers, v. 2, file 20, Ferguson to Dexter, 12 July 1941; Ferguson Papers, memoir draft; and NA, King Papers, Diaries, 10 July 1941

27 Dexter Papers, v. 2, file 20, Ferguson to Dexter, 12 July 1941. Ibid., Ferguson to Dexter, undated [July 1941]; QUA, Norman Lambert Papers, Diaries, 21 July 1941

28 Dafoe Papers, CS, 1940-2, Victor Sifton to Ralston, 1 Oct. 1941, and 1942-4, Dexter to Dafoe, 14 April 1942; Ralston Papers, v. 117, Sixth Division file, Victor Sifton to Ralston, 9 July 1941

29 Dexter Papers, v. 2, file 19, Dexter to Ferguson, 14 July 1941, and Ferguson to Dexter, 16 July 1941; file 20, Ferguson to Dexter, 12 July 1941

30 *Winnipeg Free Press*, 5, 7, 15 and 17 Oct. 1941

31 Dafoe Papers, CS, 1942–4, Dexter to Dafoe, 20 Nov. and 9 Dec. 1941

32 Ibid., 19 Nov. 1941

33 Crerar Papers, III, v. 104, Dafoe 1936–43 file, Dafoe to Crerar, 15 Nov. 1941

34 Dafoe Papers, CS, 1942–4, Dexter to Dafoe, 12 Jan. 1942

35 Ibid., 1940–2, Dafoe to Clifford Sifton, 27 Dec. 1941. Interview with Peters; Granatstein, *The Politics of Survival,* 104–5

36 Richardson Papers, v. 3, file 26, Ferguson to Richardson, 11 Dec. 1941. Dexter Papers, v. 13, file 66, Ferguson to Dexter, 9 Dec. 1941, and Dexter to Ferguson, 11 Dec. 1941

37 Crerar Papers, III, v. 104, Dafoe 1936–43 file, Dafoe to Crerar, 12 Jan. 1942

38 Claxton Papers, v. 31, Ferguson file, Claxton to Ferguson, 5 Nov. 1941

39 Dexter Papers, v. 2, file 20, memos, 5 and 9 Dec. 1941

40 Claxton Papers, v. 31, Ferguson file, Ferguson to Claxton, 27 Oct. 1941; Dexter Papers, v. 2, file 20, Ferguson to Dexter, 22 Dec. 1941, and v. 3, file 21, Ferguson to Dexter, 15 Jan. 1942

41 Crerar Papers, III, v. 104, Dafoe 1936–43 file, Crerar to Dafoe, 8 and 23 Jan. 1942; UBCA, Norman Mackenzie Papers, Main CS, v. 25, file 4, Claxton to Mackenzie, 24 Jan. 1942

42 *Winnipeg Free Press*, 16 Jan. 1942. Ibid., 23 and 24 Jan. and 2 and 10 Feb. 1942

43 Dafoe Papers, CS, 1942–4, Hutchison to Dafoe, undated [Jan. 1942]

44 Ibid., Dafoe to Stevenson, 21 March 1942. Claxton Papers, v. 27, Dafoe (2) file, Dafoe to Claxton, 21 March 1942; Dafoe Papers, CS, 1910–43, Dafoe to Macdonnell, 18 Feb. 1942

45 Claxton Papers, v. 31, Ferguson file, Ferguson to Claxton, 30 Jan. 1942

46 *Winnipeg Free Press*, 14 March 1942

47 Ibid., 28 April 1942

48 Ibid., 29 April and 1 May 1942

49 Pearson Papers, N1 Series, v. 12, Ritchie file, Pearson to Ritchie, 12 May 1942

50 Claxton Papers, v. 67, Tarr file, Claxton to Tarr, 18 May 1942; Dafoe Papers, CS, 1942–4, Dexter to Ferguson, 13 May 1942; and Lambert Papers, Diaries, 11 May and undated [May] 1942

51 *Winnipeg Free Press*, 20 June 1942. Dafoe Papers, CS, 1942–4, Dafoe to Macdonnell and Dafoe to Stevenson, 12 Feb. 1942

52 Dexter Papers, v. 3, file 22, Dafoe to Dexter, 8 May 1942; *Winnipeg Free Press*, 11 June 1942

53 Dexter Papers, v. 3, file 23, memo, 21 July 1942. Ibid., file 22, memo, 6 May 1942

54 BUA, T.W.L. MacDermot Papers, M371/1–131, Ferguson to MacDermot,
    3 June 1942
55 Dexter Papers, v. 3, file 23, Ferguson to Dexter, 16 July 1942. Ibid., v. 1, file
    5, Dafoe to Lower, 2 July 1942, and Dafoe to Dexter, 25 July 1942; Richard-
    son Papers, v. 3, file 26, Ferguson to Richardson, 19 May 1942
56 NA, Frank Scott Papers, v. 25, Plebiscite vote in Quebec file, Lower to Dafoe,
    19 July 1942
57 King Papers, Diaries, 12 June 1942
58 NA, Alexander Hume Papers, Diaries, 11 May 1942
59 Dexter Papers, v. 3, file 23, memo, 21 July 1942; QUA, C.G. Power Papers,
    v. 1a, file 1, memo, 12 July 1942
60 Lambert Papers, Diaries, 4 July 1942 (based on a conversation with Dexter)
61 Dexter Papers, v. 3, file 23, memo, 17 July 1942
62 Dafoe Papers, CS, 1942–4, Dafoe to Dexter, 15 April 1942
63 King Papers, Diaries, 9 Jan. 1944
64 Dexter Papers, v. 3, file 24, Hutchison to Dexter, 7 Jan. 1943; J.K. Nesbitt,
    'Editor Bruce Hutchison Commutes between Victoria and Winnipeg,' *Satur-
    day Night* 10 May 1947, 6–7
65 Claxton Papers, v. 20, T–W Correspondence 1931–41 file, Claxton to Wilson,
    10 Dec. 1940
66 Interviews with Susan Dexter and Pickersgill; NA, H.E. Kidd Papers, v. 4,
    file 5, Hutchison to Kidd, undated [1944]
67 Richardson Papers, v. 1, file 10, Richardson to Mrs Richardson, 18 Jan. 1944,
    and Ferguson to Richardson, 14 March 1944; v. 3, file 29, Gray to Richard-
    son, 13 March 1944
68 Claxton Papers, v. 77, G–miscellaneous file, Claxton to Gibson, 20 Feb. 1958.
    Richardson Papers, v. 3, file 29, Ferguson to Richardson, 19 June 1944
69 Ibid., Hutchison to Richardson, 17 Feb. 1944
70 Gray, *Troublemaker!* 104 and 160–1; Lambert Papers, Diaries, 2 May 1944;
    Richardson Papers, v. 3, file 27, Dafoe to Richardson, 17 July 1943
71 Dexter Papers, v. 3, file 26, memo, 22 June 1944. Scott Papers, v. 24, Personal
    correspondence 1944 file, Dexter to Scott, 8 and 31 Aug. 1944
72 Dexter Papers, v. 3, file 26, Ferguson to Dexter, 21 Sep. 1944. Ibid., 8 Sept.
    1944; Richardson Papers, v. 3, file 29, Gray to Richardson, 1 Sep. 1944, Fer-
    guson to Richardson, 8 Sep. 1944
73 C.P. Stacey, *Arms, Men and Governments: The War Policies of Canada,
    1939–45* (Ottawa 1970), 440–1
74 Crerar Papers, III, v. 119, King 1938–41 file, memo, 26 Dec. 1944; King
    Papers, Diaries, 18 and 19 Oct. 1944; Stacey, *Arms, Men and Governments,*
    444–8
75 Ralston had submitted a formal letter of resignation to the prime minister in

1942 and, although King had persuaded Ralston to stay on, he had kept the letter. It was this letter which King had tabled before a stunned cabinet on 1 November to engineer Ralston's 'resignation.'

76 Bruce Hutchison, *The Far Side of the Street* (Toronto 1976), 184
77 *Winnipeg Free Press*, 3 Nov. 1944
78 Hutchison Papers, 2.1.4., Naylor to Hutchison, 27 Dec. 1976; Power Papers, 1e, 22A, Resignation 1944 file, Power to Lower, 11 Dec. 1944, and 1c, 6, Hutchison file, Hutchison to Power, 20 May 1952
79 J.L. Granatstein, *Canada's War: The Politics of the Mackenzie King Government, 1939–1945* (Toronto 1975), 260; Norman Mackenzie Papers, Wartime Information Board Series, v. 2, file 16, memos from Dunton to the cabinet, 6 and 13 Nov. 1944
80 QUA, John Stevenson Papers, unpublished manuscript biography of Mackenzie King, file 7
81 Claxton Papers, v. 67, Tarr file, Tarr to Claxton, 3 Nov. 1944. Hutchison, *The Far Side of the Street*, 184–7
82 *Winnipeg Free Press*, 13 Nov. 1944. Ibid., 17 and 18 Nov. 1944
83 Crerar Papers, III, v. 119, King 1938–41 file, memo on the conscription crisis, 26 Dec. 1944; King Papers, Diaries, 9 Jan. 1945. Granatstein, *Canada's War*, 363–4; Stacey, *Arms, Men and Governments*, 470–2
84 King Papers, Diaries, 23 Nov. 1944
85 Ibid., 9 Jan. 1945. *Winnipeg Free Press*, 23 Nov. 1944
86 Ralston Papers, v. 86, Resignation – Vining file, Sifton to Vining, 4 Dec. 1944. *The Far Side of the Street*, Hutchison, 167; Norman Mackenzie Papers, Wartime Information Board Series, v. 2, file 16, memo from Dunton to the cabinet, 18 Dec. 1944
87 Dafoe Papers, CS, 1942–4, Dafoe to Dr Shih, 24 Feb. 1942
88 William Christian, ed., *The Idea File of Harold Adams Innis* (Toronto 1980), 100–1

CHAPTER 4: Ken Wilson and the Making of an Authoritative Voice

1 Interviews with Floyd Chalmers, Paul Deacon, Robert Fulford, and Peter Newman; AO, MHP, HHC, v. 64, '75th Anniversary Supplement' to *Newsweekly*, 26 Sept. 1962; and NA, Burton Richardson Papers, v. 4, file 36, Kreutzweiser to Richardson, 16 Feb. 1951. Circulation steadily increased from fewer than 30,000 per issue in 1942 to nearly 100,000 twenty years later. MHP, HHC, v. 64, '75th Anniversary Supplement,' 26 Sep. 1962
2 Interview with Ruth Wilson; Kenneth W. Taylor, 'Kenneth Ramsay Wilson, 1903–1952,' CJEPS 18, no. 4 (Nov. 1952): 533–4; Kenneth Wilson Papers (Toronto), biographical notes (undated); *Newsweekly*, 31 Aug. 1951; Ruth

Wilson Papers (Toronto), Chalmers to Ruth Wilson, 27 Jan. 1952; Floyd Chalmers, 'Kenneth R. Wilson – Who Was He?', *Newsweekly*, 31 Aug. 1979

3 NA, Brooke Claxton Papers, v. 20, T–W correspondence 1939–41 file, Wilson to Claxton, 19 April 1941. Interviews with Chalmers and Ruth Wilson; MHP, HHC, v. 87, Wilson file, Wilson to Hunter, 11 June 1942

4 MHP, HHC, v. 75, Wartime editorial conferences file, minutes, 13 Feb. 1943. UTA, H. A. Innis Papers, v. 2, file 5, Ferguson to Innis, 30 Sept. 1942

5 Interview with Mitchell Sharp

6 Taylor Cole, *The Canadian Bureaucracy* (Durham, NC 1949), 269. Interviews with Robert Bryce, Chalmers, Louis Rasminsky, and Sharp

7 Interviews with Chalmers and Ruth Wilson

8 QUA, Clifford Clark Papers, v. 6, file M–1–7–3, McEachern to Clark, 9 March 1944; Kenneth Wilson Papers, Wilson to Chalmers, undated [1943]. *Financial Post*, 11 Sept. 1943

9 Kenneth Wilson Papers, Wilson to Chalmers, 29 Nov. 1944. Chalmers Papers, Conversations 1943 file, memo of briefing by Clark, Towers and Robertson, 26 April 1943; Arthur Irwin Papers (Victoria), *Maclean's* – Ilsley Q012 file, Wilson to Irwin, 7 and 17 Sept. 1942; MHP, HHC, v. 75, Wartime editorial conferences file, minutes, 13 Feb. 1943, and v. 87, Wilson to Chalmers, 3 Dec. 1940

10 QUA, John Deutsch Papers, v. 122, file 1532, Deutsch to Dexter, 15 Oct. 1945; QUA, William Mackintosh Papers, v. 3, file 76, memoranda on Dominion–Provincial relations, 19 Feb. and 26 July 1945

11 QUA, Charles Dunning Papers, v. 23, file 217, memorandum prepared for the Canadian Reconstruction Association by J.S. McLean, undated [1943]. MHP, HHC, v. 83, Moore file, Hunter to Moore, 23 Jan. 1947; Michael Bliss, *Northern Enterprise: Five Centuries of Canadian Business* (Toronto 1987), 456

12 Robert Bothwell and William Kilbourn, *C.D. Howe* (Toronto 1979), 177–8; Douglas Owram, *The Government Generation: Intellectuals and the State, 1900–1945* (Toronto 1986), 259

13 MHP, HHC, v. 82, McEachern file, Hunter to McEachern, 9 Oct. 1947; v. 78, Free enterprise versus socialism file, Hunter to Chalmers, 1 and 17 Nov. 1944, and Chalmers to Hunter, 16 Nov. 1944

14 Interview with Sharp; MHP, HHC, v. 87, Wilson file, Wilson to Smith, 26 Jan. 1946, and Wilson to McEachern, 7 Feb. 1949; Kenneth Wilson Papers, text of speech on government wartime organization, 30 Oct. 1946

15 MHP, HHC, v. 78, Socialism versus free enterprise file, Hunter to Chalmers, 25 Sept. 1944, and Chalmers to Hunter, 26 Sept. 1944

16 *Financial Post*, 21 April 1945. Ibid., 5 Feb. 1944

17 William Mackintosh as quoted in Ian Drummond, Robert Bothwell and John English, *Canada since 1945* (Toronto 1981), 79

18 Interviews with Douglas Abbott, James Coyne, Rasminsky, and Sharp
19 *Financial Post,* 5 Feb., 18 March and 9 Dec. 1944, and 20 Jan. and 24 March
    1945. On early Canadian suspicions of Britain's commitment to multilateral-
    ism, see L.S. Pressnell, *External Economic Policy since the War,* vol. 1: *The
    Post–War Financial Settlement* (London 1986), 203–4.
20 *Financial Post,* 17 and 24 Nov. and 15 Dec. 1945. Bruce Muirhead, 'Canadian
    Trade Policy, 1949–57: The Failure of the Anglo–European Option' (PhD
    dissertation, York University 1986), 4–5
21 *Financial Post,* 16 March 1946. Robert Cuff and J.L. Granatstein, *American
    Dollars – Canadian Prosperity* (Toronto 1978), 29; Drummond, Bothwell,
    and English, *Canada since 1945,* 81–2. On the difficulties encountered in the
    negotiations, from a British perspective, see Pressnell, *External Economic
    Policy,* 342–52
22 Paul Wonnacott, *The Canadian Dollar, 1948–1962* (Toronto 1965), 50 and 54
23 A.F.W. Plumptre, *Three Decades of Decision: Canada and the World Mone-
    tary System, 1944–75* (Toronto 1977), 76–8. For Wilson's own assessement,
    produced for popular consumption under the auspices of the Canadian Insti-
    tute of International Affairs, see Kenneth R. Wilson, 'The External Back-
    ground to Canada's Economic Problems,' in J.D. Gibson, ed., *Canada's
    Economy in a Changing World* (Toronto 1948).
24 DEA, v. 3846, file 9100–M–40, Smith to Pierce, 23 Oct. 1946
25 Ken Wilson Papers, memo to McEachern, 27 Nov. 1947
26 *Financial Post,* 1 Feb. 1947. For Towers's concerns, expressed later that
    month, see Cuff and Granatstein, *American Dollars,* 33.
27 *Financial Post,* 5 April 1947. Ibid., 1 and 15 March and 5 and 19 April 1947;
    Drummond, Bothwell and English, *Canada since 1945,* 80; Muirhead, 'Cana-
    dian Trade Policy,' 8–9
28 Muirhead, 'Canadian Trade Policy,' 8–9; Elliot Zupnick, *Britain's Postwar
    Dollar Problem* (New York 1957), 88–9
29 DEA, v. 3845, file 9100–L–40, pt. 1, Mackenzie to MacKinnon, 18 April 1947;
    Pearson to Wilgress, 16 April 1947; Wilgress to Pearson, 19 April 1947
30 On the Pierce connection, see QUA, Dexter Papers, v. 4, file 29, Freedman to
    Dexter, undated [Nov. 1946].
31 Interview with John Holmes
32 MHP, HHC, v. 87, Wilson file, Wilson to McEachern, 17 April 1947
33 DEA, v. 3845, file 9100–L–40, pt 1, memo, 8 May 1947
34 Dexter Papers, v. 4, file 30, Dexter to Victor Sifton, 3 June 1947. DF, v. 3438,
    Exchange Problem – Import Restrictions file, memo 'Notes on Import Analy-
    sis,' 20 April 1947, and v. 3970, file B–2–8–7–2–2, Gordon to Abbott, 28 May
    1947; Bryce memo to Clark, 5 June 1947, and Abbott to Gordon, 11 June 1947
35 Kenneth Wilson Papers, memos to McEachern, 4 June and 27 Nov. 1947

36 *Financial Post,* 31 May 1947. MHP, HHC, v. 78, Fraser file, memos, 30 June and 9 July 1947
37 *Financial Post,* 31 May 1947
38 Ibid., 14 June 1947
39 Ibid., 26 July 1947. DF, v. 3970, B–2–8–7–2–2, Abbott to Gordon, 11 June 1947; Kenneth Wilson Papers, memo to McEachern, 14 June 1947
40 DF, v. 3437, file E 2(f), Bryce to Clark, 27 Aug. 1947, and v. 3438, Exchange Problem–Programs file, Wrong to Pearson, 30 July 1947; Douglas Fullerton, *Graham Towers and His Times* (Toronto 1986), 231–2; and Muirhead, 'Canadian Trade Policy,' 6–7
41 *Financial Post,* 9 Aug. 1947. DF, v. 3437, file E 2(f), Clark to Bryce, 25 Aug. 1947
42 *Financial Post,* 30 Aug. 1947
43 DF, v. 3437, file E 2(f), Clark to Bryce, 25 Aug. 1947, Clark to Pearson, 1 July 1947, and LePan to Pearson, 28 June and 9 Aug. 1947
44 *Financial Post,* 30 Aug. 1947
45 DF, v. 3992, file U–3–8, Clark to Bryce, 3 Sept. 1947. Muirhead, 'Canadian Trade Policy,' 7–9 and Zupnick, *Britain's Postwar Dollar Problem,* 87–9
46 DF, v. 3437, file E 2(f), copy of an unsigned memo for Abbott, undated [late Aug. 1947]. *Financial Post,* 6 and 13 Sept. 1947
47 DF, v. 3604, file E–05, Rasminsky to Clark, 18 Sept. 1947, and v. 3992, file U–3–8, Abbott to Clark, 11 Sept. 1947
48 MHP, HHC, v. 87, Wilson file, Wilson to McEachern, 20 Aug. 1947. Interview with Bryce
49 MHP, HHC, v. 87, Wilson file, Wilson to McEachern, 12 Sept. 1947. QUA, Thomas Crerar Papers, II, v. 88, 1947 file, Howe to Crerar, 15 Sept. 1947
50 DF, v. 3992, file U–3–8, Clark to Abbott, 16 Sept. 1947. Ibid., v. 3438, Canadian Ambassador to the United States 1947 file, Wrong to Pearson, 31 May 1947, and Exchange Problem – Programs file, Wrong to Pearson, 30 July 1947
51 Ibid., v. 3438, Canadian Ambassador to the United States 1947 file, Wrong to Clark, 19 Sept. 1947. Ibid., Clark to Wrong, 24 Sept. 1947, and Clark memo, 'Outline of Discussions during Trip to Washington and New York, September 16–20, 1947,' undated
52 MHP, HHC, v. 87, Wilson file, Wilson to McEachern, undated [Sept. 1947]. DF, v. 3438, Canadian Ambassador to the United States 1947 file, Clark to Keith, 24 Sept. 1947, and file E 2(f), secret memo, 'The Dollar Problem,' undated [Sept. 1947]
53 Kenneth Wilson Papers, memo to McEachern, 27 Nov. 1947
54 MHP, HHC, v. 78, Fraser file, memo, 17 Oct. 1947
55 *Financial Post,* 27 Sept. 1947

56 Ibid., 11 Oct. 1947. Ibid., 18 Oct. 1947; and DF, v. 3970, file B–2–8–7–2–2, Towers to Abbott, 10 Oct. 1947

57 Privy Council Office, Roll T–2365, v. 11, series 16, cabinet minutes, 10, 14, and 24 Oct. 1947

58 DF, v. 3438, Exchange Problem–Programs, Clark memo (based on discussions with Deutsch, Taylor, Bryce, and Towers, 1 Oct. 1947, and file E 2(f), memo on dollar crisis, undated [Sept. 1947], and v. 3970, file B–2–8–7–2–2, Towers to Abbott, 10 Oct. 1947

59 Plumptre, *Three Decades of Decision*, table 13, 321

60 Cuff and Granatstein, *American Dollars*, 55–9; DF, v. 3438, Canadian Ambassador to the United States 1947 file, Murray memo, 'Summary of U.S.–Canada Financial Discussions, October 28–31, 1947,' undated

61 DF, v. 3610, ITO–26 file, minutes of meeting on US–UK trade negotiations breakdown, 30 Sept. 1947, and Wilgress to Beaudry, 6 Oct. 1947; v. 3438, Canadian Ambassador to the United States 1947 file, Towers to Clark, 6 Nov. 1947

62 Kenneth Wilson Papers, memo to McEachern, 27 Nov. 1947. *Financial Post*, 18 Oct. 1947; Privy Council Office, Roll T–2365, v. 11, series 16, Cabinet Minutes, 21 Oct. 1947. Drummond, Bothwell, and English, *Canada since 1945*, 82–3

63 MHP, HHC, v. 87, Wilson file, Wilson to McEachern, 19 Jan. 1948; Kenneth Wilson Papers, memo to McEachern, 27 Nov. 1947

64 *Financial Post*, 15 Nov. 1947; DF, v. 3438, file E 2(f), memo, 'The Dollar Problem,' undated [Sept.–Oct. 1947]

65 DF, v. 3610, ITO–26 file, Wilgress to Deutsch, 14 Oct. 1947. Ibid., v. 3438, Canadian Ambassador to the United States 1947 file, Wrong to Pearson, 11 Nov. 1947, and Exchange Problem–Programs file, Wrong to Clark and Moran, 10 Nov. 1947; Deutsch to Robertson, 14 Nov. 1947; Wrong to Pearson, 19 Nov. 1947; Scully to Pearson, 20 Nov. 1947

66 *Financial Post*, 22 Nov. 1947. Kenneth Wilson Papers, memo, undated [Dec. 1947]

67 Kenneth Wilson Papers, memo to McEachern, 27 Nov. 1947. Ibid., Bateman to McEachern, 25 Nov. 1947; Dunning to McEachern, 26 Nov. 1947; Turner to Wilson, 25 Oct. 1947

68 MHP, HHC, v. 87, Wilson file, Wilson to McEachern, 4 June 1948. Drummond, Bothwell, and English, *Canada since 1945*, 89–90

69 Interviews with Deacon, Sharp, and Ruth Wilson

70 MHP, HHC, v. 87, Wilson file, Wilson to McEachern, 25 Oct. 1946

71 Interviews with Bryce, Coyne, Sharp, and Rasminsky

72 Interviews with Abbott, Coyne, and Rasminsky

73 Interviews with Bryce, Coyne, and Deacon

74 Deutsch Papers, cs, v. 2, file 9, Deutsch to Farquharson, 24 Aug. 1951. Farquharson was editor of *Saturday Night*. Interviews with Coyne and Rasminsky
75 *Financial Post,* 26 Nov. 1949. This case involved the government's suppres-
   sion until after the election of the publication of an anti–combines report in a
   case involving the milling industry. The story had been leaked to Wilson by
   one of Howe's aides. Interview with Wilfred Kesterton; Kenneth Wilson Papers,
   memo to Chalmers, 15 Nov. 1945, and memo to McEachern, 16 Nov. 1945
76 Confidential interview. Interview with Coyne; Fullerton, *Towers,* 221–4
77 Interview with Deacon; MHP, HHC, v. 74, Chipman file, Chipman to Hunter,
   28 July 1950, and v. 87, Wilson file, Wilson to McEachern, 27 Jan. 1948.
   Deutsch Papers, cs, v. 2, file 9, Gibson to Deutsch, 19 Oct. 1951
78 MHP, HHC, v. 83, Moore file, Moore to Hunter, 6 July 1949, and v. 87, Wilson
   file, Wilson to McEachern, 8 Oct. 1946, 20 Sept. 1948, and 2 Oct. 1950. Management's motives were not entirely altruistic; outside earnings, which by
   1950 made up about one–quarter of Wilson's income, enabled the company to
   pay him considerably less than his reputation and ability merited. Confidential
   interviews
79 John Porter, *The Vertical Mosaic: An Analysis of Social Class and Power in
   Canada* (Toronto 1965), 431. Peter Newman, *The Canadian Establishment,*
   vol. 1 (Toronto 1979), 165–6 and 390–1
80 MHP, HHC, v. 87, Wilson file, Wilson to Hunter, 18 June 1949, and Wilson to
   McEachern, 20 Feb. 1948. Wilson's views are clearly reflected in a speech
   delivered to the New York City Chamber of Commerce, 15 Dec. 1949. On his
   and Howe's attitudes towards the Canadian business community, see Bothwell
   and Kilborn, *C.D. Howe,* 262; and MHP, HHC, v. 87, Wilson file, Wilson to
   McEachern, 2 Oct. 1950; interview with Deacon
81 Interview with Hutchison. Interviews with Coyne, Deacon, and Maurice Jefferies
82 Interview with Coyne
83 McEacheren to Brennan, 10 July 1984. Interview with Deacon; MHP, HHC,
   v. 78, Gowdy file, Gowdy to Hunter, 7 Nov. 1949; Kenneth Wilson Papers,
   Wilson to Chalmers, 15 Nov. 1945
84 Cuff and Granatstein, *American Dollars,* 63
85 MHP, v. 26, *Annual Report on Canadian Publications, 1951;* MHP, HHC, v. 87,
   Wilson file, Hunter to Wilson, 10 Oct. 1946. Some idea of the warm regard
   in which Wilson was held in Ottawa can be gauged by the outpouring of support for the establishment of a scholarship in his name at the Carleton College
   School of Journalism. Wilson had been a close friend of the dean, Wilfrid
   Eggleston, and had frequently lectured there. The list of donors read like a
   'Who's Who' of the senior civil service. Deutsch Papers, cs, v. 2, file 10,
   Deutsch to Eggleston, 3 April 1952

86 MHP, HHC, v. 68, D–J file, memo to the editors, 30 May 1946

CHAPTER 5: Blair Fraser and *Maclean's*

1 AO, MHP, HHC, v. 78, Gowdy file, advertisement, undated (1951). Ibid., v. 4,
   Minute Books, Chalmers, 11 June 1954, and Hunter, 12 June 1956. Maclean
   Publishing had officially become Maclean–Hunter in 1945.
2 Floyd Chalmers, *A Gentleman of the Press* (Toronto 1969), 150–3; Paul
   Rutherford, *The Making of the Canadian Media* (Toronto 1978), 47–8
3 Interview with Arthur Irwin; Glen Allen Papers (Toronto), research memorandum on the career of W.A. Irwin, undated [1984]
4 Interviews with Pierre Berton and Adam Marshall; Allen Papers,
   research memorandum on the career of W.A. Irwin, undated [1984];
   Chalmers, *A Gentleman of the Press*, 252
5 Interview with Irwin; Floyd Chalmers, *Both Sides of the Street: One Man's
   Life in Business and the Arts in Canada* (Toronto 1983), 181–2; MHP, HHC,
   v. 91, *Maclean's* – editorial policy file, Chalmers to Hunter, 22 Sept. 1950
6 MHP, HHC, v. 80, Irwin file, memo, 6 Jan. 1950. Interview with Irwin; Allen
   Papers, research memorandum on the career of W.A. Irwin, undated [1984];
   Elspeth Cameron, 'Once upon a time …' *Saturday Night*, Aug. 1987, 22–3;
   David Mackenzie, *Arthur Irwin: A Biography*, (Toronto 1993)
7 Douglas Owram, *The Government Generation: Intellectuals and the State*
   (Toronto 1986), 156
8 Mackenzie, *Arthur Irwin*, and MHP, v. 27, *Annual Report on Canadian Publications, 1955*. MHP, HHC, v. 73, Chalmers file, Chalmers to Hunter, 18 July
   1944
9 MHP, v. 27, *Annual Report on Canadian Publications, 1955;* v. 4, Minute
   Books, Chalmers, 12 June 1956, and Hunter, 17 May 1955, and HHC, v. 89,
   Analysis of profit and loss file, memorandum, undated [1955]. *Saturday
   Night*, a weekly and in style and content its closest Canadian–based rival,
   had roughly one–quarter the annual circulation of *Maclean's* despite the
   latter's being published only twenty-four times a year. MHP, HHC, v. 83,
   Moore file, 'Brief Presented on Behalf of the Periodical Press Association
   to the Royal Commission on National Development in the Arts, Letters and
   Sciences,' 27 Oct. 1949
10 MHP, HHC, v. 83, Moore file, memorandum of a meeting with Finance Minister
   Abbott and Deutsch, 27 Aug. 1952; v. 91, *Maclean's* – editorial policy file,
   Chalmers to Hunter, 22 Sept. 1950; Rutherford, *The Making of the Canadian
   Media*, 45–6 and 52
11 Interviews with Berton, Robert Fulford, and Marshall; Mackenzie, *Arthur
   Irwin*

12 MHP, HHC, v. 80, Irwin file, Irwin to Hunter, 23 Dec. 1949. Confidential interviews; Chalmers, *Both Sides of the Street,* 168, 182–3, and 215

13 MHP, v. 26, *Annual Report on Canadian Publications, 1945.* Ibid., HHC, v. 75, Chipman file, Hunter to Chipman, 27 March 1946

14 MHP, HHC, v. 90, Editorial policies file, quoted in Allen to Chalmers, 10 July 1950. Mackenzie, *Arthur Irwin,* and MHP, HHC, v. 90, Editorial policies file, Chalmers to Allen, 11 July 1950

15 MHP, HHC, v. 80, Irwin file, Chipman to Hunter, 21 Nov. 1947. Ibid., v. 74, Chipman file, Chipman to Hunter, 18 Oct. 1948, and v. 75, 27 Nov. 1946. Arthur Irwin Papers (Victoria), *Maclean's* – policy memos/criticisms file, Fraser to Irwin, 27 Oct. 1948; MHP, HHC, v. 74, Chipman file, Hunter to Chalmers, 19 Oct. 1948; v. 80, Irwin file, Hunter to Irwin, 26 Nov. 1947; and v. 91, *Maclean's* – editorial policy file, Hunter to Chalmers, 26 June 1950

16 Interviews with Berton and Marshall. On Allen, Mackenzie, *Arthur Irwin*; Christina McCall–Newman, *The Man from Oxbow: The Best of Ralph Allen* (Toronto 1967), 2–6 and 83–5; Peter Newman, *Home Country: People, Places and Power Politics* (Toronto 1973), 195–6

17 For instance, the very favourable assessment in Wilfrid Eggleston's 'Special Study on the Press in Canada' prepared for the Massey Commission in 1949. UBCA, Norman Mackenzie Papers, Royal Commission Correspondence, v. 3, file 4. Also Irwin Papers, *Maclean's* – letters – Hutchison, Hutchison to Irwin, 10 Oct. 1949

18 MHP, v. 26, *Annual Report on Canadian Publications,* 1952. Interview with Fulford

19 MHP, HHC, v. 91, *Maclean's* – editorial policy file, Chalmers to Hunter, 22 Sept. 1950. Interview with Berton

20 Interviews with Marjorie (Fraser) Armitage and Graham Fraser; Graham Fraser Papers (Ottawa), Joan Fraser to Graham Fraser, 27 March and 10 April 1969; John Fraser and Graham Fraser, eds., *'Blair Fraser Reports': Selections 1944–1968* (Toronto 1969), xi–xii

21 Graham Fraser Papers, John Fraser memorandum, undated. John Fraser and Graham Fraser, eds., 'Blair Fraser Reports,' xiii–xv

22 Interviews with Donald Macdonald and Charles Peters; Graham Fraser Papers, Joan Fraser to Graham Fraser, 27 March 1969; John Fraser and Graham Fraser, eds., 'Blair Fraser Reports,' xv and xvii

23 Interviews with Isabel Dobell, Irwin, Marshall, and Peters; Graham Fraser Papers, John Fraser memo, undated, and Irwin to Graham Fraser, 28 March 1969

24 Interviews with Armitage, Dobell, and Graham Fraser; NA, Blair Fraser Papers, John Hugh Fraser to Blair Fraser, 12 Jan. 1944; Ruth Wilson Papers, Blair Fraser to Mrs Wilson, 30 Jan. 1952

25 NA, J.L. Ralston Papers, v. 86, Resignation – Vining file, Vining to Moore, 30 Nov. 1944. Interviews with Dobell and Graham Fraser; Graham Fraser Papers, Irwin to Fraser, 28 March 1969; Irwin Papers, *Maclean's* – letters – Fraser file, Fraser to Irwin, 19 Dec. 1944

26 MHP, HHC, v. 80, Irwin file, Chipman to Hunter, 21 Nov. 1947. Ibid., v. 73, Chalmers file, Chalmers to Hunter, 18 July 1944. Interview with Irwin; Irwin Papers, *Maclean's* – letters – Fraser file, Fraser to Irwin, 19 Dec. 1944; MHP, HHC, v. 91, *Maclean's* – editorial policy file, Moore to Chalmers, 15 Sept. 1950

27 Interviews with Irwin and Marshall; Jean Fraser Papers (Ottawa), Irwin to Blair Fraser, 11 Dec. 1944; Mackenzie, *Arthur Irwin,* 00–0

28 Interviews with Davidson Dunton and Graham Fraser; Ralston Papers, v. 86, Resignation – Vining file, Irwin to Vining, 20 Dec. 1944

29 Interviews with Robert Bryce, Louis Rasminsky, Mitchell Sharp, and Dr Omond Solandt; Jean Fraser Papers, Ritchie to Mrs Fraser, 15 May 1968; MHP, HHC, v. 78, Fraser file, Fraser to Chalmers, 30 June 1947

30 Interviews with Dunton, Tom Earle, Fulford, and Newman

31 Interviews with Florence Bird, Earle, Fulford, and Dr A.H.U. Lovink. NA, Brooke Claxton Papers, v. 52, MacDermot (2) file, dinner party guest list, 26 March 1954, and v. 81, MacDermot file, dinner party guest list, 23 Aug. 1955; J.L. Granatstein, *The Ottawa Men: The Civil Service Mandarins, 1935–1957* (Toronto 1982), 12–14. Other journalists who formed part of the press elite: O'Leary's colleague, Norman Smith, Jr; freelance Wilfrid Eggleston; John Bird of Southams and his broadcaster wife Florence (Anne Francis) Bird; Bruce Hutchison when he was in Ottawa; and Dexter's gallery replacement, Max Freedman.

32 Interviews with Fulford and Newman

33 Interviews with Dobell, Graham Fraser, Lovink, and Solandt; Blair Fraser, *The Search for Identity* (Toronto 1967), 314–5; Graham Fraser Papers, Morse to Fraser, 12 Nov. 1969; and Jean Fraser Papers, Olson to Mrs Fraser, 20 Sept. 1968

34 MHP, v. 401, Irwin – *Maclean's* year-end conference file, undated [Dec. 1946]

35 Ibid., v. 104, Irwin – readership surveys, 1945, 1946, 1947, and 1949. The popularity of 'Backstage' had nearly doubled during Fraser's first year as its writer

36 *Maclean's,* 15 March 1946. Interview with Graham Fraser; Irwin Papers, *Maclean's* – editorial/article memos, Fraser to Young, 21 June 1945

37 *Maclean's,* 15 Oct. 1945, 15 March and 1 Nov. 1946; MHP, v. 401, Irwin–Fraser file, Fraser to Irwin, 22 Aug. 1945

38 MHP, HHC, v. 78, Fraser file, Fraser to Irwin, 26 May 1947. Interviews with Fulford and Newman

39 Interviews with Dunton, Graham Fraser, James Gray, and Macdonald. Christina McCall Newman, *Grits* (Toronto 1982), 75–6 and 98

40 Interviews with Floyd Chalmers and Marshall; MHP, HHC, v. 73, Chalmers file, Chalmers to Hunter, 18 July 1944, and v. 81, Sévigny file, Hunter to Sévigny, 15 Aug. 1942

41 MHP, HHC, v. 402, Irwin – policy file, undated [1944]. Mackenzie, *Arthur Irwin*

42 Interview with Berton. Interview with Marshall; MHP, HHC, v. 91, *Maclean's* – editorial policy file, Allen to Chalmers, 21 Sept. 1950

43 The first, a freelance piece on the impending coal crisis, had appeared in the 1 November 1943 issue. It may have served as a trial run for both writer and editor while Fraser was pondering his future at the *Gazette*

44 *Maclean's*, 1 Jan. 1944

45 Irwin Papers, *Maclean's* – letters – Fraser file, Fraser to Irwin, 10 and 18 July 1944

46 Ibid., undated [June 1944]

47 MHP, HHC, v. 79, Donald Hunter file, Horace Hunter to Mrs. Donald Hunter, 28 Aug. 1944. *Maclean's*, 15 Aug. 1944; MHP, HHC, v. 85, Sévigny file, Hunter to Sévigny, 10 Jan. 1945, and v. 402, Irwin – staff candidates file, Fraser to Irwin, 5 Aug. 1945

48 John Fraser to Brennan, 12 Sept. 1989. Interviews with Macdonald and Peters; and MHP, HHC, v. 74, Chipman file, Chipman to Hunter, 1 Nov. 1948

49 QUA, C.G. Power Papers, Ic, 6, Hutchison file, Hutchison to Power, 29 June 1951. Interviews with Graham Fraser and Fr Georges–Henri Lévesque

50 *Maclean's*, 15 May 1947

51 Interview with Lévesque

52 *Time* (Canadian edition), 16 May 1949. Stuart Keate, *Paper Boy* (Toronto 1980), 50

53 *Maclean's*, 1 July 1949. Fraser followed this up with another article of similar tone and content in *Foreign Affairs*, a prestigious American journal widely read in elite circles in Ottawa. *Foreign Affairs* 28, 2 (Jan. 1950): 247–54

54 *Maclean's*, 1 July 1949

55 Interviews with Graham Fraser and Lévesque; Michael Behiels, 'Le père Georges-Henri Lévesque et l'établissement des sciences sociales à Laval, 1938–1955,' *Revue de l'Université d'Ottawa* 52, 3 (juil.–sept. 1982): 364–5, 372–3 and 376

56 Michael Behiels, *Prelude to Quebec's Quiet Revolution: Liberalism versus Neo–Nationalism, 1945–1960* (Montreal and Kingston 1985), 34; Conrad Black, *Duplessis* (Toronto 1977), 524 and 527–9

57 Norman Mackenzie Papers, Royal Commission Series, v. 1, file 3, Ferguson to Mackenzie, 28 Nov. 1949, and Mackenzie to Ferguson, 2 Dec. 1949

58 *Maclean's*, 15 Aug. 1944

59 Interview with Lévesque
60 *Maclean's,* 1 July 1950. Interview with Lévesque
61 Apparently Murray Ballantyne, editor of *The Ensign,* the Catholic church's national English–language publication, had urged Fraser to adopt this tack. Black, *Duplessis,* 549. Interview with Lévesque
62 Interview with Lévesque
63 MHP, HHC, v. 74, Chipman file, memo, undated [July 1950]; *Time* (Canadian edition), 10 July 1950
64 François–Albert Angers, 'Deux modèles d'inconscience: Le Premier Saint-Laurent et le Commissaire Lévesque,' *L'Action Nationale* 38, 3 (nov. 1951): 207; Behiels, *Prelude to Quebec's Quiet Revolution,* n 92, 208
65 MHP, HHC, v. 74, Chipman file, memo, undated [July 1950]
66 Newman, *Home Country,* 238
67 MHP, HHC, v. 91, *Maclean's* – editorial policy file, Allen to Chalmers, 21 Sept. 1950
68 NA, Frank Underhill Papers, v. 6, *Maclean's* file, Allen to Underhill, 23 March and 17 Nov. 1955
69 McCall–Newman, *Grits,* 201

CHAPTER 6: The Department of External Affairs and the Press

1 Interview with John Holmes; J.L. Granatstein, *The Ottawa Men: The Civil Service Mandarins, 1935–1957* (Toronto 1982), chap. 3; John W. Holmes, *The Shaping of Peace: Canada and the Search for World Order, 1943–1957,* vol. 1 (Toronto 1979), 14–15 and 25–7
2 Interview with Escott Reid
3 NA, Mackenzie King Papers, Robertson to King, 2 Feb. 1944, c 230349–50. Interview with Holmes; J.L. Granatstein, *A Man of Influence: Norman Robertson and Canadian Statecraft, 1929–1968* (Ottawa 1981), 190 and 252
4 Interviews with Reid and Holmes; NA, DEA, v. 2904, file 2349–A–6–40, pt. 1, Robertson to Rae, 11 May 1944, and minutes of press conferences, various dates
5 NA, J.W. Dafoe Papers, CS, 1940–2, Richardson to Dafoe, 29 Oct. 1941
6 Hutchison also wrote for the *Vancouver Sun* and, during the 1950s, the *Financial Post.*
7 NA, Brooke Claxton Papers, v. 52, J.W. McConnell file, Claxton to McConnell, 11 Aug. 1945. Interview with Hugh Keenleyside
8 Holmes, *Shaping of Peace,* I, 28
9 Claxton Papers, v. 52, J.W. McConnell file, Claxton to McConnell, 11 Aug. 1945. Ibid., v. 66, Smith file, Claxton to Smith, 18 Nov. 1943; DF, v. 3600, file c–09 (Deutsch); CIIA *Annual Report, 1946–7*

10 Interviews with Davidson Dunton and Keenleyside; QUA, Norman Lambert Papers, Diaries, 19 April 1943

11 NA, NLFP, v. 609, *Canadian Liberal* editorial file, 1952–3, Hutchison to Kidd, 14 Dec. 1953

12 QUA, Grant Dexter Papers, v. 3, file 26, Dexter to Victor Sifton, 8 April 1944. NA, Burton Richardson Papers, v. 3, file 29, Ferguson to Richardson, 4 Oct. 1944. Interview with Carl Goldenberg; Grant Dexter, *Canada and the Building of Peace* (Toronto 1944), 137–8 and 142–3

13 Interviews with Dunton, Holmes, and A.H.U. Lovink; Blair Fraser, 'Backstage at Ottawa,' *Maclean's*, 15 April 1952; John Fraser and Graham Fraser, eds., *'Blair Fraser Reports': Selections 1944–1968* (Toronto 1969), 143

14 *Winnipeg Free Press*, 25 April 1945. Holmes, *Shaping of Peace*, vol. 1, 245; F.H. Soward and Edgar McInnis, *Canada and the United Nations* (New York 1956), 13–15

15 DEA, v. 3756, file 7391–H–40, Aylen to MacDermot and Morrison, 18 April 1945

16 Escott Reid, *On Duty: A Canadian at the Making of the United Nations, 1945–1946* (Toronto 1983), 29, 34–5, and 110. Interviews with Holmes, George Ignatieff and Reid; Richardson Papers, v. 1, file 10, Richardson to Mrs Richardson, 18 June 1945

17 NA, Lester Pearson Papers, N1 Series, v. 52, San Francisco Conference 1945 file, Pearson to Fraser, 19 May 1945. Interview with Reid

18 Richardson Papers, v. 1, file 10, Richardson to Mrs Richardson, 7 June 1945. *Winnipeg Free Press*, 25 April, 2 May and 30 June 1945

19 DEA, v. 3653, file 4697–B–40, pt 1, Andrew to MacDermot, 25 April 1946, and Tevlin to Stephens, 17 July 1945

20 *Maclean's*, 15 Sept. and 1 Oct. 1946. Claxton Papers, v. 90, Correspondence Paris 1946 (4) file, Fraser to Mrs Claxton, 22 Sept. 1946

21 Dexter Papers, v. 4, file 29, memorandum, 17 Oct. 1946

22 UCA, Bruce Hutchison Papers, 1.2.1, Dexter to Hutchison, 23 Oct. 1946. Dexter Papers, v. 4, file 29, Victor Sifton to Dexter, 19 Oct. 1946; Hutchison Papers, 1.2.1, Dexter to Hutchison, 25 Oct. 1946

23 *Winnipeg Free Press*, 5 Dec. 1946

24 Ibid., 10 and 27 Sept. and 19, 25, and 30 Oct. 1946

25 *Maclean's*, 'Backstage at Ottawa,' 15 Oct. 1946; Pearson Papers, N1 Series, v. 25, Congratulations 1946 file, Hutchison to Pearson, undated (6 Sept. 1946); *Winnipeg Free Press*, 6 Sept. 1946. Dale C. Thomson, *Louis St. Laurent: Canadian* (Toronto 1967), 216–7

26 Interview with Goldenberg. Interviews with Florence Bird, Gerald Clark, and Dunton; Richardson Papers, v. 4, file 37, Ferguson to Richardson, 25 March 1953

27 Peter Newman, *The Canadian Establishment,* vol. 1 (Toronto 1979), 394. Interviews with Bird, David Ferguson, and Goldenberg

28 Pearson Papers, NI Series, v. 32, External Affairs Department, Personnel 1946–8 file, Robertson to King, 29 Aug. 1946. Interviews with James Gray; Holmes and Claxton Papers, v. 31, Mr and Mrs Ferguson file, Claxton to Ferguson, 23 May 1946

29 Interviews with Susan Dexter, Wilfrid Eggleston, Gray and William Metcalfe; confidential interviews; Claxton Papers, v. 67, Tarr file, Tarr to Claxton, 19 July 1948

30 Claxton Papers, R–miscellaneous file, Claxton to Reid, 7 Nov. 1958; Eayrs, *In Defence of Canada,* vol. 3: *Peacemaking and Deterrence,* 13; and Denis Smith, *Diplomacy of Fear: Canada and the Cold War, 1941–1948* (Toronto 1988), 218

31 Interviews with Holmes, Ignatieff, and J.W. Pickersgill; Don Page and Don Munton, 'Canadian Images of the Cold War, 1946–7,' IJ 32, 3 (summer 1977): 509–602

32 DEA, v. 2904, file 2349–A–60 (2), MacDermot memorandum, 24 Jan. 1946, and v. 3583, file 2349–A–1–40, memorandum on press relations, 5 April 1948

33 Interviews with Holmes and Dave McIntosh; Norman Smith, 'Pearson, People, and Press,' IJ 29, 1 (winter 1973–4): 5–8

34 DEA, box 351 (acc. 84–85/019), file 10118–40, pt 1, memorandum, 'Press Relations at International Conferences,' 8 Aug. 1951. Ibid., v. 3583, file 2349–A–1–40, press conference minutes, 27 Feb. 1947

35 Confidential interviews; DEA, box 401 (acc. 84–85/019), file 11488–40, pt 1, Anderson to LePan, 29 Aug. 1951

36 Interviews with Ignatieff, Reid, and Peter Stursberg

37 DEA, box 351 (acc. 84–85/019), file 10118–40, pt. 1, memorandum, 'Press Relations at International Conferences,' 8 Aug. 1951. Ibid., Anderson memorandum, 15 March 1951

38 Ibid., v. 1062, file 9–3–0, Charpentier to Pearson, 4 Nov. 1948

39 Ibid., T.E. to Rae, 2 Nov. 1948

40 Ibid., box 351 (acc. 84–85/019), file 10118–40, pt 1), memorandum, 'Press Relations at International Conferences,' 8 Aug. 1951. Ibid., v. 1031, file 2–C, Smith to Pearson, 15 Nov. 1946

41 Interview with Paul Martin

42 DF, v. 3438, Canadian Ambassador to the U.S. 1947 file, Clark memorandum, 'Outline of discussions during trip to Washington and New York, September 16–20, 1947.' Escott Reid, *Time of Fear and Hope: The Making of the North Atlantic Treaty* (Toronto 1977), 83; Norman Smith, 'Pearson, People, and Press,' 16–17

43 Interview with Holmes; DEA, v. 3687, file 5475–R–40, Robertson to Pearson, 8 March 1946

44 DEA, v. 3687, file 5475–R–40, Robertson to Pearson, 8 March 1946; box 401 (acc. 84–85/019), file 11488–A–40, pt. 1, Anderson to Scully, 21 Feb. 1951, and file 11488–F–6–40, Dunn to Carlisle, 2 Sept. 1949

45 Claxton Papers, v. 90, Correspondence Paris 1946 (4) file, Claxton to Fraser, 2 Oct. 1946. Dexter Papers, v. 5, file 37, Hutchison to Dexter, 4 Feb. 1950; Pearson Papers, N1 Series, External Affairs Department/administration and personnel 1943–50 file, memorandum on press relations, 11 Dec. 1954

46 DEA, box 401 (acc. 84–85/019), file 11488–40, pt 1, memorandum on UN press coverage, 28 June 1951. Confidential interview; DEA, box 351 (acc. 84–85/019), file 10118–40, pt 1, Ignatieff to Reid, 15 Oct. 1947, and Reid to Farquharson, 18 Oct. 1947

47 DEA, v. 3687, file 5475–R–40, Reid to Dexter, 25 Aug. 1947, and box 351 (acc. 84–85/019), file 10118–40, pt 1, Baldwin memorandum on Canadian newspaper coverage of the ICAO conference, 5 Dec. 1947

48 Dexter Papers, v. 5, file 37, Hutchison to Dexter, 31 Jan. 1950. DEA, box 401 (acc. 84–85/019), file 11488–A–40, pt 1, Scully to Pearson, 24 April 1951, and Norman to de Thysebaert, 16 Oct. 1952

49 Reid, *Time of Fear and Hope*, 76. Interviews with Holmes, Ignatieff, and Reid; Dennis Smith, *Diplomacy of Fear* 136–8

50 Reid, *Time of Fear and Hope*, 33

51 *Winnipeg Free Press*, 12 July 1947. Holmes, *Shaping of Peace*, vol. 2, 99; John English, *Shadow of Heaven: The Life of Lester Pearson*, vol. 1: *1897–1948* (Toronto 1989), 300–1

52 *Montreal Star*, 12 July 1947. Hutchison Papers, 1.2.1, Dexter to Hutchison, 25 Oct. 1946. *Montreal Star*, 12 June 1947 and *Maclean's*, 15 Sept. 1947

53 *Winnipeg Free Press*, 20 Dec. 1947

54 *Montreal Star*, 26 Feb. 1948. *Winnipeg Free Press*, 3 March 1948. MHP, HHC, v. 78, Fraser file, memo, 1 March 1948; *Montreal Star*, 2, 17, and 19 March 1948

55 Dexter Papers, v. 5, file 32, Freedman to Dexter, 16 March 1948 and English, *Shadow of Heaven*, 320

56 *Montreal Star*, 30 April 1948. *Winnipeg Free Press*, 1 May 1948

57 Granatstein, *Ottawa Men*, 247–9

58 *Montreal Star*, 7 Oct. 1948. *Financial Post*, 24 July, 14 Aug., and 11 Sept. 1948; *Maclean's*, 1 Nov. 1948; *Montreal Star*, 27 Oct. 1948 and 17 Jan. 1949; *Winnipeg Free Press*, 26 Aug., 14 Sept., and 5 Oct. 1948

59 *Financial Post*, 1 Jan. 1949. Ibid, 5 Feb. 1949

60 Pearson Papers, N1 Series, v. 25, Congratulations 1948 file, Ferguson to Pearson, 10 Sept. 1948, and Purcell to Pearson, 13 Sept. 1948; Irwin to Pearson

and Southam to Pearson, 13 Sept. 1948, and West to Pearson, 17 Sept. 1948. *Financial Post,* 11 and 18 Sept. 1948; *Maclean's,* 'Backstage at Ottawa,' 15 Oct. 1948

61 Dexter Papers, v. 5, file 35, Hutchison memo, dated Feb. 1949. Ibid., undated [Feb. 1949] and interview with Holmes

62 *Montreal Star,* 18 March 1949. *Winnipeg Free Press,* 19 March 1949

63 Interviews with Holmes and Reid; *Canada and the United Nations,* Soward and McInnis, 69–73

64 MHP, HHC, v. 83, Moore file, Moore to Hunter, 30 Nov. 1949. Dexter Papers, v. 5, file 37, Hutchison to Dexter, 31 Jan. 1950

65 Denis Stairs, *The Diplomacy of Constraint: Canada, the Korean War, and the United States* (Toronto 1974), 31–9

66 MHP, HHC, v. 87, Wilson file, Wilson to McEachern, 20 July 1950

67 *Montreal Star,* 26, 27, 28 and 29 June 1950; *Winnipeg Free Press,* 26, 27, and 28 June and 1 July 1950

68 Dexter Papers, v. 6, file 38, Victor Sifton to Hutchison, 21 July 1950

69 *Montreal Star,* 28 July 1950. Ibid., 17 July 1950; *Winnipeg Free Press,* 17, 20, 27, 28, and 31 July 1950

70 Stairs, *Diplomacy of Constraint,* 57 and 61. Claxton Papers, v. 67, Tarr file, Claxton to Tarr, 4 Aug. 1950

71 Pearson Papers, NI Series, v. 16, E.J. Tarr file, Pearson to Tarr, undated [Aug. 1950]. *Montreal Star,* 28 July and 5 Sept. 1950; *Winnipeg Free Press,* 8 Aug. 1950

72 MHP, HHC, v. 78, Fraser file, Hunter to Allen, 17 and 19 Jan. 1951. Dexter Papers, v. 5, file 37, Hutchison to Dexter, 31 Jan. 1950; MHP, HHC, v. 83, Moore file, Moore to Hunter, 30 Nov. 1949, and v. 91, *Maclean's* – editorial policy file, Allen to Chalmers, 21 Sept. 1950

73 Interview with Holmes

74 Dexter Papers, v. 1, file 1, Hutchison to Dexter, 13 March 1952. Interviews with Victor Mackie and Richard Malone

75 Dexter Papers, v. 6, file 43, Hutchison to Dexter, 12 Feb. 1953. Ibid., v. 5, file 36, Freedman to Dexter, 15 Oct. 1949, and Hutchison to Dexter, 5 Oct. 1949

76 Ibid., v. 5, file 32, Freedman to Dexter, 16 April 1948

77 Ibid., file 37, Hutchison to Dexter, 21 Jan. 1950. Interview with Reid

78 Dexter Papers, v. 5, file 37, Hutchison to Dexter, 21 Jan. 1950. Interview with Goldenberg; Stuart Keate, *Paper Boy* (Toronto 1980), 71

79 Interviews with Holmes and Martin

80 Interviews with Holmes and Reid

81 Holmes, *Shaping of Peace,* vol. 2, 152–5; Stairs, *Diplomacy of Constraint,* 93–4, 108–9, 140, and 150–1

82 BUA, T.W.L. MacDermot Papers, M371/1–131, Ferguson to MacDermot,

6 Dec. 1950. *Financial Post,* 23 Dec. 1950 and 13 and 20 Jan. 1951; *Winnipeg Free Press,* 1, 6, and 22 Dec. 1950

83 Soward and McInnis, *Canada and the United Nations,* 133

84 *Winnipeg Free Press,* 11 Jan. 1951

85 Stairs, *Diplomacy of Constraint,* 168–74; Dennis Stairs, 'Present in Moderation: Lester Pearson and the Craft of Diplomacy,' IJ 29, 1 (winter 1973–4): 150. *Montreal Star,* 24 Jan. 1951

86 *Winnipeg Free Press,* 27 Jan. 1951. NA, Frank Underhill Papers, v. 9, *Winnipeg Free Press* file, Underhill to Dexter, 19 March 1951

87 *Montreal Star,* 8 Feb. 1951. Ibid., 5 Feb. 1951. *Maclean's,* 'Backstage at Ottawa,' 1 March 1951

88 Richardson Papers, v. 4, file 36, Ferguson to Richardson, 13 and 16 Feb. 1951

89 Ibid.

90 QUA, T.A. Crerar Papers, II, v. 88, Correspondence 1951 file, Freedman to Dexter, 23 Jan. 1951

91 Dexter Papers, v. 6, file 39, Freedman to Dexter, 3 Feb. 1951. Interview with Holmes

92 Crerar Papers, III, v. 105, Dexter 1951–9 file, Dexter to Crerar, 27 March 1951. Pearson Papers, NI Series, v. 6, Hutchison file, Hutchison to Pearson, 1 June 1951

93 Pearson Papers, NI Series, v. 6, Hutchison file, undated [Jan. 1951]

94 John Fraser to Brennan, 20 July 1984

95 Holmes, *Shaping of Peace,* vol. 2, 119

96 Interviews with Holmes, Ignatieff, and Reid

97 QUA, J.M. Macdonnell Papers, v. 6, Correspondence E–F 1954 file, Macdonnell to Fleming, 6 April 1954. NA, Arnold Heeney Papers, v. 2, Canadian ambassador to NATO correspondence 1952–3 file, Heeney to Pearson (based on conversation with Fleming), 14 Oct. 1952; Pearson Papers, N2 Series, v. 24, MacDermot file, Pearson to MacDermot, 2 June 1959; QUA, John Stevenson Papers, Outgoing correspondence 1940–58, file 3, Stevenson to Percy, 1 Dec. 1951

98 Interviews with Dunton, Keenleyside, and Stursberg

99 Interviews with Keenleyside and Martin

100 Interviews with Dunton and Keenleyside; Hutchison Papers, 1.2.1, Hutchison to Dexter, 15 Nov. 1947

101 Pearson Papers, N1 Series, v. 6, Hutchison file, Hutchison to Pearson, 21 Jan. 1953

CHAPTER 7: The Emergence of a Liberal Press Establishment

1 *Maclean's,* 22 June 1957. John Fraser to Brennan, 12 Sept. 1989

2 John Stevenson, Grattan O'Leary, George Bain, and John Bird being the most notable of these exceptions
3 QUA, Norman Lambert Papers, Diaries, 29 Nov. 1943; QUA, C.G. Power Papers, 1a, 1, Roberts to Power, 23 Sept. 1943, Power to King, 15 Oct. 1943
4 NA, H.E. Kidd Papers, v. 1, file 9, Kidd to Claxton, 19 June 1944; Reginald Whitaker, *The Government Party: Organizing and Financing the Liberal Party of Canada, 1930–1958* (Toronto 1977), 139–40, 143 and 154
5 Dalton Camp, *Gentlemen, Players and Politicians* (Toronto 1970), 7; NA, Brooke Claxton Papers, v. 31, Mr and Mrs George Ferguson file, Claxton to Mrs Ferguson, 22 Jan. 1946
6 Camp, *Gentlemen,* 7
7 NA, PCPP, v. 313, file P–2–G, Charters to Eastman, 17 March 1947
8 NA, Thomas Crerar Papers, III, v. 105, Dexter 1940–1950 file, Dexter to Crerar, 24 Feb. 1948; QUA, Grant Dexter Papers, v. 5, file 33, Lambert to Dexter, 20 June 1948; Power Papers, 1e, 24, *Winnipeg Free Press* articles 1948 file, Dexter to Power, 29 March 1948
9 Dexter Papers, v. 4, file 30, Dexter to Victor Sifton, 30 May 1947; Power Papers, 1e, 18, National Liberal Convention 1948 file, Power to Dexter, 27 April 1948
10 Power Papers, 1b, 2, General Correspondence file, Power to Armour, 21 Feb. 1956
11 UCA, Bruce Hutchison Papers, 1.2.1, Hutchison to Dexter, undated [Nov. 1947]. Lambert Papers, General Correspondence, 1923–65, file 2, Lambert to Mackenzie, 28 Feb. 1947. Claxton Papers, v. 122, Prime Minister's file (2), Claxton to King, 8 Jan. 1947; Kidd Papers, v. 1, file 13, Kidd to Wright, 14 June 1948
12 *Winnipeg Free Press,* 3 and 9 Aug. 1948
13 *Maclean's,* 1 Aug. 1948; ibid., 'Backstage at Ottawa,' 15 Sept. 1948
14 *Financial Post,* 18 Aug. 1948
15 NA, Burton Richardson Papers, v. 4, file 34, Ferguson to Richardson, 1 July 1948. *Montreal Star,* 4 and 9 Aug. 1948
16 PCPP, v. 313, file P–2–G, McCloskey to Trimble, 4 Nov. 1947
17 *Maclean's,* 'Backstage at Ottawa,' 1 Aug. 1947. *Montreal Star,* 11 Sept. and 26 Oct. 1948; NA, Lester Pearson Papers, N1 Series, v. 25, Congratulations 1948 file, Hunter to Pearson, Irwin to Pearson, and Southam to Pearson, 13 Sept. 1948, and West to Pearson, 17 Sept. 1948
18 PCPP, v. 306, file M–5–G, Charters to Macdonnell, 24 Sept. 1948
19 Ibid., v. 313, file P–2–G, Gazley to Homuth, 5 Jan. 1948. The best analysis of the Conservatives' internal leadership problems and the impact this had on their public image and press relations is M. Ann Capling, 'Political Leader-

ship in Opposition: The Conservative Party of Canada, 1920–1948' (PhD dissertation, University of Toronto 1991).

20 NA, Blair Fraser Papers, Fraser to Jean Fraser, undated [Sept. 1948]. John Kendle, *John Bracken: A Political Biography* (Toronto 1979), 222, 229, and 233

21 *Maclean's*, 1 Sept. 1948

22 *Winnipeg Free Press*, 4 Oct. 1948

23 Camp, *Gentleman*, 170; J.W. Pickersgill, *My Years With Louis St. Laurent: A Political Memoir* (Toronto 1975), 86; and Whitaker, *The Government Party*, 237

24 Claxton Papers, v. 155, 1949 Election Correspondence file (20), Claxton to Dexter, 17 May 1949 and 1949, Election – Dexter file, Claxton to Dexter, 12 May 1949; Dexter Papers, v. 5, file 35, Hutchison to Dexter, undated [Feb.–March 1949]

25 *Winnipeg Free Press*, 21 June 1949

26 *Montreal Star*, 24 June 1949

27 *Maclean's*, 'Backstage at Ottawa,' 1 June 1949

28 *Winnipeg Free Press*, 29 June 1949. *Montreal Star*, 28 June 1949

29 Interview with Peter Newman. *Financial Post*, 2 July 1949; NA, Clifford Sifton, Jr Papers, v. 4, Victor Sifton June–Dec. 1945 file, Clifford to Victor Sifton, 4 July 1945

30 QUA, J.M. Macdonnell Papers, v. 44, PC Party public relations file, memorandum on public relations, undated [late 1948]

31 Clifford Sifton, Jr Papers, v. 6, Victor Sifton 1949 file, Clifford to Victor Sifton, 7 March 1949

32 Macdonnell Papers, v. 44, PC Party public relations file, memorandum on public relations, undated [late 1948]

33 Quoted in Pickersgill, *My Years*, 75. Interview with Paul Martin; Fleming, *So Very Near* (Toronto, 1985), vol. 1, 172; Grattan O'Leary, *Recollections of People, Press and Politics* (Toronto 1977), 102; *Ottawa Evening Citizen*, 4 Oct. 1948; Pickersgill, *My Years*, 75–6

34 Interviews with David Ferguson, Newman, and Peter Stursberg

35 PCPP, v. 310, file N–5–G, Nowlan to Kidd, 23 July 1951. Margaret Conrad, *George Nowlan: Maritime Conservative in National Politics* (Toronto 1986), 106–7 and 133–4

36 Interview with Edgar Collard; Conrad, *Nowlan*, 107

37 PCPP, v. 310, file N–5–G, Kidd to Nowlan, 8 March 1951

38 Interviews with Pierre Berton and Stursberg

39 NLFP, v. 636, Newspapers: dailies and weeklies file, Kidd to Donnelly, 11 Dec. 1956; v. 615, *Liberal News of Canada* – Claude Sanagan (editor) file, Sanagan to Kidd, 31 Jan. 1949, and v. 623, Prime Minister's Office 1951–2 file, Kidd

to Martin, 5 Aug. 1952; Whitaker, *The Government Party*, 156, 191, and 205
40 NLFP, v. 613, Dexter file, Kidd to Fogo, 6 Sept. 1948; v. 646, Newspapers: dailies and weeklies file, memo, undated
41 *Maclean's,* 'Backstage at Ottawa,' 1 Sept. 1950. Interviews with George Ignatieff, Martin, and J.W. Pickersgill; Camp, *Gentlemen,* 137
42 Interview with Eugene Griffin. Interview with Pickersgill; Dexter Papers, v. 5, file 37, Hutchison to Dexter, 2 Feb. 1950; and I. Norman Smith, *A Reporter Reports* (Toronto 1954), 21–3
43 Dexter Papers, v. 5, file 37, Hutchison to Dexter, 2 Feb. 1950. Interview with Gerald Waring
44 Interviews with Douglas Abbott, Robert Bryce, Paul Martin, and Newman; QUA, John Deutsch Papers, Personal Correspondence, v. 2, file 13, Fortier to Deutsch; and Peter Dempson, *Assignment Ottawa: Seventeen Years in the Press Gallery* (Toronto 1968), 29–30
45 Interviews with Abbott and Davidson Dunton
46 Interviews with Fraser MacDougall and Dave McIntosh; Richardson Papers, v. 4, file 39, Campbell to Richardson, 3 Feb. 1955
47 Interviews with Abbott, Bryce, Wilfrid Eggleston, Arthur Irwin, and Victor Mackie
48 Hutchison Papers, 1.2.3, Hutchison to Dexter, undated [Oct. 1955] and NLFP, v. 609, *The Canadian Liberal* editorial 1950–1 file, Jefferies to Munro, 7 April 1950
49 Claxton Papers, v. 44, Kidd file, Kidd to Claxton, 5 Feb. 1948; NLFP, v. 613, Dexter file, Kidd to Fogo, 6 Sept. 1948
50 NLFP, v. 615, *Liberal News of Canada* – Sanagan file, Sanagan to Kidd, 17 Feb. 1949. Claxton Papers, v. 60, National Liberal Federation (1) file, Fogo to Claxton, 23 Feb. 1949; NLFP, v. 618, Pickersgill file, Kidd to Pickersgill, 17 July 1953
51 Dexter Papers, v. 7, file 44, memo, 27 May 1954. NLFP, v. 616, Claxton file, memorandum, undated [May 1950], and v. 619, Winters file, Kidd to Winters, 30 Sept. 1952
52 Crerar Papers, II, v. 88, Correspondence 1952 file, Freedman to Hutchison, 6 Jan. 1952; Dexter Papers, v. 6, file 41, Hutchison to Dexter, 23 Jan. 1952; and Hutchison Papers, 2.1.6, Power to Hutchison, 21 May 1951
53 Dexter Papers, v. 6, file 43, Hutchison memorandum, 1 March 1953. Power Papers, 1c, 6, Hutchison file, Hutchison to Power, 1 April 1952
54 BUA, Terrence MacDermot Papers, M 371/1–131, Ferguson to MacDermot, 1 March 1952
55 *Maclean's,* 'Backstage at Ottawa,' 1 June 1949 and 15 July 1950
56 MacDermot Papers, M 371/1–131, Ferguson to MacDermot, 17 June 1953. NLFP, v. 616, Claxton file, Kidd to Claxton, 6 July 1953

57 NA, Arnold Heeney Papers, v. 2, Ambassador to the United States – Correspondence 1953–7 file, Barkway to Heeney, 14 June 1953
58 NLFP, v. 609, *The Canadian Liberal* editorial policy, 1952–3 file, Hutchison to Kidd, 8 Dec. 1952
59 Dexter Papers, v. 6, file 43, Hutchison to Dexter, 3 June 1953. Heeney Papers, v. 2, Ambassador to the United States – Correspondence 1953–7 file, Hutchison to Heeney, 25 June 1953
60 Arthur Irwin Papers (Victoria), *Maclean's* – letters – Hutchison file, Hutchison to Irwin, undated [1953]
61 MacDermot Papers, M 371/1–131, Ferguson to MacDermot, 12 July 1953. *Financial Post*, 3 July 1953
62 MacDermot Papers, M 371/1–131, Ferguson to MacDermot, 1 March 1953. Heeney Papers, v. 1, NATO Ambassadorship, congratulations 1952 file, Ferguson to Heeney, 19 March 1952
63 *Maclean's,* 'Backstage at Ottawa,' 1 Aug. 1953. Interview with Isabel Dobell
64 *Maclean's,* 15 Aug. 1953
65 Camp, *Gentlemen,* 137 and 209. Macdonnell Papers, v. 6, Correspondence J–M 1954 file, 20 Feb. 1954
66 *Financial Post,* 15 Aug. 1953; Bruce Hutchison, 'Is the Two-Party System Doomed?' *Maclean's,* 15 Oct. 1953; *Maclean's,* 'Backstage at Ottawa,' 1 Oct. 1953; and *Montreal Star,* 11 Aug. 1953
67 NLFP, v. 616, Claxton file, Claxton to Kidd, 18 July 1953
68 Ibid., v. 636, Minister of Finance 1954 file, Kidd to Harris, 23 Feb. 1955
69 Crerar Papers, III, v. 117, Hutchison 1941–64 file, Crerar to Hutchison, 24 Jan. 1956. Ibid., v. 120, Lambert 1946–65 file, Lambert to Crerar, 18 July 1955; Hutchison Papers, 1.2.3, Hutchison to Dexter, 6 June 1955
70 Hutchison Papers, 1.2.3, Hutchison to Dexter, 1 July 1955
71 *Financial Post,* 23 July 1955. Ibid., 18 June and 13 Aug. 1955
72 *Winnipeg Free Press,* 11 July 1955
73 *Montreal Star,* 7 July 1955
74 Crerar Papers, II, v. 89, Correspondence 1955 file, Ferguson to Crerar, 27 July 1955
75 *Maclean's,* 'Backstage at Ottawa,' 20 Aug. 1955. NLFP, v. 633, Minister of Citizenship and Immigration file, Kidd to Pickersgill, 13 Aug. 1954
76 PCPP, v. 309, file M–5–G, Clark to Macdonnell, 28 June 1955. Conrad, *Nowlan,* 166–7; NA, Frank Underhill Papers, v. 6, Macdonnell file, Macdonnell to Underhill, 13 July 1955
77 Interviews with Maurice Jefferies, Mackie, and McIntosh
78 Hutchison Papers, 1.2.3, Hutchison to Dexter, undated [Dec. 1955]
79 Charles Ritchie, *Diplomatic Passport: More Undiplomatic Diaries, 1946–1962* (Toronto 1981), entry for 22 April 1956, 107–8. The publication

in 1955 in *Queen's Quarterly* of J.E. Hodgetts's article 'The Liberal and the Bureaucrat,' sharply critical of the relationship that had evolved between the Liberals and the mandarins, offered further evidence that such doubts were becoming more widespread in intellectual circles.

80 Crerar Papers, II, v. 89, Correspondence 1956 file, Howe to Crerar, 21 March 1956. NA, Alexander Hume Papers, Diaries, 23 March 1956
81 Crerar Papers, II, v. 89, Correspondence 1956, Crerar to Mr and Mrs Naylor, 11 May 1956
82 *Financial Post*, 19 May 1956. Interviews with Paul Deacon and Mackie
83 *Winnipeg Free Press*, 9 and 15 May 1956. *Montreal Star*, 16 May 1956
84 Interviews with Eggleston and Martin; Macdonnell Papers, v. 60, Recollections file, memo, undated, 28; Peter C. Newman, *Renegade in Power: The Diefenbaker Years* (Toronto 1963), 34–5
85 Interviews with Florence Bird, Jefferies, and McIntosh
86 Interviews with Alice Dexter, Tom Earle, Newman, and Mitchell Sharp
87 Crerar Papers, II, v. 89, Correspondence 1956 file, Sifton to Crerar, 13 June 1956
88 *Winnipeg Free Press*, 25 May 1956
89 *Montreal Star*, 29 May 1956. Interviews with Gerald Clark and David Ferguson; *Montreal Star*, 2 June 1956
90 *Financial Post*, 2 June 1956. Ibid., 9 and 16 June 1956
91 John Bird, 'When the Liberals Lost the Press,' *Canadian Commentator* 1, 6 (June 1956): 3
92 *Winnipeg Free Press*, 4 June 1956. *Montreal Star*, 4 June 1956
93 Richardson Papers, v. 4, file 40, Ferguson to Richardson, 13 July 1956. *Montreal Star*, 6 June 1956
94 Crerar Papers, Additions, v. 199, Correspondence transcripts 1936–75 file, Crerar to Mr and Mrs Naylor, 15 June 1956; Paul Martin, *A Very Public Life*, vol. 2, *So Many Worlds* (Ottawa 1985), 289
95 *Winnipeg Free Press*, 5 June 1956
96 *Maclean's*, 7 July 1956. Interview with Berton
97 John Fraser to Brennan, 12 Sept. 1989. Interviews with Dunton and Newman
98 *Maclean's*, 'Backstage at Ottawa,' 7 July 1956
99 Camp, *Gentlemen*, 201–4; PCPP, v. 429, Research reports 51–54 file, Report 54, 'Parliament and the Trans–Canada Pipeline,' 31 July 1956; Richardson Papers, v. 4, file 40, Richardson to Nicholson, 29 May 1956
100 Interviews with Robert Fulford, Mackie, Newman, and Waring
101 Whitaker, *The Government Party*, 209
102 *Financial Post*, 29 Dec. 1956
103 *Maclean's*, 'Backstage at Ottawa,' 23 June, 18 Aug., and 15 Sept. 1956. Heeney Papers, v. 3, Diaries, 28 Nov. 1956

104 NLFP, v. 640, Election statistics 1957 file, memorandum 'Liberal Organization in the 1957 Campaign,' undated; Power Papers, IC, 7, Meisel file, draft of Power to Meisel, undated [1959]

105 Claxton Papers, v. 81, MacDermot file, Claxton to MacDermot, 3 July 1957. John Meisel, *The Canadian General Election of 1957* (Toronto 1962), 38–9, 158, and 165–6

106 Camp, *Gentlemen*, 271; Claxton Papers, v. 77, Gordon file, Claxton to Gordon, 20 March 1957

107 *Financial Post*, 22 Dec. 1956, and 30 March, 4 and 11 May 1957; Macdonnell Papers, v. 7, Hutchison correspondence 1957 file, Hutchison to Macdonnell, 27 Feb. 1957

108 *Financial Post*, 13 April 1957

109 Meisel, *Canadian General Election*, 155–6 and 181–7; Newman, *Renegade in Power*, 49–55; and Whitaker, *The Government Party*, 248–51

110 *Winnipeg Free Press*, 27 May 1957

111 Power Papers, IC, 6, Hutchison file, Hutchison to Power, 4 June 1957. Ibid., 14 May 1957. *Financial Post*, 25 May 1957; *Winnipeg Free Press*, 21 May 1957

112 *Winnipeg Free Press*, 29 May 1957. Crerar Papers, III, v. 105, Dexter 1948–61 file, Dexter to Crerar, 23 May 1957

113 QUA, J.A. Corry Papers, Series I, Additions, v. 2, Correspondence May–December 1957 file 24, Ferguson to Corry, 25 Aug. 1957. *Montreal Star*, 1 and 8 June 1957

114 *Financial Post*, 8 June 1957

115 *Winnipeg Free Press*, 3 June 1957

116 *Maclean's*, 'Backstage at Ottawa,' 8 June 1957. Interviews with Berton and Graham Fraser

117 The final opinion poll, taken on 7 June, three days before the vote, gave the Liberals a six-point lead. Newman, *Renegade in Power*, 56. Interviews with Jefferies, Pickersgill, and Escott Reid; Hume Papers, Diaries, 31 May 1957

118 *Maclean's*, 'Backstage at Ottawa,' 6 July 1957

119 PCPP, v. 347, Newspapers 1957–9 file, Davey to Grosart, 10 July 1957

120 Corry Papers, I, Additions, v. 2, Correspondence May–December 1957 file 24, Ferguson to Corry, 25 Aug. 1957. Interview with Ferguson

121 *Montreal Star*, 17 Aug. 1957. Power Papers, IC, 5, Crerar file, Power to Crerar, 14 June 1957

122 Hutchison Papers, 1.2.4, Hutchison to Dexter, 12 Dec. 1957. *Financial Post*, 6 July 1957

123 Crerar Papers, III, v. 105, Dexter 1948–61 file, Dexter to Crerar, 5 Sept. 1957

124 *Montreal Star*, 2 Oct. 1957. *Maclean's*, 'Backstage at Ottawa,' 17 Aug. 1957. *Financial Post*, 29 Dec. 1956

125 Stuart Keate, *Paper Boy* (Toronto 1980), 197; Power Papers, 1c, 6, Hutchison file, Power to Hutchison, 9 June 1958
126 Dexter Papers, v. 7, file 46, Dexter to Kent, 9 Oct. 1957. Thomas Kent, *A Public Purpose: An Experience of Liberal Opposition and Canadian Government* (Montreal and Kingston 1988), 47–8
127 *Financial Post*, 30 Nov. 1957; *Maclean's*, 'Backstage at Ottawa,' 17 Aug. 1957. Interviews with Dr Carl Goldenberg and Martin; Hutchison Papers, 1.2.3, Hutchison to Dexter, 8 Nov. 1957, and 1.2.4, 12 Nov., 12 Dec. 1957, and undated [late 1957]
128 Hutchison Papers, 1.2.4, 12 Dec. 1957. Power Papers, IV, 86, Memoirs – transcripts (2), Meisel interview, 17 May 1960
129 *Winnipeg Free Press*, 17 Jan. 1958
130 *Financial Post*, 25 Jan. 1958. Richardson Papers, v. 4, file 42, Ferguson to Richardson, 24 Jan. 1958; *Montreal Star*, 11 and 17 Jan. 1958
131 Dexter Papers, v. 6, file 43, Dexter to Victor Sifton, 22 May 1953
132 *Montreal Star*, 22 Jan. 1958. *Financial Post*, 25 Jan. 1958. *Winnipeg Free Press*, 21 Jan. 1958
133 Hutchison Papers, 1.2.4, Hutchison to Dexter, 3 March 1958. *Maclean's*, 'Backstage at Ottawa,' 29 March 1958; Richardson Papers, v. 4, file 42, Richardson to Agnew, 3 March 1958
134 Crerar Papers, II, v. 89, Correspondence 1958 file, Dexter to Crerar, 19 March 1958
135 Newman, *Renegade in Power*, 70–5. Interviews with Abbott and Bryce; Richardson Papers, v. 4, file 42, Richardson to Agnew, 3 March 1958
136 *Maclean's*, 'Backstage at Ottawa,' 15 Feb. and 1 March 1958. *Financial Post*, 8 Feb. 1958
137 *Montreal Star*, 21 March 1958
138 Interview with Reid
139 Interviews with Fulford, Goldenberg, Ben Malkin, and Newman
140 *Toronto Telegram*, 27 Jan. 1970
141 Claxton Papers, v. 77, H–miscellaneous file, Harris to Claxton, 30 Nov. 1955; NLFP, v. 613, Dexter file, Kidd to Fogo, 6 Sept. 1948. Paul W. Rutherford, *The Making of the Canadian Media* (Toronto 1978), 125; Whitaker, 200

CONCLUSION: A Responsible, Civilized Relationship

1 UCA, Bruce Hutchison Papers, 1.2.4, Hutchison to Dexter, undated [late 1957]. Interview with Maurice Jefferies; Frank Underhill, 'If Our Politics Are Dull – Blame Our Dull Press,' *Maclean's*, 27 Feb. 1960, 50 and 52
2 The statistics are for the period 1947–57. Wilfred Kesterton, 'The Growth of the Newspaper in Canada,' in Benjamin D. Singer, ed., *Communication in*

Canadian Society (Toronto 1983), 9, and *A History of Canadian Journalism* (Toronto 1978), 69–71; Paul Rutherford, *The Making of the Canadian Media* (Toronto 1978), 38 and 64

3 NA, Frank Underhill Papers, v. 8, *Winnipeg Free Press* file, Underhill to Kent, 23 Aug. 1956. A Gallup poll taken in December 1946 asking Canadians which of the media they relied on most in forming their opinions on political matters ranked newspapers and magazines at 48.2 per cent (newspapers alone stood at 36.6 per cent) and radio at 30.0 per cent. NA, Clifford Sifton, Jr Papers, v. 5, Victor Sifton May–Dec. 1947 file, Clifford to Victor Sifton, 9 Sept. 1947

4 NA, NLFP, v. 623, Prime Minister's Office 1951–2 file, Kidd to W. Ross Martin, 1 Oct. 1952. NA, Brooke Claxton Papers, v. 77, H–misc. file, Harris to Claxton, 30 Nov. 1955, and Claxton to Harris, 1 Dec. 1955

5 Interviews with Jefferies and Escott Reid

6 QUA, Grant Dexter Papers, v. 5, file 37, Hutchison to Dexter, 2 Feb. 1950

7 Interviews with Arthur Irwin and Jefferies; UBCA, Norman Mackenzie Papers, Royal Commission on Arts, Letters and Sciences Correspondence, v. 3, file 4, Wilfrid Eggleston, 'Special Study on the Press in Canada,' undated [1949]

8 NA, Burton Richardson Papers, v. 1, file 10, Burton to Wanda Richardson, 11 June 1945; Anthony Westell, 'The Press: Adversary or Channel of Communication?' in Harold D. Clarke et al., eds., *Parliament, Policy and Representation* (Toronto 1980), 25

9 Interview with Edgar Collard

10 Hutchison Papers, 2.1.3, Garson to Hutchison, 11 Feb. 1955; Norman Mackenzie Papers, Main Correspondence, v. 32, file 4, Mackenzie to Claxton, 3 May 1954

11 Dexter Papers, v. 6, file 38, Hutchison to Dexter, 17 Oct. 1950, and file 40, 1 May 1951

12 Interview with Carl Goldenberg

13 Charles Lynch, *You Can't Print That: Memoirs of a Political Voyeur* (Edmonton 1983), 244. Dexter Papers, v. 6, file 42, Hutchison to Dexter, 5 Nov. 1952; Wilfrid Eggleston, 'Leaves from a Pressman's Log,' QQ 63, 4 (Winter 1957): 563–4

14 Interviews with Douglas Abbott and Collard

15 J.E. Hodgetts, 'The Liberal and the Bureaucrat,' QQ 62, 2 (summer 1955): 182–3. QUA, T.A. Crerar Papers, II, v. 88, Correspondence 1949 file, Tarr to Crerar, 28 Oct. 1949; Dexter Papers, v. 3, file 27, memo, 1 March 1945, and v. 5, file 37, Hutchison to Dexter, 3 Feb. 1950; *Financial Post,* 3 Jan. 1953; Christina McCall–Newman, *Grits: An Intimate Portrait of the Liberal Party* (Toronto 1982), 193–4 and 197–203; and *Montreal Star,* 20 Jan. 1949 and 29 Dec. 1952

16 J.L. Granatstein, *The Ottawa Men: The Civil Service Mandarins, 1935–1957* (Toronto 1982), xi. Interviews with Pierre Berton and James Coyne

17 Quoted in J.E. Hodgetts, 'The Civil Service and Policy Formation,' CJEPS 23, 4 (Nov. 1957): 467. Interviews with Berton, Coyne, and David Ferguson

18 John Diefenbaker, *One Canada: Memoirs of the Rt Hon. J.G. Diefenbaker: The Crusading Years, 1895-1956* (Toronto 1975), 278

19 Interviews with Wilfrid Eggleston and Victor Mackie; NA, Arthur Meighen Papers, Forsey to Meighen, 20 Oct. 1952, 146011; and NLFP, v. 627, *Canadian Liberal* editorial file, Kidd to Kelly, 7 Dec. 1955

20 Richardson Papers, v. 5, file 47, Ferguson to Richardson, 21 Dec. 1961

21 QUA, C.G. Power Papers, IC, 6, Hutchison file, Hutchison to Power, 26 May 1952. Interview with Susan Dexter; Hutchison Papers, 2.1.1, Bassett to Hutchison, 5 Dec. 1952

22 Hutchison Papers, 1.2.4, Hutchison to Dexter, 18 Feb. 1958

23 Crerar Papers, III, v. 105, Dexter 1948-61 file, Dexter to Crerar, 18 Sept. 1960; Hutchison Papers, 1.2.4, Hutchison to Dexter, 24 Feb. 1958

24 Hutchison Papers, 1.2.4, Hutchison to Dexter, undated [April 1958]

25 Richardson Papers, v. 4, file 36, Ferguson to Richardson, 29 March 1951

26 Confidential interview. Interviews with Gerald Clark and Ferguson; NLFP, v. 596, Fogo – President of the NLF file, McLean to Fogo, 22 Sept. 1948

27 Interviews with Clark, Goldenberg, and John Holmes

28 Interview with Ferguson; UTA, Harold Innis Papers, v. 4, file 5, Ferguson to Innis, 20 March 1949

29 Dexter Papers, v. 10, file 11, Freedman to Dexter, 8 Jan. 1952. Interviews with Floyd Chalmers, Paul Deacon, Louis Rasminsky, and Mitchell Sharp

30 This pro-Liberal quality was clear enough to *Maclean's* associate editor Pierre Berton, who occasionally had Fraser rewrite portions of 'Backstage' columns. Ever the professional, Fraser never balked at these requests. Interview with Berton. Graham Fraser Papers (Ottawa), memo, 4 Feb. 1969. Interviews with Robert Fulford, Irwin, David McIntosh, and Peter Newman

31 Interviews with Davidson Dunton, Tom Earle, Fulford, and Newman

32 Richardson Papers, v. 4, file 40, Richardson to Bassett, undated. Graham Fraser Papers, Fulford to Fraser, 7 Nov. 1977; Norman Mackenzie Papers, Main Correspondence, v. 32, file 4, Mackenzie to Claxton, 3 May 1954

33 Dalton Camp, *Gentlemen, Players and Politicians* (Toronto 1970), 232

34 Reginald Whitaker, *The Government Party: Organizing and Financing the Liberal Party of Canada, 1930-58* (Toronto 1977), 166-7

35 Interviews with Berton, Fulford, and Adam Marshall; Wilfrid Eggleston, *While I Still Remember: A Personal Record* (Toronto 1968), 563-4; and Robert Fulford, 'The Press in the Community,' in D.L.B. Hamlin, ed., *The Press and the Public* (Toronto 1962), 27

36 On the shift to 'critical style' journalism, see Geoffrey Stevens, 'The Influence and Responsibilities of the Media in the Legislative Process,' in W.A.W.

Neilson and J.C. Macpherson, eds., *The Legislative Process in Canada: The Need for* Reform (Montreal 1978), 235; David Taras, *The Newsmakers: The Media's Influence on Canadian Politics* (Toronto 1990), 53–65; and Anthony Westell, 'Reporting the Nation's Business,' in G. Stuart Adam, ed., *Journalism, Communication and the Law* (Toronto 1976), 67

37 NLFP, v. 646, Newspapers – daily and weekly file, Kidd to Fraser, 5 June 1959

Bibliography

PRIMARY SOURCES

Archival Sources

Archives of Ontario, Toronto (AO)
Maclean-Hunter Papers

Bishop's University Archives, Lennoxville (BUA)
T.W.L. MacDermot Papers

National Archives of Canada, Ottawa (NA)
Douglas Abbott Papers
Florence Bird Papers
John Bird Papers
Brooke Claxton Papers
J.W. Dafoe Papers
Blair Fraser Papers
Gordon Graydon Papers
Arnold Heeney Papers
C.D. Howe Papers
Alexander Hume Papers
Robert Inch Papers
H.E. Kidd Papers
Mackenzie King Papers
Ian Mackenzie Papers
Paul Martin Papers
Arthur Meighen Papers

National Liberal Federation Papers
Progressive Conservative Party Papers
Raleigh Parkin Papers
Lester Pearson Papers
J.L. Ralston Papers
Burton Richardson Papers
Norman Robertson Papers
Frank Scott Papers
Clifford Sifton, Jr Papers
Sir Clifford Sifton Papers
John Stevenson Papers
Frank Underhill Papers
Sir John Willison Papers
Department of External Affairs Records
Department of Finance Records
Department of Munitions and Supply Records
Department of Trade and Commerce Records
Privy Council Office Records
Wartime Information Board Records

Queen's University Archives, Kingston (QUA)
Clifford Clark Papers
J.A. Corry Papers
T.A. Crerar Papers
John Deutsch Papers
Grant Dexter Papers
Charles Dunning Papers
Donald Gordon Papers
Norman Lambert Papers
J.M. Macdonnell Papers
W.A. Mackintosh Papers
C.G. Power Papers
Norman Rogers Papers

University of British Columbia Archives, Vancouver (UBCA)
Norman Mackenzie Papers
Alan Plaunt Papers

University of Calgary Archives, Calgary (UCA)
Bruce Hutchison Papers

University of Toronto Archives, Toronto (UTA)
H.A. Innis Papers

Private Collections
Glen Allen Papers, Ottawa
Floyd Chalmers Papers, Toronto
Wilfrid Eggleston Papers, Ottawa
George Ferguson Papers, Toronto
Jean Fraser Papers, Ottawa
Eugene Griffin Papers, Ottawa
Arthur Irwin Papers, Victoria
Kenneth Wilson Papers, Toronto
Ruth Wilson Papers, Toronto

Interviews

Ablett, Jack. Winnipeg, 11 Oct. 1984
Abbott, The Hon. Douglas. Ottawa, 11 May 1984
Armitage, Majorie (Fraser). Ottawa, 7 Nov. 1984
Bird, Sen. Florence. Ottawa, 10 May 1984 and 15 July 1990
Bryce, R.B. Ottawa, 9 March 1984
Campbell, Douglas. Winnipeg, 10 Oct. 1984
Chalmers, Floyd. Toronto, 23 Nov. 1983
Clark, Gerald. Montreal, 7 Aug. 1985
Collard, Edgar. Ottawa, 13 Aug. 1985
Coolican, Denis. Ottawa, 19 July 1990
Coyne, James. Winnipeg, 10 Oct. 1984
Deacon, Paul. Ottawa, 8 Nov. 1985
Deutsch, Stephanie. Kingston, 18 May 1985
Dexter, Alice. Ottawa, 17 Nov. 1983 and 10 Sept. 1984
Dexter, Susan. Toronto, 3 June 1986 and 8 July 1989
Dobell, Isabel. Montreal, 21 May 1986 and 10 Nov. 1990
Drury, The Hon. C.M. Ottawa, 25 June 1984
Dunton, Davidson. Ottawa, 28 June 1984
Earle, Thomas. Ottawa, 14 Feb. 1984
Eggleston, Wilfrid. Ottawa, 19 Oct. 1983
Ferguson, David. Toronto, 6 April 1985 and 10 July 1989
Fisher, Douglas. Ottawa, 15 June 1990
Fraser, Graham. Quebec City, 15 and 16 March 1984, and Ottawa, 22 June 1990
Fraser, Jean. Ottawa, 25 June 1984
Fraser, John. Ottawa, 3 June 1990
Fraser, Norman. 9 Nov. 1990
Freedman, Justice Samuel. Winnipeg, 11 Oct. 1984
Fulford, Robert. Toronto, 10 July 1985

Fullerton, Douglas. Ottawa, 15 June 1990
Goldenberg, Carl. Montreal, 3 Aug. 1984
Gray, James. Calgary, 4 and 7 June 1985
Griffin, Eugene. Ottawa, 14 Feb. 1985
Handy, Edouard. Ottawa, 26 June 1984
Holmes, John. Toronto, 3 May 1985
Hutchison, Bruce. Shawnigan Lake, BC, 21 Aug. 1984
Ignatieff, George. Toronto, 24 April 1985
Irwin, Arthur. Victoria, 20 Aug. 1984 and 9 Nov. 1989
Jefferies, Maurice. Ottawa, 15 Feb. 1984
Keenleyside, Hugh. Victoria, 18 Aug. 1984
Kesterton, Wilfred. Ottawa, 15 Feb. 1984
Lévesque, Père Georges-Henri. Montreal, 30 April 1985
Lovink, A.H.U. Ottawa, 7 Nov. 1984
Macdonald, Donald S. Toronto, 31 Oct. 1985
MacDougall, Fraser. Ottawa, 1 Dec. 1984
Mackie, Victor. Ottawa, 9 March 1985
Malkin, Ben. Ottawa, 10 May 1984
Malone, Richard. Toronto, 7 Nov. 1983
Marshall, Adam. Toronto, 10 Aug. 1984
Marsters, Jack. Montreal, 16 July 1985
Martin, The Hon. Paul. Windsor, 9 and 10 Nov. 1983
McIntosh, David. Ottawa, 17 Feb. 1984
Metcalfe, William. Winnipeg, 11 Oct. 1984
Newman, Peter. Toronto, 15 May 1984
Peters, Charles. Montreal, 29 April 1986
Pickersgill, The Hon. J.W. Ottawa, 10 May 1984
Rasminsky, Louis. Ottawa, 10 May 1984
Reid, Escott. Ste-Cécile-de-Masham, Que, 27 July 1986
Richardson, Burton. Toronto, 28 Nov. 1983
Scott, Marian. Montreal, 9 Nov. 1990
Sharp, The Hon. Mitchell. Ottawa, 9 May 1984
Smith, Norman. Ottawa, 12 Oct. 1983
Solandt, Omond. Bolton, Ont., 12 July 1984
Stursberg, Peter. West Vancouver, 22 Aug. 1984
Turnbull, Walter. Ottawa, 15 Aug. 1986
Waring, Gerald. Ottawa, 27 June 1985
Wilson, Ruth. Toronto, 16 April, 4 May and 5 July 1984

Government of Canada Documents

Parliament. House of Commons. *Debates,* 1936–1958

Report of the Royal Commission on National Development in the Arts, Letters and Sciences (Massey Commission). Ottawa, 1950
Report of the Royal Commission on Publications (O'Leary Commission). Ottawa, 1961
Report of the Royal Commission on Newspapers (Kent Commission). Ottawa, 1981

SECONDARY SOURCES

Dissertations and Theses

Black, Hawley L. 'The Role of the Canadian Press News Agency in Gatekeeping Canada's News.' PhD dissertation, McGill University, 1979
Capling, M. Ann. 'Political Leadership in Opposition: The Conservative Party of Canada, 1920–1948.' PhD dissertation, University of Toronto, 1991
Clippingdale, Richard. 'J.S. Willison, Political Journalist: From Liberalism to Independence, 1881–1905.' PhD dissertation, University of Toronto, 1970
Muirhead, Bruce. 'Canadian Trade Policy, 1949–57: The Failure of the Anglo-European Option.' PhD dissertation, York University, 1986
Slobodin, Thomas B. 'A Tangled Web: The Relationship between Mackenzie King's Foreign Policy and National Unity.' PhD dissertation, Queen's University, 1986
Young, William R. 'Making the Truth Graphic: The Canadian Government's Home Front Information Structure and Programmes during World War II.' PhD dissertation, University of British Columbia, 1978

Books

Beck, J. Murray. *Pendulum of Power: Canada's Federal Elections* (Toronto: Prentice-Hall 1968)
Behiels, Michael. *Prelude to Quebec's Quiet Revolution: Liberalism versus Neo-Nationalism, 1945–1960* (Montreal and Kingston: McGill-Queen's University Press 1985)
Bilkey, Paul. *Persons, Papers and Things* (Toronto: Ryerson 1940)
Bird, Florence. *Anne Francis* (Toronto: Clarke, Irwin 1974)
Bissell, Claude. *The Imperial Canadian: Vincent Massey in Office* (Toronto: University of Toronto Press 1986)
Black, Conrad. *Duplessis* (Toronto: McClelland and Stewart 1977)
Bliss, Michael. *Northern Enterprise: Five Centuries of Canadian Business* (Toronto: McClelland and Stewart 1987)
Bothwell, Robert, Ian Drummond, and John English. *Canada since 1945: Power, Politics, and Provincialism* (Toronto: University of Toronto Press 1981)

Bothwell, Robert, and Norman Hillmer, eds. *The In-Between Time: Canadian External Policy in the 1930s* (Toronto: Copp Clark 1975)

Bothwell, Robert, and William Kilbourn. *C.D. Howe* (Toronto: McClelland and Stewart 1979)

Bowman, Charles A. *Ottawa Editor: The Memoirs of Charles A. Bowman* (Sidney, BC: Gray's Publishing 1966)

Bruce, Charles. *News and the Southams* (Toronto: Macmillan 1968)

Bryce, Robert B. *Maturing in Hard Times: Canada's Department of Finance through the Great Depression* (Montreal and Kingston: McGill-Queen's University Press 1986)

Camp, Dalton. *Gentlemen, Players and Politicians* (Toronto: McClelland and Stewart 1970)

Chalmers, Floyd. *Both Sides of the Street: One Man's Life in Business and the Arts in Canada* (Toronto: Macmillan 1983)

– *A Gentleman of the Press* (Toronto: Doubleday 1969)

Charlesworth, Hector. *Candid Chronicles: Leaves from the Notebook of a Canadian Journalist* (Toronto: Macmillan 1925)

– *More Candid Chronicles: Further Leaves from the Notebook of a Canadian Journalist* (Toronto: Macmillan 1928)

Christian, William, ed. *The Idea File of Harold Adams Innis* (Toronto: University of Toronto Press 1980)

Cole, Taylor. *The Canadian Bureaucracy* (Durham, NC: Duke University Press 1949)

Colquhoun, A.H.U. *Press, Politics and People: The Life and Letters of Sir John Willison* (Toronto: Macmillan 1935)

Conrad, Margaret. *George Nowlan: Maritime Conservative in National Politics* (Toronto: University of Toronto Press 1986)

Cook, Ramsay. *The Politics of J.W. Dafoe and the Free Press* (Toronto: University of Toronto Press 1963)

Creighton, Donald. *The Forked Road: Canada, 1939–1957* (Toronto: McClelland and Stewart 1976)

Cuff, Robert, and J.L. Granatstein. *American Dollars – Canadian Prosperity* (Toronto: Samuel Stevens 1978)

Dawson, R. MacGregor. *The Conscription Crisis of 1944* (Toronto: University of Toronto Press 1961)

Dempson, Peter. *Assignment Ottawa: Seventeen Years in the Press Gallery* (Toronto: General Publishing 1968)

Dexter, Grant. *Canada and the Building of Peace* (Toronto: Canadian Institute of International Affairs 1944)

Diefenbaker, John. *One Canada: Memoirs of the Rt Hon. J.G. Diefenbaker, vol. 1: The Crusading Years, 1895–1956* (Toronto: Macmillan 1975)

Donnelly, Murray. *Dafoe of the Free Press* (Toronto: Macmillan 1968)

Eayrs, James. *In Defence of Canada*, vol. 2: *Appeasement and Rearmament* (Toronto: University of Toronto Press 1965)
- *In Defence of Canada*, vol. 3: *Peacemaking and Deterrence* (Toronto: University of Toronto Press 1972)
Eggleston, Wilfrid. *While I Still Remember: A Personal Record* (Toronto: Ryerson 1968)
English, John. *Shadow of Heaven: The Life of Lester Pearson, 1897–1948* (Toronto: Lester and Orpen Dennys 1989)
- *The Worldly Years: The Life of Lester Pearson, 1949–1972* (Toronto: Alfred A. Knopf Canada 1992)
Ferguson, George. *John W. Dafoe* (Toronto: Ryerson 1948)
Ferns, H.S. *Reading from Left to Right* (Toronto: University of Toronto Press 1983)
Fetherling, Douglas. *The Rise of the Canadian Newspaper* (Toronto: Oxford University Press 1990)
Fleming, Donald. *So Very Near*, vols. 1 and 2 (Toronto: McClelland and Stewart 1985)
Ford, Arthur. *As the World Wags On* (Toronto: Ryerson 1950)
Fraser, Blair. *The Search for Identity: Canada, 1945–1967* (Toronto: Doubleday 1967)
Fraser, John, and Graham Fraser, eds. *'Blair Fraser Reports': Selections 1944–1968* (Toronto: Macmillan 1969)
Fulford, Robert. *Best Seat in the House: Memoirs of a Lucky Man* (Toronto: Collins 1988)
Fullerton, Douglas. *Graham Towers and His Times* (Toronto: McClelland and Stewart 1986)
Gordon, Walter. *A Political Memoir* (Toronto: McClelland and Stewart 1977)
Graham, Roger. *Arthur Meighen*, vol. 3: *No Surrender* (Toronto: Clarke, Irwin 1965)
Granatstein, J.L. *Canada 1957–1967: The Years of Uncertainty and Innovation* (Toronto: McClelland and Stewart 1986)
- *Canada's War: The Politics of the Mackenzie King Government, 1939–1945* (Toronto: Oxford University Press, 1975)
- *A Man of Influence: Norman Robertson and Canadian Statecraft, 1929–1968* (Ottawa: Deneau 1981)
- *The Ottawa Men: The Civil Service Mandarins, 1935–1957* (Toronto: Oxford University Press 1982)
- *The Politics of Survival: The Conservative Party of Canada, 1939–1945* (Toronto: University of Toronto Press 1967)
Granatstein, J.L., and J.M. Hitsman. *Broken Promises: A History of Conscription in Canada* (Toronto: Oxford University Press 1977)

Gray, James. *Troublemaker! A Personal History* (Toronto: Macmillan 1978)

Gwyn, Sandra. *The Private Capital* (Toronto: McClelland and Stewart 1984)

Hall, D.J. *Clifford Sifton*, vol. 2: *A Lonely Eminence, 1901–1929* (Vancouver: University of British Columbia Press 1985)

Harkness, Ross. *J.E. Atkinson of the Star* (Toronto: University of Toronto Press 1963)

Heeney, Arnold. *The Things That Are Caesar's* (Toronto: University of Toronto Press 1972)

Hodgetts, J.E. *The Canadian Public Service: A Physiology of Government, 1967–1970* (Toronto: University of Toronto Press 1973)

Holmes, John. *The Better Part of Valour: Essays on Canadian Diplomacy* (Toronto: McClelland and Stewart 1970)

– *The Shaping of Peace: Canada and the Search for World Order, 1943–1957*, vols. 1 and 2 (Toronto: University of Toronto Press 1979, 1982)

Hutchison, Bruce. *The Far Side of the Street* (Toronto: Macmillan 1976)

– *The Incredible Canadian* (Toronto: Longmans, Green 1952)

– *The Unfinished Country* (Vancouver: Douglas and McIntyre 1985)

Keate, Stuart. *Paper Boy* (Toronto: Clarke, Irwin 1980)

Keenleyside, Hugh. *Memoirs of Hugh L. Keenleyside*, vol. 1: *Hammer the Golden Day* (Toronto: McClelland and Stewart 1981)

Kendle, John. *John Bracken: A Political Biography* (Toronto: University of Toronto Press 1979)

Kent, Tom. *A Public Purpose: An Experience of Liberal Opposition and Canadian Government* (Montreal and Kingston: McGill-Queen's University Press 1988)

Kesterton, Wilfred. *A History of Journalism in Canada* (Toronto: Macmillan 1978)

Kyba, Patrick. *Alvin: A Biography of the Hon. Alvin Hamilton P.C.* (Regina: Canadian Plains Research Centre 1989)

LePan, Douglas V. *Bright Glass of Memory* (Toronto: McGraw-Hill Ryerson 1979)

Lynch, Charles. *You Can't Print That: Memoirs of a Political Voyeur* (Edmonton: Hurtig 1983)

Mackay, R.A., and E.B. Rogers. *Canada Looks Abroad* (Toronto: Oxford University Press 1938)

Mackenzie, David. *Arthur Irwin: A Biography* (Toronto: University of Toronto Press 1993)

Malone, Richard S. *Missing from the Record* (Toronto: Collins 1946)

– *A Portrait of War, 1939–1943* (Toronto: Collins 1983)

– *A World in Flames, 1943–1945* (Toronto: Collins 1984)

Mansergh, Nicholas. *Survey of British Commonwealth Affairs: Problems of External Policy* (London: Oxford University Press 1952)

Martin, Paul. *A Very Public Life,* vol. 1: *Far from Home* (Ottawa: Deneau 1983)
– *A Very Public Life,* vol. 2: *So Many Worlds* (Toronto: Deneau 1985)
McCall-Newman, Christina. *Grits: An Intimate Portrait of the Liberal Party*
    (Toronto: Macmillan 1982)
– *The Man from Oxbow: The Best of Ralph Allen* (Toronto: McClelland and
    Stewart 1967)
McNaught, Carlton. *Canada Gets the News* (Toronto: Ryerson/Canadian Institute
    of International Affairs 1940)
McPhail, Thomas L., and Brenda M. McPhail. *Communication: The Canadian
    Experience* (Toronto: Copp Clark Pitman 1990)
Meisel, John. *The Canadian Election of 1957* (Toronto: University of Toronto
    Press 1962)
Metcalfe, William. *The View from Thirty* (Winnipeg: William Metcalfe 1984)
Neatby, H. Blair. *William Lyon Mackenzie King,* vol. 3: *1932–39, The Prism of
    Unity* (Toronto: University of Toronto Press 1976)
Newman, Peter C. *The Canadian Establishment,* vol. 1 (Toronto: McClelland and
    Stewart 1979)
– *Home Country: People, Places and Power Politics* (Toronto: McClelland and
    Stewart 1973)
– *Renegade in Power: The Diefenbaker Years* (Toronto: McClelland and Stewart
    1963)
Nichols, N.E. *(CP): The Story of the Canadian Press* (Toronto: Ryerson 1938)
O'Leary, Grattan. *Recollections of People, Press and Politics* (Toronto: Macmil-
    lan 1977)
Owram, Douglas. *The Government Generation: Intellectuals and the State,
    1900–1945* (Toronto: University of Toronto Press 1986)
Parisé, Robert. *Georges-Henri Lévesque: père de la renaissance québécois*
    (Montreal: Alain Stanké 1976)
Peers, F.W. *The Politics of Canadian Broadcasting* (Toronto: University of
    Toronto Press 1969)
Pearson, Lester. *Mike: The Memoirs of the Rt Hon. Lester B. Pearson,* vol. 1:
    1897–1948 (Toronto: University of Toronto Press 1972)
– *Mike:* vol. 2: *1948–1957,* with John A. Munro and Alex I. Inglis, eds. (Toronto:
    University of Toronto Press 1973)
Pickersgill, J.W. *My Years with Louis St. Laurent: A Political Memoir* (Toronto:
    University of Toronto Press 1975)
Pickersgill, J.W., and D.F. Forster, eds. *The Mackenzie King Record,* vol. 2:
    1944–45 (Toronto: University of Toronto Press 1968)
– *The Mackenzie King Record,* vol. 3: *1945–46* (Toronto: University of Toronto
    Press 1970)
– *The Mackenzie King Record,* vol. 4: *1947–48* (Toronto: University of Toronto
    Press 1976)

Plumptre, A.F.W. *Three Decades of Decision: Canada and the World Monetary System, 1944–75* (Toronto: McClelland and Stewart 1977)

Pope, Maurice. *Soldiers and Politicians* (Toronto: University of Toronto Press 1962)

Porter, John. *The Vertical Mosaic: An Analysis of Social Class and Power in Canada* (Toronto: University of Toronto Press 1965)

Poulton, Ron. *Paper Tyrant: John Ross Robertson of the Toronto Telegram* (Toronto: Clarke, Irwin 1971)

Pressnell, L.S. *External Economic Policy since the War*, vol. 1: *The Postwar Financial Settlement* (London: HMSO 1986)

Reid, Escott. *On Duty: A Canadian at the Making of the United Nations, 1945–1946* (Toronto: McClelland and Stewart 1983)

– *Time of Fear and Hope: The Making of the North Atlantic Treaty* (Toronto: McClelland and Stewart 1977)

Ritchie, Charles. *Diplomatic Passport: More Undiplomatic Diaries, 1946–1962* (Toronto: Macmillan 1981)

– *The Siren Years: A Canadian Diplomat Abroad, 1937–1945* (Toronto: Macmillan 1974)

Roberts, Leslie. *C.D.: The Life and Times of Clarence Decatur Howe* (Toronto: Clarke, Irwin 1957)

Ross, Philip Dansken. *Retrospects of a Newspaper Person* (Toronto: Oxford University Press 1931)

Rutherford, Paul. *The Making of the Canadian Media* (Toronto: McGraw-Hill Ryerson 1978)

– *A Victorian Authority: The Daily Press in Late Nineteenth-Century Canada* (Toronto: University of Toronto Press 1982)

Scott, F.R. *Canada Today* (Toronto: Oxford University Press 1939)

Seymour-Ure, Colin. *The Political Impact of the Mass Media* (London: Constable 1974)

Shea, Albert. *Broadcasting the Canadian Way* (Montreal: Harvest House 1963)

Smith, Denis. *Diplomacy of Fear: Canada and the Cold War, 1941–1948* (Toronto: University of Toronto Press 1988)

Smith, I. Norman. *A Reporter Reports* (Toronto: Ryerson 1954)

Soward, F.H. *Canada in World Affairs: The Pre-War Years* (Toronto: Ryerson 1941)

Soward, F.H., and Edgar McInnis. *Canada and the United Nations* (New York: Manhattan Publishing/Canadian Institute of International Affairs 1956)

Stacey, C.P. *Arms, Men and Governments: The War Policies of Canada, 1939–45* (Ottawa: Canadian Government Publishing Centre 1970)

– *Canada in the Age of Conflict*, vol. 2: *1921–1948, The Mackenzie King Era* (Toronto: University of Toronto Press 1981)

– *Six Years of War: The Army in Canada, Britain and the Pacific* (Ottawa: Queen's Printer 1966)

Stairs, Dennis. *The Diplomacy of Constraint: Canada, the Korean War, and the United States* (Toronto: University of Toronto Press 1974)

Stratford, Philip, ed. *André Laurendeau: Witness for Quebec* (Toronto: Macmillan 1975)

Stursberg, Peter. *Lester Pearson and the Dream of Unity* (Toronto: Doubleday 1978)

Swettenham, John. *McNaughton*, vol. 2: *1939–1943*, and vol. 3: *1944–1966* (Toronto: Ryerson 1969)

Taras, David. *The Newsmakers: The Media's Influence on Canadian Politics* (Toronto: Nelson 1990)

Thomson, Dale C. *Jean Lesage and the Quiet Revolution* (Toronto: Macmillan 1984)

– *Louis St. Laurent: Canadian* (Toronto: Macmillan 1967)

Thompson, John Herd, with Allen Seager. *Canada, 1922–1939: Decades of Discord* (Toronto: McClelland and Stewart 1985)

Underhill, Frank. *In Search of Canadian Liberalism* (Toronto: Macmillan 1960)

Vipond, Mary. *The Mass Media in Canada* (Toronto: James Lorimer 1989)

Wade, Mason. *The French Canadians*, rev. ed., vol. 2: *1911–1967* (Toronto: Macmillan 1968)

Ward, Norman, ed. *A Party Politician: The Memoirs of Chubby Power* (Toronto: Macmillan 1966)

Ward, Norman, and David Smith. *Jimmy Gardiner: Relentless Liberal* (Toronto: University of Toronto Press 1990)

Whitaker, Reginald. *The Government Party: Organizing and Financing the Liberal Party of Canada, 1930–58* (Toronto: University of Toronto Press 1977)

Wilgress, Dana. *Memoirs* (Toronto: Ryerson 1967)

Williams, John R. *The Conservative Party of Canada: 1920–1949* (Durham, NC: Duke University Press 1956)

Willison, John S. *Reminiscences: Political and Personal* (Toronto: McClelland and Stewart 1919)

Wonnacott, Paul. *The Canadian Dollar* (Toronto: University of Toronto Press 1965)

Zupnick, Elliot. *Britain's Postwar Dollar Problem* (New York: Columbia University Press 1957)

Articles and Papers

Angers, François-Albert. 'Deux modèles d'inconscience: le Premier Saint-Laurent et le Commissionaire Lévesque,' *L'Action Nationale* 38, no. 3 (nov. 1951)

Behiels, Michael. 'Le père Georges-Henri Lévesque et l'établissment des sciences sociales à Laval, 1938–1955,' *Revue de l'Université d'Ottawa* 52, no. 3 (juil.-sept. 1982)

Betts, Robin. 'George Ferguson, Canada and Appeasement,' *The Historian* 7 (summer 1985)

Bird, John. 'When the Liberals Lost the Press,' *Canadian Commentator* 1, no. 6 (June 1957)

Bothwell, Robert. '"Who's Paying for Anything These Days": War Production in Canada, 1939–45,' in N.F. Dreisziger, ed., *Mobilization for Total War* (Waterloo: Wilfrid Laurier University Press 1981)

Callwood, June. 'The Truth about Parliament,' *Maclean's*, 17 April 1965

Cameron, Elspeth. 'Once upon a time …' *Saturday Night*, Aug. 1987

Cook, Ramsay. 'J.W. Dafoe at the Imperial Conference of 1923,' *Canadian Historical Review* 51, no. 1 (spring 1960)

Cox, Corolyn. 'News Makes the Newspaperman,' *Saturday Night*, 19 Dec. 1942

Cross, Austin. 'Oligarchs at Ottawa, Part I,' *Public Affairs* 14, no. 1 (autumn 1951)

– 'Oligarchs at Ottawa, Part II,' *Public Affairs* 15, no. 2 (winter 1952)

Dafoe, J.W. Review of 'Press, Politics and People,' *Canadian Historical Review* 17, no. 1 (March 1936)

Deutsch, J.J. 'Canadian Views,' in A.L.K. Acheson, J.F. Chant, and M.F.J. Prachowny, eds., *Bretton Woods Revisited* (Toronto: University of Toronto Press 1972)

Dexter, Grant. 'Politics, Pipeline and Parliament … A Salutary Lesson?' *Queen's Quarterly* 63, no. 3 (autumn 1956–7)

Eayrs, James. '"A Low Dishonest Decade": Aspects of Canadian External Policy, 1931–1939,' in H.L. Keenleyside, ed., *The Growth of Canadian Policies in External Affairs* (Durham, NC: Duke University Press 1960)

Eggleston, Wilfrid. 'Leaves from a Pressman's Log,' *Queen's Quarterly* 63, no. 4 (winter 1957)

Ferguson, George. 'Freedom of the Press,' in *Press and Party in Canada: Issues of Freedom* (Toronto: Ryerson 1955)

– 'The Prairie Provinces and Canadian Foreign Policy,' *Foreign Affairs* 18, no. 1 (Oct. 1939)

Fetherling, Douglas. 'Divided Empire,' *Saturday Night*, Dec. 1983

Fletcher, Fred. 'The Prime Minister as Public Persuader,' in T.A. Hockin, ed., *Apex of Power: The Prime Minister and Political Leadership in Canada*, 2nd ed. (Toronto: Prentice-Hall 1977)

Fraser, Blair. 'Labour and the Church in Quebec,' *Foreign Affairs* 28, no. 2 (Jan. 1950)

Fulford, Robert. 'The Press in the Community,' in D.L.B. Hamlin, ed., *The Press and the Public* (Toronto: University of Toronto Press 1962)

Graham, W.R. 'Can the Conservatives Come Back?' *Queen's Quarterly* 62, no. 4 (winter 1955–6)

Granatstein, J.L. 'King and His Cabinet: The War Years,' in John English and J.O. Stubbs, eds., *Mackenzie King: Widening the Debate* (Toronto: Macmillan 1977)

Granatstein, J.L., and Robert Bothwell. '"A Self-Evident National Duty": Canadian Foreign Policy, 1935–1939,' *Journal of Imperial and Commonwealth History* 3, no. 2 (Jan. 1973)

Hodgetts, J.E. 'The Civil Service and Policy Formation,' *Canadian Journal of Economics and Political Science* 23, no. 4 (Nov. 1957)

– 'The Liberal and the Bureaucrat,' *Queen's Quarterly* 62, no. 2 (summer 1955)

Holmes, John. 'The Second World War and After,' in "Canadian Foreign Policy: Four Introductory Lectures" (unpublished manuscript)

Hooker, M.A. 'Serving Two Masters: Ian Mackenzie and Civil-Military Relations in Canada, 1935–1939,' *Journal of Canadian Studies/Revue d'études canadiennes* 21, no. 1 (spring/print. 1986)

Hudson, Robert V. 'John Wesley Dafoe: Canada's Liberal Voice,' *Journalism Quarterly* 47, no. 1 (spring 1970)

Hutchison, Bruce. 'Canada's Gadfly: The *Winnipeg Free Press*,' *Harper's,* April 1963

– 'The Greatest Man in Canada,' *Fortune* 25 (June 1942)

Keenleyside, T.A. 'Lament for a Foreign Service: The Decline of Canadian Idealism,' *Journal of Canadian Studies/Revue d'études canadiennes* 15, no. 4 (winter 1980–1 hiver)

Kesterton, Wilfred. 'The Growth of the Newspaper in Canada,' in Benjamin Singer, ed., *Communications in Canadian Society* (Toronto: Addison-Wesley 1983)

– 'A Short History of the Press in Canada,' *Gazette* 15, no. 2 (1969)

Le Cocq, Thelma. 'Editor Ferguson,' *Maclean's,* 1 April 1947

Mackenzie, David. 'The Bren Gun Scandal and the Maclean Publishing Company's Investigation of Canadian Defence Contracts, 1938–1940,' *Journal of Canadian Studies/Revue d'études canadiennes* 26, no. 3 (fall/automne 1991)

Mackintosh, William A. 'Canadian Views,' in A.L.K. Acheson, J.F. Chant, and M.F.J. Prachowny, eds., *Bretton Woods Revisited* (Toronto: University of Toronto Press 1972)

McInnis, Edgar. 'Canadian Opinion and Foreign Policy,' *Queen's Quarterly* 62, no. 4 (winter 1955–6)

McNaught, K.W. 'Canadian Foreign Policy and the Whig Interpretation: 1936–1939,' in Bruce Hodgins and Robert Page, eds., *Canadian History since Confederation: Essays and Interpretations* (Georgetown, Ont.: Irwin-Dorsey 1972)

Meisel, John. 'The Formulation of Liberal and Conservative Programmes in the 1957 Canadian General Election,' *Canadian Journal of Economics and Political Science* 26, no. 4 (Nov. 1960)

Munro, John A. 'Loring Christie and Canadian External Relations, 1935–1939,' *Journal of Canadian Studies/Revue d'études canadiennes* 7, no. 2 (May/mai 1972)

Neatby, H. Blair. 'Mackenzie King and National Unity,' in H.L. Dyck and H.P. Krosby, eds., *Essays in Honour of Frederic P. Soward* (Toronto: University of Toronto Press 1969)

Nesbitt, J.K. 'Editor Bruce Hutchison Commutes between Victoria and Winnipeg,' *Saturday Night*, 10 May 1947

Page, Donald. 'The Development of a Western Peace Movement,' in Susan Trofimenkoff, ed., *The Twenties in Western Canada* (Ottawa: National Museum 1972)

– 'The Institute's "Popular Arm": The League of Nations Society in Canada,' *International Journal* 33, no. 3 (winter 1977–8)

Page, Donald, and Don Munton. 'Canadian Images of the Cold War, 1946–7,' *International Journal* 32, no. 3 (summer 1977)

Pelletier, Gérard. 'The Strike and the Press,' in Pierre Elliott Trudeau, ed., *The Asbestos Strike,* trans. James Boake (Toronto: James Lewis and Samuel 1974)

Rutherford, Paul. 'The Emergence of the New Journalism in Canada, 1869–99,' *Canadian Historical Review* 61, no. 2 (June 1975)

Scott, F.R. 'A Policy of Neutrality for Canada,' *Foreign Affairs* 17, no. 2 (Jan. 1939)

Smith, I. Norman. 'Pearson, People and Press,' *International Journal* 29, no. 1 (winter 1973–4)

Stairs, Dennis. 'Present in Moderation: Lester Pearson and the Craft of Diplomacy,' *International Journal* 29, no. 1 (winter 1973–4)

Stevens, Geoffrey. 'The Influence and Responsibilities of the Media in the Legislative Process,' in W.A.W. Neilson and J.C. MacPherson, eds., *The Legislative Process in Canada: The Need for Reform* (Montreal: Institute for Research on Public Policy 1978)

Taylor, Kenneth W. 'Kenneth Ramsay Wilson, 1903–1952,' *Canadian Journal of Economics and Political Science* 18, no. 4 (Nov. 1952)

Underhill, Frank. 'Canadian Liberal Democracy in 1955,' in *Press and Party in Canada: Issues of Freedom* (Toronto: Ryerson 1955)

– 'If Our Politics Are Dull … Blame Our Dull Press,' *Maclean's,* 27 Feb. 1960

Vipond, Mary. 'Canadian Nationalism and the Plight of Canadian Magazines in the 1920s,' *Canadian Historical Review* 58, no. 1 (March 1977)

Ward, Norman. 'The Liberals in Convention,' *Queen's Quarterly* 65, no. 1 (spring 1958)

- 'Patronage and the Press,' in Kenneth M. Gibbons and Donald C. Rowat, eds., *Political Corruption in Canada: Causes and Cures* (Toronto: McClelland and Stewart 1976)
Westell, Anthony. 'The Press: Adversary or Channel of Communication?' in Harold D. Clarke et al., eds., *Parliament, Policy and Representation* (Toronto: Methuen 1980)
- 'Reporting the Nation's Business,' in G. Stuart Adam, ed., *Journalism, Communication and the Law* (Toronto: Prentice-Hall 1976)
Willison, John S. 'Journalism and Public Life in Canada,' *Canadian Magazine,* Oct. 1905
Wilson, Kenneth R. 'The External Background of Canada's Economic Problems,' in J.D. Gibson, ed., *Canada's Economy in a Changing World* (Toronto: Macmillan/Canadian Institute of International Affairs 1948)
Winn, Conrad. 'Mass Communications,' in Conrad Winn and J. McMenemy, *Political Parties in Canada* (Toronto: McGraw-Hill Ryerson 1975)
Young, Scott. 'The Men Behind the Front Page,' *Maclean's,* 15 Dec. 1948
Young, William R. 'Academics and Social Scientists vs. the Press: The Politics of the Bureau of Public Information and the Wartime Information Board, 1939–45,' Canadian Historical Association, *Report* 1978

Newspapers and Magazines

Canadian Forum
Financial Post
Financial Times
Maclean's
Montreal *Gazette*
Montreal Star
Ottawa Citizen
Ottawa Journal
Saturday Night
Time (Canadian edition)
Toronto Daily Star
Toronto *Globe and Mail*
Toronto *Telegram*
Winnipeg Free Press

Picture Credits

Index

War, 136; Korean War, criticism of
External Affairs over policy,
139–41; Liberal government,
influence with, 5; Liberal government, his postwar basis of support
for, 145, 172, 179; Liberal party,
leftward drift of, 146, 156; Liberalism of, 145, 152, 161, 165, 171,
176–7, 179; and mandarins, 55;
and Paul Martin, 168; post-Munich
attitudes of, 29–30; nationalism of,
18, 123; NATO, 135; Ottawa role of,
53–4; and Mike Pearson, 22–3,
25, 27, 31; and Mike Pearson's
Liberal leadership aspirations,
167–8; pipeline debate, 162; press
gallery, 10; and J.L. Ralston, 69;
St Laurent government, disillusion
over decline, 160, 161; and Victor
Sifton, 67; sources, closeness to,
23; United Nations, 125–6, 132.
See also Dafoe, Ferguson, *Winnipeg Free Press*
Diefenbaker, John, 164, 166, 169,
176; Liberal underestimation of,
164
Dion, Fr Gérard, 116
dollar crisis: Canadian, 81–94;
British, 85–6
Drew, George, 35, 164; 1949 election,
149; journalists' perception
of, 176; pipeline debate, 160; press
reaction to his election as Conservative leader, 148–9; and press
relations, 148, 151. *See* Progressive Conservative party
Drew-Duplessis axis, 149, 155
Dunton, Davidson, 109
Duplessis, Maurice, 114, 115, 116

Eggleston, Wilfrid, 5

Ethiopian crisis, 19
European Recovery Program, 85, 86,
89, 90, 91, 93, 94, 132, 134, 138

Federal Aircraft, 42, 44
federal election:
– 1940, 39, 52, 56
– 1945, 145
– 1949, 149–50; Drew's lack of
appeal, 149; St Laurent's appeal,
149
– 1953, 155–7
– 1957, 164–7
– 1958, 169
Ferguson, George, 4, 5, 14–15, 23,
56, 57, 65, 69, 101, 122; 1949
election, 150; 1953 election,
156–7; 1957 election, reaction to
Conservative victory, 167; 1958
election, neutrality during, 169;
and appeasement, 24, 26–7; and
CCF, 147; and Cold War, 133; collective security, 18, 31–2; and
conscription, 50, 58, 59–60, 63,
70; on conscription plebiscite,
1942, 62; and Conservative party,
151, 162; relationship with J.W.
Dafoe, 15–16, 18; and George
Drew, 151; editorial role with *Winnipeg Free Press*, 21, 53; External
Affairs, contacts within, 127;
French Canada, 52, 64; internationalism of, 18, 122–3, 142–3;
journalism, philosophy of, 142–3;
journalist-politician relationship,
proper boundaries of 177–8; and
Mackenzie King, 69; Mackenzie
King government, 56, 61, 68;
Korean War, 136, 139, 140; Liberal government, influence with, 5;
Liberal government, postwar basis

Pearson's Liberal leadership aspirations, his support of, 167; political allegiances of, 106, 157, 171, 179; political ideology of, 178–9; Progressive Conservative party, 151, 157, 166; and Quebec, 111, 114, 115, 118; and Louis St Laurent, 147; St Laurent government, disillusion with its decline, 158, 159, 161, 163, 166. *See also* Irwin, *Maclean's*
Fraser, Jean, 106, 107
Freedman, Max, 122, 132, 137, 138, 141; links to External Affairs, 138
Fulton, Davie, 161

Gardiner, James, 61
General Agreement on Tariffs and Trade, 92–3
Gibson, J.D., 97
Globe (Toronto), 6, 10
Globe and Mail (Toronto), 28, 106, 150, 151
Gordon, Donald, 78, 89, 94
Gordon, Walter, 167
'Government party,' 146, 157, 171, 173. *See* Liberal party
Gray, James, 111
Groulx, Abbé Lionel, 113

Harris, Walter, 160
Heeney, Arnold, 109, 125, 131, 141; and Blair Fraser, 132; and Ken Wilson, 132, 135
Holmes, John, 129, 141, 142
Howe, C.D., 40, 41, 42, 43, 44, 54, 61, 70, 77, 78, 111, 127, 155, 178; and business community, 45, 78–9; as declining force in Liberal party, 159; Defence Production Act, debate on extension of, 157;

attack on *Financial Post*, 44–5; and H.R. MacMillan, 41–3; organizing war economy, 41–5; pipeline debate, 159–63; press relations of, 153; press support for, 145, 176; wartime administration of, 41, 44, 46, 47; and Ken Wilson, 89, 98. *See* Department of Munitions and Supply
Hume, Alex, 162
Hunter, Horace, 35, 37, 39, 44, 45, 47, 75, 99, 101; Bren gun affair, editorial involvement in, 36; business sympathies of, 34, 104; Conservative party, attitude towards, 39; editorial ideas of, 34; and Arthur Irwin, 43; and Mackenzie King, 37, 39; Mackenzie King government, 36, 45; management style of, 33; and Quebec, 112, 114; and socialism, 79; support of reconstruction planning, 104
Hutchison, Bruce, 4, 5, 53, 66, 68, 69, 122, 132, 134, 137, 174; 1957 election, reaction to Conservative victory, 167; American affairs, coverage of, 138; cabinet links, 69; Cold War, 126; conscription, 67; Defence Production Act, debate on extension, 158; and George Drew, 149, 156; and External Affairs, 123–5, 138; influence with government officials, 5; internationalism of, 123, 142–3; journalism, his philosophy of, 142–3; journalism, on weakness of Canadian, 173; and Mackenzie King, 70; Korean War, 141; Liberal government, postwar basis of his support for, 145, 172, 179; and Liberal party, 66, 138; Liberal